Concise Introduction to Comparative Law

D1344170

LIVERPOOL JMU LIBRARY

3 1111 01423 5020

Europa Law Publishing, Groningen 2013

Concise Introduction to Comparative Law

Prof. Dr. Michael Bogdan

Europa Law Publishing is a publishing company
specializing in European Union law, international trade
law, public international law, environmental law and
comparative national law.
For further information please contact Europa Law
Publishing via email: info@europalawpublishing.com
or visit our website at: www.europalawpublishing.com.

All rights reserved. No part of this publication may
be reproduced or transmitted, in any form or by any
means, or stored in any retrieval system of any nature,
without the written permission of the publisher.
Application for permission for use of copyright material
shall be made to the publishers. Full acknowledgement
of author, publisher and source must be given.

Voor zover het maken van kopieën uit deze uitgave
is toegestaan op grond van artikel 16h t/m 16m
Auteurswet 1912 *juncto* het Besluit van 27 november
2002, Stb. 575, dient men de daarvoor wettelijk
verschuldigde vergoedingen te voldoen aan de Stichting
Reprorecht (Postbus 3060, 2130 KB Hoofddorp).
Voor het overnemen van (een) gedeelte(n) uit
deze uitgave in bloemlezingen, readers en andere
compilatiewerken (artikel 16 Auteurswet 1912) dient
men zich tot de uitgever te wenden.

© Europa Law Publishing, Michael Bogdan, 2013

Typeset in Scala and Scala Sans, Graphic design by
G2K Designers, Groningen/Amsterdam

NUR 828
ISBN 978-90-8952-125-5

Foreword

This book is intended primarily to be used as an elementary and conveni-
ent introductory textbook on foreign and comparative law. It may be too simple
for elective courses on the subject, chosen by students with special interest in
acquiring a more in-depth knowledge; its target are rather students taking more
general courses, such as jurisprudence or legal history, that should include
an introduction to comparative law but do not do so because of the lack of a
suitably concise course literature. The book can also be used by legal practitioners and others who wish to acquire basic knowledge about the most important
legal systems of the world and about the methodological problems that arise in
connection with the study of or work with foreign law in general.

The book is intended, despite the use of the English language, also for law
students and jurists in countries with Roman-Germanic legal traditions. In fact,
somewhat more attention is paid to English and American law than to French
and German law as most readers likely have less previous knowledge of the
common-law legal systems. Citations to legal literature are extensive in the first
part of the book, which deals with the often controversial general issues, while
in the second part, which is descriptive, references to further materials have
generally been omitted.

My employer, the Faculty of Law at the University of Lund, has enabled me to
devote a substantial portion of my working hours to research and writing. The
Institute for Research in Legal Science (*Institutet för rättsvetenskaplig forskning*)
has provided financial support that made this book possible. I wish to express
my sincere gratitude to the above-mentioned, as well as to extend my anticipated
thanks to all those readers who will share with me their suggestions for future
improvements.

Lund, 1 January 2013

Michael Bogdan

Abbreviations

A.B.A.	American Bar Association
ABGB	Allgemeines Bürgerliches Gesetzbuch
Act.Jur.Hung.	Acta Juridica Academiae Scientiarum Hungaricae
AG	Amtsgericht, Aktiengesellschaft
A.J.C.L.	American Journal of Comparative Law
A.J.I.L.	American Journal of International Law
Ann.Univ.Budapest.	Annales Universitatis Scientiarum Budapestiensis. Sectio Juridica
BGB	Bürgerliches Gesetzbuch
BGH	Bundesgerichtshof
BverfG	Bundesverfassungsgericht
B.Y.I.L.	British Yearbook of International Law
C.A.	Court of Appeal(s)
C.c.	Code civil
C.com.	Code de commerce
Clunet	Journal du droit international
C.P.	Code pénal
C.P.C.	Code de procédure civile
C.P.P.	Code de procédure pénale
D.C.	District of Columbia
E.J.C.L.	Electronic Journal of Comparative Law (www.ejcl.org)
EU	European Union and/or the former European Community
Eur.Rev.Priv.L.	European Review of Private Law
FJFT	Tidskrift, utgiven av Juridiska föreningen i Finland
Gaz.Pal. (or G.P.)	Gazette du Palais
GmbH	Gesellschaft mit beschränkter Haftung
HGB	Handelsgesetzbuch
I.C.L.Q.	International and Comparative Law Quarterly
J.O.	Journal officiel
JR	Juristische Rundschau
JT	Juridisk tidskrift vid Stockholms universitet
JZ	Juristenzeitung
KG	Kammergericht
LG	Landgericht
L.J.	Law Journal
L.Q.R.	Law Quarterly Review
L.R.	Law Review
MDR	Monatschrift für Deutsches Recht
M.L.R.	Modern Law Review
N.C.P.	Nouveau code pénal
N.C.P.C.	Nouveau code de procédure civile
NILR	Netherlands International Law Review
NJW	Neue Juristische Wochenschrift
NordTIR	Nordisk tidsskrift for international ret / Nordic Journal of International Law

NU	Nordisk utredningsserie
OLG	Oberlandesgericht
Q.C.	Queen's Counsel
RabelsZ	Rabels Zeitschrift für ausländisches und internationales Privatrecht
RG	Reichsgericht
Rev.dr.int.dr.comp.	Revue de droit international et de droit comparé
Rev.int.dr.comp.	Revue internationale de droit comparé
Rev.roumaine	Revue roumaine des sciences sociales. Série de sciences juridiques
Sc.St.L.	Scandinavian Studies in Law
SOU	Statens offentliga utredningar
StGB	Strafgesetzbuch
StPO	Strafprozessordnung
SvJT	Svensk Juristtidning
TfR	Tidsskrift for rettsvitenskap
TSA	Tidskrift för Sveriges advokatsamfund
U.C.C.	Uniform Commercial Code
VwGO	Verwaltungsgerichtsordnung
VwVfG	Verwaltungsverfahrensgesetz
ZaöRV	Zeitschrift für ausländisches öffentliches Recht und Völkerrecht
ZeuP	Zeitschrift für Europäisches Privatrecht
ZfRV	Zeitschrift für Rechtsvergleichung, Int. Privatrecht und Europarecht
ZPO	Zivilprozessordnung
ZvglRW	Zeitschrift für vergleichende Rechtswissenschaft

PART I

General Part

CHAPTER I

Introduction

1.1 The Name of the Subject

Most systematic presentations of law courses and fields of legal research tend to reflect the usual way of dividing the legal system. Each legal subject is concerned with a particular branch of law dealing with particular legal relationships and problems; consequently penal law deals with the rules concerning the punishment of crimes, procedural law is concerned with the rules of trial proceedings, etc. Some fields of legal science are however of another nature, as they are concerned with certain overall problems that affect the entire, or almost the entire, legal system. Theoretical subjects, such as legal history, sociology of law and jurisprudence, belong in this group, and the same is true of comparative law, which is the topic of this book.

The term "comparative law" may be as misleading as it would be to speak of legal history as "historical law", or of sociology of law as "sociological law", as there are no separate parts of the legal system which can be denoted using these designations.[1] Nevertheless the term "comparative law" has been established to such a degree for so many years that it can legitimately be used in literature, as the title of courses or books, etc.[2] Its counterpart in French is *droit comparé* (literally "compared law") and in German *Rechtsvergleichung* (literally "comparison of law").

1.2 An Attempt to Define the Subject

It is difficult to define comparative law, largely due to the fact that ideas about the meaning of the concept vary greatly.[3] For the purpose of facilitating the continued reading of this book, an attempt has to be made to provide a working definition of the subject. According to this definition, the study of comparative law encompasses:

a) the comparison of general features or detailed provisions of different legal systems with the purpose of ascertaining their similarities and differences;

b) the processing of the similarities and differences that have been ascertained, for instance by explaining their origin, evaluating of the solutions

---

[1] See Ancel, *Festschrift Rheinstein*, vol. 1, p. 212; Constantinesco, *Rechtsvergleichung*, vol. 1, p. 20, note 1; David, *Traité*, pp. 3-4; Faiziev, *Sovetskoe sravnitelnoe pravovedenie*, p. 77; Gutteridge, *Comparative Law*, p. 1; Kamba, 23 *I.C.L.Q.* 486-487 (1974); Malmström, *Festskrift Sundberg*, p. 277; Schwarz-Liebermann von Wahlendorf, *Droit*, p. 171; Tokarczyk, *Wprowadzenie*, pp. 19-24; Winizky, *Problèmes contemporains*, vol. 2, pp. 527-528.

[2] On the history and development of comparative law see e.g. Ancel, *Utilité*, pp. 12-28; Constantinesco, *Rechtsvergleichung*, vol. 1, pp. 69-201; David & Brierley, *Major Legal Systems*, pp. 1-4; Gutteridge, *Comparative Law*, pp. 11-22; Rheinstein, *Einführung*, pp. 37-76; Sarfatti, *Mélanges Maury*, vol. 2, pp. 237-241; Schnitzer, *Vergleichende Rechtslehre*, vol. 1, pp. 7-21; Sola Cañizares, *Iniciación*, pp. 47-93; Winterton, 23 *A.J.C.L.* 87-97 (1975); Zweigert/Kötz, *Introduction*, pp. 48-62.

[3] See e.g. the brief overview in Schnitzer, *Vergleichende Rechtslehre*, vol. 1, pp. 106-118.

LIVERPOOL JOHN MOORES UNIVERSITY
LEARNING SERVICES

utilized in the different legal systems, grouping of legal systems into families of law, or searching for the common core of the legal systems; and
c) the treatment of the methodological problems that arise in connection with
these tasks, including methodological problems arising in connection with
the study of foreign law.

From this definition it is clear that, in principle, comparative law is without
borders and that it can never be treated in an exhaustive manner. One can
hardly imagine all of the conceivable bilateral and multilateral comparisons
between all combinations of existing legal systems. Research efforts in comparative law are therefore normally limited to a particular question and to a few
countries. Those works, which in common with Part I of this book concern
general problems in comparative law and methodology, naturally occupy a
special position in this respect.[4]

1.3 Comparative Law and Studies of Foreign Law

From the definition above, it is clear that studies of foreign law
in and of themselves alone do not fall within the framework of comparative law.
The relationship of the subject to such studies deserves, however, further comment.

Members of the human race live in organized societies. The degree of
organization in these societies is normally very high. Virtually all societies have
adopted rules for human conduct, enforced by the organized power of the society, i.e. normally by the state. Such rules can be regarded as having the character
of legal rules (for reasons of space it is not possible to go into a more detailed
discussion here on what is meant by "law", as such a discussion alone could fill
many books of this size).[5]

---

[4] Some comparatists suggest that comparative law can be divided into different subjects depending
upon the purpose or degree of ambition. Thus, Loeber, *RabelsZ* 1961, pp. 211-216 speaks of descriptive,
dogmatic, applied (legislative) and contrasting comparative law. Szabó, *Recueil Ancel*, vol. 1, pp. 59-67
distinguishes between internal and external comparative law, depending upon whether one compares
legal systems in countries with the same or with different types of societies. Strömholm, *SvJT* 1971,
pp. 251-253 and in *SvJT* 1972, p. 462 distinguishes between two types of comparative legal research.
In one type, the foreign law has a subservient task, i.e. it is used to attain purposes that are typical for
traditional legal research limited to a single legal system. The other type gives the comparison an independent meaning and it is the national systems being compared that are subservient: they are studied
for another purpose than to find an answer to a question within the framework of one or othe other legal
system. The comparison becomes here the dominant element.

[5] Some authors have criticized the mainstream comparative law for dealing only with state law (disregard-
ing such phenomena as, for example, the "law" of the Roma communities) and focusing merely on
Western law. Twining, *Maastricht Journal of European and Comparative Law* 1999, pp. 233-238, speaks in
this context about "the Country and Western tradition".

Despite all the similarities in people's way of life in large parts of the world, there are important differences between the legal rules of the different societies. There are hundreds of legal systems on Earth: in the United States of America alone there are more than fifty individual legal systems. The problems in societies that require legal regulation are often identical, or at the least very similar. They can, for instance, concern the determination of the seller's responsibility for the quality of a product sold, the distribution of an estate of a deceased person, or the punishment of a person who has taken the life of another human being. Despite the similarity of the problems, they have normally been regulated completely independently in the various countries, often without having considered how other countries deal with the same problem. Even today one sometimes encounters the attitude that it is not very relevant to study foreign law: foreign legislation and judicial decisions are not ordinarily regarded as a source of law in one's own country and therefore are not followed by the courts and other authorities, apart from the relatively few cases where foreign law is applied due to the conflict-of-laws rules of private international law.

The reality is, however, that many jurists will in one way or another come into contact with foreign law in connection with their professional activities, for instance when advising or representing clients involved in international business.[6] To acquire knowledge of foreign law can of course have its own practical value, such as when a Swedish lawyer gives advice to Swedes intending to purchase real property in Spain. But even apart from any immediate practical value, and regardless of whether one is a practicing lawyer or a legal scholar, it is natural to become interested in how the legal issues one works with at home are regulated in other countries. Even jurists who do not come into direct contact with foreign law have begun to realize that a jurist just like a doctor, computer scientist, or any other qualified professional cannot limit his attention only to what occurs within the borders of his own country.

The practical and theoretical value of knowledge of foreign law increases substantially if one goes one step further and begins to compare the different legal rules in different countries, especially when comparing foreign legal rules with those in one's own country. It is only in connection with the comparison between legal systems that one can speak of comparative legal knowledge in the real sense.[7] It is however clear that even the study of, and providing others with information on, foreign law contains certain comparative elements. If, for example, a German lawyer desires to explain the English institute of trust to his compatriots, he must do so by using German terminology, which already in and of itself involves a form of comparison.[8]

---

[6] Cf. Baade, 31 *A.J.C.L.* 499-505 (1983).

[7] See e.g. Ancel, *Festschrift Rheinstein*, vol. 1, p. 215; Hanisch, *Beihefte zur Zeitschrift für schweizerisches Recht*, no. 16, 1994, pp. 126-127; Kamba, 23 *I.C.L.Q.* 505-506 (1974); Reitz, 46 *A.J.C.L.* 618-620 (1998); Schnitzer, *ZfRV* 1976, p. 15; Sola Cañizares, *Iniciación*, p. 99; Rodière, *Introduction*, p. 34.

[8] See Lando, *FJFT* 1966, pp. 262-263. Se också Knapp, *Mélanges Malmström*, pp. 139-140; Siesby, *TfR* 1967, pp. 489-490; Winterton, 23 *A.J.C.L.* 69-70 (1975).

Naturally, an accurate knowledge of the foreign rule(s) to be compared is a basic precondition for every meaningful comparison. The study of foreign law is consequently the first step within the comparative work process, even though the problems and difficulties that come up in connection with the study of foreign law are the same regardless of whether the knowledge is sought for comparative or for other purposes. It is therefore appropriate for a presentation of comparative law intended for beginners to direct attention to these problems and difficulties as well as to the basic features of the most important legal systems in the world. In fact, most introductory comparative law courses and textbooks provide primarily an introduction to the most important legal systems and cultures, whereas the comparison itself is paid only limited attention. This is natural considering that the majority of beginners ordinarily lack a basic knowledge of foreign law, but it does not change the fact that one cannot begin to speak about comparative law until the purpose is to ascertain (and possibly also to further process) the similarities and differences between the legal systems, i.e. when the comparison is at the heart of the work and not merely an incidental by-product.[9]

1.4 Comparative Law – Method or Science?

The question of whether comparative law is an independent branch of legal science or only a method, which can be used by legal scholars within all the traditional fields of legal research, can be regarded as being of purely theoretical interest if one disregards such practical aspects as the allocation of research grants and the curriculum of law schools. Despite this, or perhaps because of it, many legal authors have expended significant effort to discussions of the status of comparative law in this respect.[10] In this book, however, this question cannot be given more than a few lines.

---

[9] See e.g. Kamba, 23 I.C.L.Q. 489 (1974); Schmidt, TfR 1951, p. 474. Cf. also Strömholm, SvJT 1971, pp. 251-253 and SvJT 1972, p. 462.

[10] See e.g. Ancel, Utilité, pp. 35-38 and in Act.Jur.Hung. 1971, p. 196; Arminjon, Nolde & Wolff, Traité, vol. 1, pp. 23-41; Blagojevič, Rev.int.dr.comp. 1953, pp. 649-657; Blomeyer, RabelsZ 1934, pp. 1-16; Constanti-nesco, Rechtsvergleichung, vol. 1, pp. 217-253; David, Traité, pp. 5-7; Engström & Wesslau, Anteckningar, pp. 103-111; Faiziev, Sovetskoe sravnitelnoe pravovedenie, pp. 10-11; Gordley, 46 A.J.C.L. 607-615 (1998); Jeschek, Entwicklung, pp. 36-37; Kahn-Freund, 82 L.Q.R. 41 (1966); Kamba, 23 I.C.L.Q. 487-489 (1974); Knapp, Mélanges Malmström, pp. 132-135; Legrand, 58 M.L.R. 264-265 (1995); Malmström, Festskrift Sundberg, pp. 276-279; Mansouri, Rev.dr.int.dr.comp. 2006, pp. 176-196 ; Rozmaryn i Rotondi, ed., Inch-ieste, pp. 590-591; Schmitthoff, 7 Cambridge L.J. 94-96 (1941); Schnitzer, ZfRV 1976, pp. 13-19; Schwarz-Liebermann von Wahlendorf, Droit, pp. 172-178; Souto, Da inexistência; Strömholm, Allmän rättslära, p. 91; Szabó, Ann.Univ.Budapest. 1964, pp. 91-108 and in Act.Jur.Hung. 1973, pp. 131-133; Tchkhikvadze & Zivs, Livre du Centenaire, vol. 2, pp. 594-596; Winizky, Problèmes contemporains, vol. 2, pp. 524-527; Winterton, 23 A.J.C.L. 70-71 (1975); Yokaris, Revue hellénique de droit international 1982-1983, pp. 65-96; Zivs, Act.Jur.Hung. 1971, pp. 175-176.

It appears to be clear that highly qualified work in comparative law has a scientific character, even if there is no universally accepted definition of "scientific".[11] An entirely different question is whether comparative law can be regarded as constituting an *independent* branch of legal science. There are no generally accepted criteria for what constitutes an independent field of scientific research.[12] Nor are there any clear divisions between the established traditional legal disciplines; their borders are instead normally based on practical considerations, which are often more dependent on pedagogical rather than scientific or theoretical grounds. But regardless of which position one takes, the fact is that comparative legal research is normally of such degree of difficulty and has to deal with so many unique tasks that its independent treatment in the form of, for instance, books and courses is well justified.[13] This applies particularly to the comparative law's general and methodological questions which are usually deemed to constitute the subject's general part.[14] Even the basic introduction to the general characteristics of the most important foreign legal systems should, due to pedagogical reasons, be provided in a continuous and coherent form, rather than be divided among courses and books in different branches of law.

If one compares corresponding legal institutions or legal rules in different legal systems, for instance if one compares the appealability of administrative decisions in Sweden and England, one is still within the legal field wherefrom the compared legal rules originate (in this example, probably within administrative law) even though one is working at the same time with comparative law. The same is true about the processing of the results of the comparison, for example trying to explain the ascertained similarities and differences. One should perhaps speak of comparative administrative law, or of research in administrative law using the comparative method.[15] Comparative law is consequently open for jurists working in all fields of law.[16]

It may be easier to designate comparative law as an independent science to the extent it concerns questions that lie on a higher level of abstraction, for instance when one searches for the common core of all legal systems, or when one attempts to group legal systems into families of law. However, here one touches upon the general theory of law (jurisprudence)[17] and it is equally correct

---

[11] I agree with Strömholm, *SvJT* 1971 sid. 251, who considers science to be an activity that attempts, with at least a certain minimum of rational and conscious method, to resolve one or more selected problems of a fairly advanced nature.

[12] Cf. Malmström, *Festskrift Sundberg*, p. 276.

[13] See e.g. Lando, *FJFT* 1966, pp. 264-271.

[14] See e.g. Engström & Wesslau, *Anteckningar*, p. 99.

[15] Concerning the question whether comparative legal research requires its own method of working, see Strömholm, *SvJT* 1972, pp. 456-465. According to Lando, *FJFT* 1966, sid. 263, the comparative method is the technique one uses to collect information on foreign law, to present foreign law and to make comparisons between legal systems.

[16] See e.g. Malmström, *Festskrift Sundberg*, p. 277; *NU* 17/70, pp. 9 och 14.

[17] Se t.ex. Agge, *SvJT* 1969, pp. 164-166; Samuel, 47 *I.C.L.Q.* 817-836 (1998); Strömholm, *Allmän rättslära*, pp. 89-91.

to say that such studies belong to jurisprudence but require the use of the comparative method. Jurisprudence seems to encompass even those questions that have to do with the comparative method as such, for example the question whether legal rules from countries with entirely different types of society are at all comparable.

An investigatory or research work in comparative law consequently normally also involves working within some other field of legal research. It distinguishes itself however by using the comparative method. This method of course consists not of one particular technique, but rather a number of different techniques (it is thus more appropriate to speak of comparative methods).[18] It is perhaps possible to say that comparative legal research constitutes a specialization within each field of law, while having so many unique features of its own that it can even be conducted across the borders separating the various branches of law.

Not long ago, comparative law was regarded as being a play-house for escapist theoreticians having rather peculiar interests. This was not quite without grounds. If legal writers and teachers can be divided into complicators and simplifiers, too many of the comparative legal scholars have belonged to the former category, trying almost desperately to provide comparative law with a theoretical framework of their own, to invent new concepts and use a terminology that is too abstract and complicated for practical use.[19] Today however, it is generally recognized that comparative studies can greatly contribute to legal education and research. Comparative law is nowadays a required or optional course in many law schools. Research focusing on comparative law is conducted at numerous scientific institutions such as the Max Planck Institute for Foreign Private Law and Private International Law (*Max-Planck-Institut für ausländisches und internationales Privatrecht*) in Hamburg (there are corresponding Max Planck institutes in other German cities for e.g. foreign and comparative criminal law, public law and social law), the British Institute of International and Comparative Law in London, *Institut suisse de droit comparé* in Lausanne, and the Parker School of Foreign and Comparative Law at Columbia University in New York. A number of non-governmental international scientific associations devote themselves to comparative legal research. The climax of international co-operation in comparative legal research is reached at the great international congresses arranged once every four years by the International Academy of Comparative Law (*Académie internationale de droit comparé*); the first congress took place in 1932 in The Hague and the most recent in 2010 in Washington D.C. At each congress about forty topics, determined long in advance, are discussed, proceeding from a comparative general report prepared by a general rapporteur on the basis of a number of national reports from different jurisdictions.

---

[18] See e.g. Husa, *RabelsZ* 2003, pp. 444; Göranson, *Festskrift Agell*, p. 195; Örücü in Smits, ed., *Elgar Encyclopedia*, p. 451; Palmer, 53 *A.J.C.L.* 261-290.

[19] This is not the only criticism that can be directed against some comparative legal scholars, who used to be jokingly defined by their colleagues as jurists who, when in their own country, pretend to be experts on foreign law, while abroad representing themselves as experts on the law of their home country.

Among the specialized legal periodicals focusing on comparative law, one may mention American Journal of Comparative Law (USA), *Revue internationale de droit comparé* (France), International and Comparative Law Quarterly (United Kingdom) and *Zeitschrift für vergleichende Rechtswissenschaft* (Germany). The largest but so far unfinished comparative law research project is the production of the International Encyclopedia of Comparative Law, which has been in progress for several decades in the form of installments written by a great number of legal experts from many different countries.[20]

---

[20] For more details on this project see e.g. Drobnig, *Festschrift Rheinstein*, vol. 1, pp. 221-233; Simmonds, 16 *I.C.L.Q.* 816-820 (1967). The project may be too ambitious and will probably never be completed, but this does not affect the value of the contributions published so far, see Knapp, *Velké právní systémy*, pp. 11-12.

CHAPTER 2

The Uses of Comparative Law

2.1 General Education

In the same way as, for example, legal history and general legal theory do contribute to the quality of a jurist's all-round education, so does comparative law. It increases his knowledge and understanding of the culture and way of life of other peoples, makes possible meaningful communication with foreign colleagues, is an interesting and useful intellectual exercise, stimulates knowledge and use of foreign languages, and as a result of all this contributes to an increased understanding between people in general.[1]

Comparative legal research increases our knowledge of the legal system as a social phenomenon. One interesting example of a possible generally instructive research project would be to study how resource-weak legal systems in countries having very few trained jurists, precedent-setting courts, experts on legislating, and lacking own law schools and juridical research, can adequately deal with situations that arise in today's modern society. Another example worth mentioning is the comparative study of those numerous legal systems, whose legal heritage consists of a mixture of legal rules and institutes originating from different families of law, for example the mixture of English and Islamic legal traditions in Pakistan or of French and English legal traditions in the Canadian province of Québec.

2.2 Obtaining a Better Understanding of One's Own Legal System

Even if it would be an exaggeration to say that the study limited to a single legal system is meaningless,[2] comparative studies are undoubtedly useful also for a jurist who is interested merely in learning more about and achieving a better understanding of his own law.[3] They may demonstrate that many legal rules and legal institutions, which one previously took for granted and unavoidable in every civilized society, actually have arisen in one's own legal system more or less accidentally or because of special historical or geographical

---

[1] See e.g. Ancel, *Mélanges Malmström*, pp. 4 and 12; Constantinesco, *Rechtsvergleichung*, vol.2, pp. 367-370; David, *Rev.int.dr.comp.* 1950, pp. 682-685; David & Brierley, *Major Legal Systems*, pp. 4-6 and 8; Glendon, Gordon & Carozza, *Comparative Legal Traditions*, pp. 4-5; Glenn in Smits, ed., *Elgar Encyclopedia*, pp. 57-59; Graveson, *Rev.int.dr.comp.* 1958, pp. 501-509; Kamba, 23 *I.C.L.Q.* 504-505 (1974); Schmitthoff, 7 *Cambridge L.J.* 100-101 (1941); Sola Cañizares, *Iniciación*, pp. 122-123; Tunc, *Essays Yntema*, pp. 80-90 and in *Rev.int.dr.comp.* 1964, pp. 46-67; Winterton, 23 *A.J.C.L.* 111-112 (1975).

[2] See Gordley, *De lege* 1995, p. 37.

[3] See e.g. Constantinesco, *Rechtsvergleichung*, vol. 2, pp. 335-337; David & Brierley, *Major Legal Systems*, pp. 6-8; Glendon, Gordon & Carozza, *Comparative Legal Traditions*, pp. 5-7; Gordley, 46 *A.J.C.L.* 607-615 (1998); Hazard, 79 *Harvard L.R.* 281 (1965-1966); Kahn-Freund, 82 *L.Q.R.* 59-60 (1966); Rheinstein, *Einführung*, pp. 191 and in 1 *A.J.C.L.* 104 (1952); Rodière, *Introduction*, pp. 47-48; Schnitzer, *Vergleichende Rechtslehre*, vol. 1, p. 42; Sola Cañizares, *Iniciación*, p. 110-111.

factors and that many, possibly most, other legal systems survive quite well without such rules. Foreign legal systems may in fact resolve similar problems in a quite different way, perhaps even simpler and better.[4] Other legal rules and legal institutions, which one previously regarded as being original to one's own legal system, are shown in fact to have foreign roots.

Comparative law thus makes it possible for a jurist to see his own legal system from a new point of view and from a certain distance.[5] In this new perspective one can obtain a better and more critical[6] understanding of the function and value of old and well-known legal phenomena in one's own law.

2.3 Working *de lege ferenda*

This increased understanding of one's own legal system also means that the jurist can look at this system without consciously or instinctively being bound by certain legal solutions which for other jurists, who do not have the benefit of comparative knowledge, seem obvious and irreplaceable, since they have never seen or heard of other methods used to resolve the same problem.[7] This is especially important in connection with the work on new legislation, but also in other cases where jurists work *de lege ferenda*, for example in the case of judges creating precedents or legal scholars recommending a law reform.

The importance of learning from the experience of other countries is obvious within the fields of natural science, medicine, and technology. The same compelling need to make use of the experience of others should also be recognized within the legal field.[8] In many countries, reports of legislative committees and doctoral dissertations usually contain at least a few pages consisting of a brief overview of the relevant legal rules in some of the most important foreign legal systems.[9] The problem is that this is seldom followed by profiting from the foreign solutions and experience; the reader often gets the impression that the excursion into foreign law was done more for the purpose of complying with a formality, or a traditional obligation, than to actually take into consideration

---

[4] Many years ago, a committee within the Association of American Law Schools expressed this in the following way: "Every law student should be introduced to a legal system other than his own. He should understand that there is nothing 'God-given' in the solutions of the common law [...]". See A.A.L.S. Proceedings 178 (1960).

[5] See e.g. Peters & Schwenke, 49 *I.C.L.Q.* 830 (2000).

[6] See e.g. Muir Watt, *Rev.int.dr.comp.* 2000, pp. 503-527

[7] See e.g. Zwarensteyn, 10 *American Business L.J.* 20 (1972-1973).

[8] See e.g. Arminjon, Nolde & Wolff, *Traité*, vol. 1, pp. 18-20; David, *Traité*, pp. 113-140; Kamba, 23 *I.C.L.Q.* 495-498 (1974); Marsh, *RabelsZ* 1977, pp. 649-668; Schmitthoff, 7 *Cambridge L.J.* 103-107 (1941); Siesby, *TfR* 1967, pp. 493-495; Zajtay, 7 *The Comparative and International L.J. of Southern Africa* 324-325 (1974); *NU* 17/70, p. 9.

[9] About the situation in Sweden, see Lögdberg, *Mélanges Malmström*, pp. 163-167; Strömholm, *SvJT* 1971, pp. 251-263.

foreign experiences by means of evaluating and attempting to learn from them. The review of foreign law is, besides, usually limited to a few of the most important legal systems, such as English, American, French and German law, even though other, smaller but equally accessible, legal systems, such as Australian or Austrian law, may be more interesting due to original modern solutions found there.

Foreign experience should, naturally, not be studied uncritically. Legal rules and institutions, which function well under certain conditions specific for one country, can be entirely inappropriate or perhaps even harmful if "transplanted" into another country with other traditions, another type of society, etc.[10] Especially great care should be taken when taking over in bulk a significant part of a foreign legal system (reception of law).[11] It is a fact, however, that large-scale legal transplants are commonplace and have been used for centuries, often with considerable success, for various reasons: they may save time and costs that would otherwise have to be spent on elaborating "own" rules, may give prestige and legitimacy to the new order or simply be dictated by political or economic necessity.[12]

In recent years many developing countries and the former socialist countries have been receiving extensive expert assistance in the field of law from the developed industrialized countries in the West, regarding first but foremost the law which is needed for the market economy and the development of political democracy. This assistance, provided by Western legal experts, is not without problems and gives rise to many interesting questions of comparative law,[13] including the issue of competition between various foreign models.[14]

---

[10] See Chapter 6 below and e.g. Arvind, 59 *I.C.L.Q.* 65-88 (2010); de Cruz, *Comparative Law*, pp. 510-513; Henrÿ, *ZfRV* 1997, pp. 45-55; Fedtke in Smits, ed., *Elgar Encyclopedia*, pp. 434-437; Graziadei in Reimann & Zimmermann, eds, *The Oxford Handbook*, pp. 441-475; Kahn-Freund, 37 *M.L.R.* 1-27 (1974); Legrand, *Maastricht Journal of European and Comparative Law* 1997, pp. 111-124; Markesinis, *RabelsZ* 1993, p. 445; Shen, *Rev.int.dr.comp.* 1999, pp. 853-857; Nelken in Legrand & Munday, eds, *Comparative Legal Studies*, pp. 437-466; Smits in Reimann & Zimmermann, eds, *The Oxford Handbook*, pp. 513-538; Watson, 92 *L.Q.R.* 79-84 (1976); Örücü, 51 *I.C.L.Q.* 205-223 (2002); Xanthaki, 57 *I.C.L.Q.* 659-673 (2008).

[11] See e.g. Doucet & Vanderlinden, eds, *La réception*; Eörsi, *Comparative Civil Law*, pp. 562-569.

[12] See e.g. Miller, 51 *A.J.C.L.* 839-885 (2003); Watson, *E.J.C.L.*, vol. 4.4 (December 2000).

[13] See e.g. Ajani, *Rev.int.dr.comp.* 1994, pp. 1087-1105 and in 43 *A.J.C.L.* 93-117 (1995); Bogdan, *SvJT* 1991, pp. 784-792, in *Essays Štěpán*, pp. 7-15 and in *Festskrift Lando*, pp. 69-81; Burg, 25 *A.J.C.L.* 492-530 (1977); Chanturia, *RabelsZ* 2008, pp. 114-135; de Cruz in Harding & Örücü, eds, *Comparative Law*, pp. 102-119; Fuchs, *ZvglRW* 1981, pp. 355-372; Merryman, 25 *A.J.C.L.* 457-491 (1977) and in 48 *A.J.C.L.* 713-727 (2000); Nelken in Harding & Örücü, eds, *Comparative Law*, pp. 19-34; Smits in Harding & Örücü, eds, *Comparative Law*, pp. 137-154; Teubner, 61 *M.L.R.* 11-32 (1998); Waelde & Gunderson, 43 *I.C.L.Q.* 347-378 (1994); a number of papers in Sevastik, ed., *Legal Assistance*.

[14] See e.g. Chanturia, *RabelsZ* 2008, pp. 116-120; Ogus, 48 *I.C.L.Q.* 405-418 (1999).

2.4 Harmonization and Unification of Laws

Comparative law is of central importance in connection with the harmonization of law, i.e. with intentionally making the legal rules of two or more legal systems more alike, as well as with the unification of law, i.e. the intentional introduction of identical legal rules into two or more legal systems.[15] Such harmonization or unification is desirable primarily where it facilitates trade and other contacts between the countries involved. Harmonization or unification of law should not be done for its own sake, without bringing about any significant practical advantages. Law is one of the aspects of the culture of a given society, like music or food. Just as we want to preserve and do not want to harmonize or unify the culinary traditions or the musical tastes of the peoples of the world, we should not merely tolerate but also support the preservation of their national legal heritage to the extent this does not undermine the efforts to achieve aims that democratically have been agreed to carry more weight.[16]

The harmonization and unification of law is often a difficult process, where not only the differences between the various opinions but also the lack of understanding of each other's way of legal thinking and legal concepts may frequently constitute the greatest difficulty.[17] Comparative law can therefore be of great value here. Despite all the difficulties arising in connection with harmonization and unification, there have been some important successes, primarily within related countries that cooperate closely with each other, such as the Nordic countries, the Benelux countries and the Member States of the European Union, and within certain fields of law such as international sales law, transportation law, intellectual property law and the law of negotiable instruments. Selected parts of private law of the Member States of the EU, for example provisions on product liability, self-employed commercial agents and consumer protection, consist today of rules that have to a significant degree been unified or harmo-

---

[15] See e.g. Ancel, *Utilité*, pp. 70-86; Banakas in Harding & Örücü, eds, *Comparative Law*, pp. 179-191; Bartels, *RabelsZ* 1981, pp. 106-123; Constantinesco, *Rechtsvergleichung*, vol. 2, pp. 421-431; David, *Traité*, pp. 141-185; David & Brierley, *Major Legal Systems*, pp. 10-11; Engström & Wesslau, *Anteckningar*, pp. 13-19 and 45-98; Ferid, *ZfRV* 1962, pp. 193-213; Gutteridge, *Comparative Law*, pp. 145-184; Kamba, 23 *I.C.L.Q.* 501-504 (1974); Kropholler, *Internationales Einheitsrecht*, pp. 30-32 and 254-258; Kötz, *De lege* 1995, pp. 21-36; Lando, 25 *A.J.C.L.* 641-657 (1977); Malmström, *Festskrift Sundberg*, pp. 287-288; Matteucci, *Rev.int.dr.comp.* 1973, pp. 865-872; Møller, *NordTIR* 1974-1975, pp. 229-263; Neuhaus & Kropholler, *RabelsZ* 1981, pp. 73-90; Philipps, *Erscheinungsformen*; Rodière, *Introduction*, pp. 82-136; Sandrock, *Sinn und Methode*, p. 28; Schmitthoff, 7 *Cambridge L.J.* 108-110 (1941); Schnitzer, *Vergleichende Rechtslehre*, vol. 1, pp. 74-97; Schwarz-Liebermann von Wahlendorf, *Droit*, pp. 225-250; Siesby, *TfR* 1967, p. 494; Tokarczyk, *Wprowadzenie*, pp. 137-138 and 142-167; Vallindas, *Festgabe Gutzwiller*, pp. 189-199; Vicente, *Direito*, pp. 567-601; Winterton, 23 *A.J.C.L.* 103-104 (1975); Zweigert, *RabelsZ* 1951, pp. 387-397; Zweigert & Kötz, *Einführung*, vol. 1, pp. 23-27; *NU* 17/70, p. 9. See further a number of papers in *RabelsZ* 1986, pp. 1-250.

[16] About law as a cultural phenomenon, see e.g. Jayme, *RabelsZ* 2003, pp. 211-230.

[17] These difficulties have, in a humorous manner, been described by Eörsi, 25 *A.J.C.L.* 658-662 (1977).

nized by means of EU directives; in the pipeline there are several other projects in this ongoing process of "Europeanization" of law,[18] including a proposal for a common European sales law[19].

While some harmonization or unification efforts have merely regional ambitions, other aspire to produce world-wide effects. A relatively significant unification achievement is the United Nations Convention on Contracts for the International Sale of Goods (CISG) of 1980.[20] There is also a specialized international organization called Unidroit (International Institute for the Unification of Private Law) with its seat in Rome.[21]

Of course, it is much easier to harmonize or unify rules dealing with a particular issue or detail of substantive law than to achieve convergence of different legal cultures as a whole, characterized e.g. by their different fundamental approaches to law as such. This has made one scholar to pronounce emphatically that in spite of the ongoing European integration process European legal systems have so different "mentalities" that they "have not been converging, are not converging and will not be converging".[22] Whether this statement is right or wrong depends on what is meant by "converging" and "legal systems". For legal theoreticians who are interested merely in phenomena of legal culture, the impact of European integration may indeed seem to be limited. A judge or legal practitioner dealing with commercial matters may be of a different view and the same is true about a businessman doing business or a legally untrained European citizen visiting, shopping or working in another Member State, who notes there that in more and more areas his legal rights and obligations as a businessman, consumer or employee are identical or similar to those in his home country.

Unfortunately it happens that the adopted uniform or harmonized rules are not interpreted in the same manner by the courts in the various countries, so that the whole effort fails to produce the desired effect. The European Union has avoided or rather limited this risk by entrusting the final interpretation of EU law to a single institution, the Court of Justice of the EU in Luxemburg. The above-mentioned CISG Convention is, on the other hand, satisfied with providing in Article 7 that when interpreting its provisions, regard shall be had to the Convention's international character and "the need to promote uniformity in its application". Such a need exists, of course, even when it is not explicitly stated in the text of a treaty. For example, the 1958 New York Convention on the Recognition and Enforcement of Foreign Arbitral Awards, which has been ratified by almost all countries, has given rise to an extensive body of judicial decisions

---

[18] See e.g. Niglia, *Maastricht Journal of European and Comparative Law* 2010, pp. 116-136.

[19] COM(2011)635 final. The enactment of a complete "European Civil Code" is, on the other hand, hardly realistic, but it has some supporters, see e.g. Schmid, *Maastricht Journal of European and Comparative Law* 2001, pp. 277-298.

[20] See Kreuzer, *Festschrift 600 Jahre Würzburger Juristenfakultät*, pp. 247-295.

[21] See <www.unidroit.org>.

[22] See Legrand, 45 *I.C.L.Q.* 61-62 (1996).

from many national courts concerning its interpretation. Considering that the national rules, which are based on this Convention, to the greatest possible extent should be interpreted and applied in the same way in all countries, it can be of value for national courts to know how the Convention is interpreted in other countries and by means of a comparison arrive at the currently prevailing interpretation.[23]

2.5 Working *de lege lata*

Comparative law can be of value even when courts and other authorities interpret and apply the legal rules of their own legal system.[24] This is of course especially true when one interprets and applies rules, which are the result of international unification or harmonization or rules transplanted from another legal system. In the countries that have more or less literally taken over legal rules from the law of other states (as for instance the Swiss Civil Code was adopted by Turkey[25]), the comparison between how the imported legal rules are applied by the courts of the receiving country and the courts in their country of origin may be of great practical significance.[26]

Courts in certain countries seem to make use of the comparative method even when they interpret and apply legal rules which are entirely autonomous and lack any direct international background or connection.[27] It may also be appropriate that when filling in a gap in the domestic legal system, the courts seek the assistance of comparative law. It is certainly not unusual that courts in such cases examine the solutions used in foreign countries and evaluate the foreign experiences, even if this is not always apparent in the judicial reasoning of the judgments.[28] Such filling-in of gaps may be considered to be on the borderline between exploits *de lege lata* and *de lege ferenda*.

2.6 Public International Law and EU Law

Article 38 of the Statute of the International Court of Justice (ICJ) in The Hague lists the sources of law that this Court may use. Among the

---

[23] Cf. Bernhardt, *ZaöRV* 1964, p. 448; Kropholler, *Internationales Einheitsrecht*, pp. 278-285; Sundberg, 10 *Sc.St.L.* 221-238 (1966).

[24] Se Zweigert, *RabelsZ* 1949-1950, pp. 5-21.

[25] This reception is discussed and evaluated by Hirsch, *ZvglRW* 1968, pp. 182-223.

[26] Cf. Kamba, 23 *I.C.L.Q.* 499 (1974).

[27] See Aubin, *RabelsZ* 1970, pp. 458-480; Glenn, *Rev.int.dr.comp.* 1999, pp. 844-848; Koopmans, 45 *I.C.L.Q.* 545-556 (1996); Lando, *Kort indføring*, pp. 196-199; Lögdberg, *Mélanges Malmström*, pp. 161-163; Markesinis, 61 *Cambridge L.J.* 386-404 (2002); Schulze, *ZfRV* 1997, pp. 192-195.

[28] See e.g. Kamba, 23 *I.C.L.Q.* 499 (1974); Sandrock, *Sinn und Methode*, pp. 75-78; Zajtay, 7 *The Comparative and International L.J. of Southern Africa* 325-326 (1974).

sources are "general principles of law recognized by civilized nations". What is primarily meant by this are the legal principles in the domestic, national law of the nations of the world and the only scientifically acceptable manner to determine such legal principles is to compare existing legal systems.[29] Until now judges and legal scholars have however, for the most part, merely guessed at what should be regarded as a universally accepted general legal principle, not infrequently be pinning this label on such rules which for them appeared to be necessary and natural. There has never been a large-scale comparative investigation of which legal principles are truly universally accepted.

In certain cases, the contribution of comparative law may be necessary to determine a point of customary public international law, consisting of legal rules which have arisen in the practice of the states. For instance, customary public international law obligates states to treat foreign citizens in accordance with "the international minimum standard", which can be determined only with the assistance of comparative investigations of existing legal systems.[30] The same applies to the customary rule of public international law according to which states are obligated to pay "appropriate compensation" for expropriation of foreign-owned property.[31]

Comparative law can be of significant value for public international law in many other connections. It is sufficient here to mention that in the drafting and interpretation of agreements (conventions, treaties) between states, difficulties with terminology and concepts often arise because the negotiators have their roots in various legal systems and bring their legal terms and concepts to the negotiating table. Comparative studies of the legal systems of the countries involved make it possible, when drafting the agreement, to be aware of the risk of different interpretations and misunderstandings. Furthermore, such studies help one, at the subsequent interpretation of the agreement, to arrive at the result that as far as possible is in accord with the intentions and expectations of the parties at the time the agreement was entered into.[32]

Comparative law plays an important role for "European Law" consisting of both the European Convention for the Protection of Human Rights and Fundamental Freedoms of 1950 (as amended) and the law of the EU. For example,

---

[29] See e.g. Banakas, *Revue hellénique de droit international* 1982-1983, pp. 121-129; Bogdan, *NordTIR* 1977, pp. 49-51; Bothe, *ZaöRV* 1976, pp. 281-299; Constantinesco, *Rechtsvergleichung*, vol. 2, pp. 396-399; de Cruz, *Comparative Law*, pp. 25-26; David, *Traité*, pp. 100-104; Eustathiades, *Festschrift Zepos*, vol. 2, pp. 139-143; Gutteridge, 21 *B.Y.I.L.* 1-10 (1944) and in *Comparative Law*, pp. 61-71; Hailbronner, *ZaöRV* 1976, pp. 190-215; Kamba, 23 *I.C.L.Q.* 504 (1974); Kiss, *Rev.int.dr.comp.* 1972, pp. 6-10; Lando, *Kort indføring*, pp. 212-213; Rabel, *RabelsZ* 1927, pp. 17-20; Ress, *ZaöRV* 1976, pp. 253-279; Sandrock, *Sinn und Methode*, pp. 26-28; Serick, *Festschrift Heidelberg*, pp. 228-229; Zemanek, *ZaöRV* 1964, pp. 457-458; Zweigert & Kötz, *Introduction*, pp. 7-8.

[30] See e.g. Eustathiades, *Festschrift Zepos*, vol. 2, pp. 133-139; Serick, *Festschrift Heidelberg*, pp. 229-230.

[31] See e.g. Bring, *Det folkrättsliga investeringsskyddet*, Stockholm 1979.

[32] See e.g. Constantinesco, *Rechtsvergleichung*, vol. 2, pp. 380-396; Eustathiades, *Festschrift Zepos*, vol. 2, pp. 143-147; Hailbronner, *ZaöRV* 1976, pp. 222-225; Rabel, *RabelsZ* 1927, pp. 10-17.

Article 7(2) of the European Human Rights Convention speaks of an act or omission that was criminal "according to the general principles of law recognised by civilised nations" and a number of other articles, for instance Article 9(2), permit certain limitations of human rights provided the limitation fulfils certain specific conditions, among them the condition of being "necessary in a democratic society". Whether a certain restriction is necessary in a democratic society can only be established by checking and comparing the laws of countries that are considered to be democratic. Concerning EU law, reference can be made to Article 340 of the Treaty on the Functioning of the European Union, stipulating that in the case of non-contractual liability, the Union shall make good any damage caused by its institutions or by its servants in the performance of their duties "in accordance with the general principles common to the laws of the Member States".[33] Comparisons between the legal systems of the Member States play an important role also in the everyday work of the institutions of the EU, such as the development of secondary legislation (Regulations and Directives) and in the decisions of the Court of Justice of the EU.[34] When interpreting EU instruments, this Court tends to give their words an autonomous meaning, independent of national legal terminology and based on the objectives of the instrument in question as well as on "the general principles which stem from the corpus of the national legal systems".[35]

2.7 Private International Law and International Penal Law

Private international law rules (rules on conflict of laws) result at times in the application of foreign law by courts and other authorities. Such application presupposes, of course, that the court or authority possesses or will obtain information on the contents of the applicable foreign legal system. To acquire this information and to apply foreign law does not in itself amount to comparative work, but the application of foreign law requires, all the same, in an indirect way certain comparisons between the foreign law and the *lex fori* (the law of the country of the forum, i.e. of the adjudicating court), even though these comparisons are not always discussed explicitly in the judgment or decision.[36]

---

[33] See e.g. Germer, *Juristen* 1967, pp. 449-463; Lando, *Kort indføring*, p. 214.

[34] See Bogdan, *Festskrift Lassen*, pp. 207-208; Grossfeld & Bilda, *ZfRV* 1992, pp. 421-433; Kakouris, *Revue hellénique de droit international* 1994, pp. 331-345; Koopmans, 45 *I.C.L.Q.* 546-548 (1996); Lando, *Kort indføring*, pp. 213-214; Lenaerts, 52 *I.C.L.Q.* 873-906 (2003); Pescatore, *Rev.int.dr.comp.* 1980, pp. 337-359; Schulze, *ZfRV* 1997, pp. 188-192; Schwarz-Liebermann von Wahlendorf, *Droit*, pp. 87-89.

[35] See e.g. *LTU* v. *Eurocontrol*, case 29/76, [1976] ECR 1541.

[36] See e.g. Arminjon, Nolde & Woff, *Traité*, vol. 1, pp. 20-22; Battiffol, *Livre du Centenaire*, vol. 1, pp. 131-142 and in *Rev.int.dr.comp.* 1970, pp. 661-674; Bendermacher-Geroussis, *Revue hellénique de droit international* 1979, pp. 54-61; Constantinesco, *Rechtsvergleichung*, vol. 2, pp. 407-411; David, *Traité*, pp. 107-111; Fauvarque-Cosson, *Rev.int.dr.comp.* 2000, pp. 797-818 and in 49 *A.J.C.L.* 407-427 (2001); van

In this context one can mention the notorious characterization problem. Suppose that a court has to decide whether a will made by a foreign citizen is invalid due to the alleged lack of capacity of the testator and that the conflict rules of the forum designate the law of the testator's country as applicable. It thus becomes necessary to turn to the applicable foreign legal system in order to find the substantive rules on the capacity to make a will. One cannot blindly rely upon the terminology and concepts in the foreign law in question; it may for instance occur that a foreign requirement concerning the validity of a will relates, in view of the country of the court, to the capacity of the testator whereas in the foreign country in question it is regarded as pertaining to the form of the will.

Similar questions may arise in connection with the recognition and enforcement of foreign judgments and decisions. For example, the forum country may have enacted a provision on the recognition of foreign adoptions. For a foreign decision to be recognized in accordance with this provision, it is naturally required that the decision is a decision on adoption and not on something else. One must therefore investigate whether the decision concerns such legal phenomenon in the foreign legal system that corresponds to adoption existing in the law of the forum country. To fulfil this requirement, the foreign legal institution does not have to be termed "adoption" and its contents can be different on various points from the legal effects of adoption in the *lex fori*, but if the differences exceed a certain degree, one can no longer speak about adoption and the provision on the recognition of foreign adoptions ceases to be applicable, for example if the foreign decision makes an orphan into an "adopted" child of a whole village.

The application of foreign law and the recognition and enforcement of foreign judgments and decisions requires, consequently, conscious or instinctive comparisons between foreign and domestic legal rules and institutions. Such a comparison must also be made in another respect. Normally, foreign legal rules cannot be applied and foreign judgments and decisions cannot be recognized or enforced if it would be manifestly incompatible with the fundamental legal principles in the forum country, i.e. if it would be against the forum's public policy (*ordre public*). This can hardly be determined without comparing the foreign law with the principles of the *lex fori*.

Certain comparisons between foreign and domestic law may be necessary also within the framework of international penal law. Even though the courts in most countries can only apply their own penal law, a person normally cannot be punished for acts committed abroad if the act is not punishable according to the

---

Ginsbergen, *ZfRV* 1970, pp. 1-9; Grossfeld, *The strength*, pp. 19-23; Kamba, 23 I.C.L.Q. 500-501 (1974); Kropholler, *ZvglRW* 1978, pp. 1-20; Lando, *Kort indføring*, pp. 214-215; Loussouarn, *Revue critique de droit international privé* 1979, pp. 307-339; Makarov in Rotondi, ed., *Inchieste*, pp. 467-480; von Mehren, 23 A.J.C.L. 751-758 (1975) and in *Rev.int.dr.comp.* 1977, pp. 493-500; Sandrock, *Sinn und Methode*, pp. 23-26; Schnitzer, *Vergleichende Rechtslehre*, vol. I, pp. 32-35; Schwarz-Liebermann von Wahlendorf, *Droit*, pp. 90-93; Vicente, *Direito*, pp. 25-27; Zweigert & Kötz, *Introduction*, pp. 6-7.

law in the place where it was committed, and the punishment imposed normally must not be more severe than the most severe penalty which is provided for in the place of commission. Furthermore, extradition to a foreign state may usually only take place if the act for which the extradition is sought corresponds to a crime of a certain gravity according to the law of the requested country. What is meant by a more severe punishment or a corresponding crime cannot, of course, be ascertained without a comparison between the domestic law and the law of the foreign country in each individual case.

2.8   Use for Pedagogical Purposes

It has previously been mentioned that comparative legal studies contribute to the jurist's general education and to an increased understanding of his own legal system. This illustrates the pedagogical value of comparative law and recommends the introduction of comparative elements into the curriculum of the law schools.[37] For obvious reasons, however, comparative law is of even greater value for those who intend to study or work with foreign law.

For a jurist who, for one reason or another, needs to become acquainted with certain rules in foreign law, it is of great value if there is no need to start the study from the beginning. It is often possible to start out with making use of the knowledge of one's own legal system and concentrate on the differences.[38] This presupposes, however, that someone has previously investigated both legal systems and ascertained their similarities and differences by means of comparative studies.

Of great pedagogical value in this connection is that numerous comparatists have reviewed and compared the most important legal systems and grouped them into "families of law" (see Chapter 7 below). Legal systems that are related to each other show great fundamental similarities and it is therefore often possible to save much effort by means of using knowledge of one legal system when studying other legal systems belonging to the same family. If one has for instance become acquainted with English law, and the need arises for knowledge of New Zealand law, one can avoid having to study New Zealand law from the scratch. As the New Zealand legal system is based upon English law, it is often sufficient to concentrate on the relatively few significant differences between the two legal systems.

---

[37] See e.g. Bogdan, 55 *Journal of Legal Education* 484-487 (2005); Blanc-Jouvan, *Rev.int.dr.comp.* 1996, pp. 347-367; Bullier, *Rev.dr.int.dr.comp.* 2008, pp. 163-172; Fauvarque-Cosson, *Rev.int.dr.comp.* 2002, pp. 293-309; Grosswald Curran, 46 *A.J.C.L.* 659-663 (1998); Gutteridge, *Comparative Law*, pp. 127-144; Kamba, 23 *I.C.L.Q.* 490-494 (1974); Lando, *Kort indføring*, pp. 220-225; Tokarczyk, *Wprowadzenie*, pp. 129-132; Winterton, 23 *A.J.C.L.* 69-118 (1975).

[38] See e.g. Zweigert & Puttfarken, *Act.Jur.Hung.* 1973, p. 111.

2.9   Other Areas of Use

It is not possible to discuss in an exhaustive manner all the fields in which comparative legal work can be of value. In addition to the areas discussed previously, one may mention its use within legal history research, where one can by means of comparisons between different present-day legal systems attempt to trace the development of certain legal institutions (the so-called "legal archeology").[39] There are comparatists who believe that the primary task of comparative law is to study and work with the historical ties between legal systems.[40] Additionally, most questions and problems that arise in connection with comparisons between currently existing legal systems can even arise in connection with time-related comparisons within one single legal system, for instance a comparison between English law in the fifteenth century and today. Some authors think that comparative law should also include this type of comparison.[41]

Comparative law is a rich and necessary source of knowledge needed in connection with translations of legal texts and the production of bi-lingual or multi-lingual law dictionaries.[42]

Finally it can be mentioned that comparative legal studies should be of great value for sociologists of law, as these studies show how different alternative legal solutions interact with the society. In this manner, comparative law can to a certain extent replace sociological experiments, which for obvious reasons are almost impossible to carry out in the field of law. On the other hand, sociologists of law can in many connections help the comparatists, for instance concerning the question of how the formally valid legal rules function in reality in their respective countries (cf. sections 3.6 and 3.7 below), the question of whether certain legal rules are comparable at all (cf. section 4.2 below), the explanation of similarities and differences between the compared legal systems (cf. Chapter 5 below), and the comparative evaluation of the different national legal solutions (cf. Chapter 6 below).[43]

---

[39]   See e.g. Constantinesco, *Rechtsvergleichung*, vol. 2, pp. 350-354; Genzmer in Rotondi, ed., *Inchieste*, pp. 235-254; Gilissen in Rotondi, ed., *Inchieste*, pp. 257-297; Gordley in Reimann & Zimmermann, eds, *The Oxford Handbook*, pp. 753-Lando, *Kort indføring*, pp. 219-220; Schmitthoff, 7 *Cambridge L.J.* 101-102 (1941).

[40]   See e.g. Watson, [1978] *Cambridge L.J.* 321.

[41]   See e.g. Del Vecchio, *Rev.int.dr.comp.* 1960, p. 493; Schnitzer, *ZfRV* 1973, pp. 187-188. See also a number of papers on the relationship between legal history and comparative law in *ZEuP* 1999, pp. 494-582.

[42]   See e.g. Constantinesco, *Rechtsvergleichung*, vol. 2, pp. 357-366; de Groot in Smits, ed., *Elgar Encyclopedia*, pp. 423-433; Gutteridge, *Comparative Law*, pp. 124-126; Reynolds, 34 *A.J.C.L.* 551-558 (1986).

[43]   About the relationship between comparative law and the sociology of law and about how they can assist each other, see e.g. Constantinesco, *Rechtsvergleichung*, vol. 2, pp. 261-276; Cotterrell in Legrand & Munday, eds, *Comparative Legal Studies*, pp. 131-153; David & Brierley, *Major Legal Systems*, pp. 13-14; Drobnig, *RabelsZ* 1953, pp. 295-309 and 1971, pp. 496-504; Feldbrugge in Rotondi, ed., *Inchieste*, pp. 213-224; Gessner, *RabelsZ* 1972, pp. 229-260; Heldrich, *RabelsZ* 1970, pp. 427-442; Lando, *Kort*

indføring, pp. 216-218; Lukic in Rotondi, ed., *Inchieste*, pp. 455-463; Recaséns-Siches in Rotondi, ed., *Inchieste*, pp. 525-544; Rheinstein, *Einführung*, pp. 143-186; Rotter, *Osteuropa-Recht* 1970, pp. 81-97; Sacco, 39 *A.J.C.L.* 388-389 (1991); Schwarz-Liebermann von Wahlendorf, *Droit*, pp. 44-62; Tokarczyk, *Wprowadzenie*, pp. 107-109; Vicente, *Direito*, pp. 37-41; Ziegert, *RabelsZ* 1981, pp. 51-72; Zweigert, *RabelsZ* 1974, pp. 299-316 and in *Recueil Ancel*, vol. 1, pp. 81-93; Zweigert & Kötz, *Introduction*, pp. 10-12. Some of these and several additional papers have been published by Drobnig & Rehbinder, eds, *Rechtssoziologie und Rechtsvergleichung*.

CHAPTER 3

Some Problems Connected with the Study or Foreign Law

3.1   General Remarks

A basic precondition for any meaningful comparison between different legal systems is that it is possible to obtain current and accurate information on the legal rules and the legal institutions one is seeking to compare. This of course applies equally to the comparative jurist's own legal system, if it is included in the legal systems being compared, but it is as a rule, because of obvious reasons, much more difficult to learn the details of foreign law. The same difficulties can of course also arise when one is studying foreign law for other than comparative purposes.

The simplest and often also the most efficient manner of obtaining information on a foreign legal system is to take direct contact with knowledgeable colleagues in the foreign country whose law is being studied. This is one of the reasons why bigger law firms often participate in international networks. If one is not fluent in the language and legal terminology of the foreign country in question, it is essential to rely upon a colleague who is able to "translate" the foreign law to the legal concepts which one is familiar with. The greatest advantage of direct contacts is that a dialogue can take place, so that specific and detailed questions can be raised, which focus on the points which are difficult to comprehend, thus making sure that the two lawyers understand one another. The risk of misunderstandings increases when two jurists are compelled by necessity to exchange information in a third language, for example when a Swedish and an Italian lawyer discuss and compare their legal systems in English and thereby use terminology that is foreign to both of their countries.

A comparatist must often, however, obtain the necessary knowledge exclusively by means of his own study of foreign legal materials, such as statutes, judicial decisions, preparatory legislative materials, books and legal periodicals. This requires, of course, that one be somewhat fluent in the language and have a certain basic knowledge of the legal system of the country being studied, particularly its sources of law, fundamental legal concepts, and the legal terminology used. Despite such background knowledge, anyone who attempts to study foreign law will be faced with a number of pitfalls. It is impossible to list all these traps and unfortunately also to avoid them completely.[1]

The greatest danger facing a student of foreign law is that he consciously or instinctively starts with the assumption that the legal concepts, legal institutions and methods of working with the law that he is familiar with in his own legal system also exist in the foreign legal system being studied. Such assumptions can often conform with reality, but it is just as often that they are wrong. An English jurist studying French law might tend to give more weight to judicial decisions than they have in the French legal system, whereas a French jurist studying English law might commit the opposite error. It is therefore necessary to study foreign law without such assumptions or presumptions.[2] In other

---

[1]   See e.g. Zweigert, *Mélanges Maury*, vol. 1, p. 588.

[2]   See e.g. Constantinesco, *Rechtsvergleichung*, vol. 2, p. 154.

words, it is essential to remove oneself from one's own legal system and its way of thinking (one is almost inclined to speak of the removal of the "handcuffs" of one's own law). This is, however, easier said than done. The legal education a jurist obtained in his own country influences to a large extent his basic attitudes as well as his way of thinking and approaching a legal problem. It is therefore not an exaggeration to suggest that an educated foreign lawyer runs a greater risk of *certain* types of mistakes and misunderstandings than a student who has just begun his legal studies. One need not, however, subscribe to the words of the German-American comparatist Max Rheinstein, who gave the following words of warning when welcoming young European jurists to the University of Chicago for their postgraduate studies:[3]

> Try to forget that you have ever studied law. Never approach a problem in the way in which you would approach it at home. You are likely to go astray.

There can be no doubt that good knowledge of one's own legal system substantially facilitates the study of foreign law. This applies not only when one is looking at a legal system that is related to one's own, but also when studying a legal system which is very different from what one is used to. Without the knowledge of at least one legal system it may be difficult to comprehend the issue under scrutiny. Imagine that the question concerning the protection of the purchaser's title to property against the creditors of the seller is resolved in the foreign legal system in an entirely different manner than what one is accustomed to at home. But would the problem be noticed and raised at all if it had not already been encountered in one's own legal system?

Incorrect factual knowledge concerning foreign law leads naturally to qualitatively poor and factually incorrect legal comparisons, and these can at times be worse than no comparison at all. These potential difficulties should however not discourage one from studying foreign law and making comparison between legal systems. As it has been expressed by two very respected German legal writers,[4]

> the cleverest comparatists sometimes fall into error; when this happens the good custom among workers in the field is not to hound the forgivable miscreant with contumely from the profession, but kindly to put him right.

3.2 Availability and Reliability of the Sources of Information

It goes without saying that a fundamental precondition of every study of foreign law is the ability to obtain accurate and up-to-date knowledge about that law, which means that one should have access to reliable sources of

---

[3] Rheinstein in Rotondi, ed., *Inchieste*, p. 553.

[4] Zweigert & Kötz, *Introduction*, p. 36.

information. It is often considered best to study the primary sources, i.e. the official sources of law (the texts of statutes, judicial precedents, etc.) from the country whose legal system is being studied.[5] This however cannot be regarded as an absolute necessity. To begin with, it presupposes a good knowledge of the language of the country, which may be a serious obstacle, especially for the studies of more exotic legal systems.[6] Foreign statutes and judicial decisions are also often difficult to obtain, even if much reliable information is these days available on the Internet. Of course much depends on the level of ambition, which is related to the purposes of the study. A foreign comparatist who has written a monograph, such as a doctoral dissertation, on French criminal law using merely secondary sources can hardly be forgiven with the excuse that he does not read French or that the law library's only copy of the French Penal Code has disappeared; in the first case he has chosen an unsuitable subject, in the second case it could not have been too difficult for him to procure a copy of the Code from another source. The same demands however cannot be placed on a law student writing a comparative paper on how a particular detail is treated by the criminal law of the EU Member States without focusing on French law; in this case the reliance on secondary sources concerning certain countries can be tolerated, as it would be excessive to demand working knowledge of all the official languages of the EU.

In fact, there are at times clear advantages in using secondary sources of law, such as textbooks, manuals, articles in periodicals, etc. To begin with, judges and practicing lawyers in the foreign country itself read and allow themselves to be influenced by well-regarded works of these types. Additionally, it may be difficult to understand the primary sources and make full use of them without having a substantial amount of background knowledge. It is more rational to first read an overview of the legal issues in a recent article or reference book than to delve directly into the text of statutes and judicial decisions. The article or book shows the entire issue in perspective and will normally contain references to other sources where one can acquire a deeper understanding of the state of the law in the country in question. This is true, in particular, if the author is aware of the fact that the text will be read by foreign readers and adds, therefore, information and explanations normally not included in texts addressed to domestic readers.

It can at times be advantageous to use books written by jurists from outside the legal system they are writing about, although this is an exception. For a German jurist studying English law, an introductory book or article about English law written by a German comparatist can be an excellent means of assistance, as it may be especially adapted to German readers, with the focus on the similarities and the differences between German and English law and their legal terminology.

---

5   See e.g. Constantinesco, *Rechtsvergleichung*, vol. 2, pp. 156-159.

6   See e.g. Constantinesco, *Rechtsvergleichung*, vol. 2, pp. 164-172; Reitz, 46 A.J.C.L. 631-633 (1998).

It is an elementary and self-evident requirement that the legal materials being studied must be current. Legal literature in the developed countries has a tendency to become out of date very quickly. Outdated sources lose their value and can even be dangerous: the reader is invited to make the experiment of imagining the picture of his own legal system a foreign colleague would obtain by studying today the course literature that was used at the law schools in, say, 2000. On the other hand, books and legal periodicals are expensive and financial and space constraints make it often impossible, even for law libraries, to procure the latest editions of foreign standard works and subscribe to all leading legal journals and collections of statutes and case law, especially regarding other than the most important legal systems. These days it is often possible to obtain much valuable and current information electronically by means of various computer databases, but not everything on the Internet can be trusted.

Much depends naturally upon what one is interested in. Certain fundamental features of a legal system change very infrequently. This applies for instance to the hierarchy of the sources of law and how they are used. A foreign jurist who wishes to know the methods of interpreting judicial precedents in English law can perhaps rely on the assumption that these methods have not changed dramatically in the last few years. Of course even such fundamental principles can and do change over time. They may even change abruptly and even very recent books may lose their value when a country has undergone a drastic change in the society, such as has occurred with the fall of the communist regimes in Eastern Europe. In the majority of situations where there is a sudden change in the regime, including situations where the change is accomplished by force, almost the entire legal system remains substantially unchanged, especially if there has not been a deeper change in the society. The once frequent military coups in Latin America are a good example of this.

The requirement of up-to-date sources can be relaxed somewhat when foreign law is being studied merely as an exercise just for obtaining the experience of studying foreign law, for instance when a student writes a paper within the framework of a university course on comparative law. Since the availability of current foreign legal sources in the law libraries is often limited, the student may be allowed to get by without the latest legal books, decisions or legislative changes, provided it is the purpose of the paper to train the student rather than to investigate and present the most recent developments of the law in the foreign country in question.

3.3 Interpretation and Use of Foreign Sources of Law

Foreign legislation, judicial decisions, legislative preparatory materials (*travaux préparatoires*), legal writings and other sources of law must be used in precisely the same manner as they are used in the country where they originate from, if one desires to obtain an accurate picture of the foreign legal system. It is a fundamental principle that when studying foreign law one must respect the system and the hierarchy of sources that exist in the foreign country in question.[7] It often occurs, however, that one unconsciously violates this self-evident principle. It is, for instance, common that Anglo-American jurists, when studying Continental European law, approach even clear and unambiguous statutory text with suspicion if its interpretation has not become settled and confirmed by higher courts, while Continental jurists when studying an Anglo-American legal system tend to place too much emphasis on the statutes.[8] An English jurist might, when studying Swedish law, risk underrating the significance of legislative preparatory materials, just as a Swedish student of English law might risk making a mistake in the opposite direction.[9]

This problem is further complicated by the fact that it is difficult to obtain accurate knowledge about the importance of the various sources of law in the daily practice of law without observing, over a substantial period of time, how they function in reality. The role of precedents or of legislative preparatory materials in a particular legal system is usually not so simple that one can explain it in a few sentences, without constantly using reservations such as "most likely", "as a rule", "usually", etc. The foreign jurist consequently receives no clear instructions and it may easily happen that he in his uncertainty becomes inclined to rely more on the types of sources of law that he is accustomed to working with in his own country.

No less dangerous is, however, to attempt to avoid this risk by means of exaggerating to the opposite extreme, for instance if a Continental jurist would believe that when studying Anglo-American law he should rely exclusively on precedents, or if an English jurist would think that in the Continental legal systems one only needs to be concerned with the text of the statutes without the need to consider judicial decisions. The truth is that both on the European Continent and in the Anglo-American legal systems statutory texts as well as judicial decisions are taken into consideration, even if the weight accorded to them varies.[10] In both systems one can arrive at very similar conclusions even if one starts out from different points of view; it has for instance been said that a Continental jurist pays attention to precedents because the legislation allows it, while a common law jurist pays attention to statutes because the courts do the same.[11]

An important thing to keep in mind is that the real importance of the various sources of law is by no means always officially recognized in the country's

---

[7] See Constantinesco, *Rechtsvergleichung*, vol. 2, pp. 179-188 and 203-205; David, *Traité*, pp. 9-12; Göranson, *Festskrift Agell*, pp. 203-204; Lando, *TfR* 1998, pp. 398-401; Zweigert, *Mélanges Maury*, vol. 1, p. 587.

[8] See Ehrenzweig, *Mélanges Malmström*, pp. 77-78.

[9] Cf. Gutteridge, *Comparative Law*, p. 116.

[10] On prejudices concerning differences between common law and Continental European law, see Mayda, *Rev.int.dr.comp.* 1970, pp. 72-74; Sweeney, *Rev.int.dr.comp.* 1960, pp. 685-700; Zweigert & Kötz, *Introduction*, pp. 256-275.

[11] See Ehrenzweig, *Mélanges Malmström*, p. 76.

judicial decisions and described in the country's legal literature. The case law and legal writing in Latin America is often extremely theoretical and entirely neglects to refer to and discuss previous cases. A European jurist visiting his Latin American colleagues has therefore frequently become astonished when he observed that the practising lawyers and judges regularly consult their comprehensive collections of judicial decisions.[12]

Foreign sources of law should be interpreted as they are interpreted in the country where they originate. If one desires accurately to understand the meaning of a foreign statute or of a foreign judicial decision, one cannot interpret them in the same manner as if they had originated in one's own legal system.[13] Anglo-American courts, for instance, tend to interpret legislative rules restrictively in accordance with the exact literal meaning of the words, while Continental judges are normally inclined to interpret the wording more flexibly, taking into consideration the purposes of the statute. This has influenced the wording of statutes in e.g. England and the USA. Where a Continental European legislature would be satisfied to say that the act concerns "banks", the text of an Anglo-American statute might prefer to speak of "a bank, banking corporation or other organization or association for banking purposes"; nor would it be satisfied to refer to "foreign laws" without more comprehensibly stating, for instance, "all acts, decrees, regulations and orders promulgated or enforced by a dominant authority asserting governmental, military or police power", etc.[14]

Even among countries which in theory accord a certain source of law approximately the same value, there may be substantial differences. For example, even if the role of precedents in general terms is the same in two countries, they may have different approaches concerning the weight of *obiter dicta* or the importance of concurring or dissenting opinions.

Not even when interpreting a foreign legal rule resulting from international legislative cooperation, or taken over from another country, one can be certain that it is interpreted in the same manner in all of the countries concerned. For example, the Belgian Civil Code originates from the French Civil Code and the rules are, to a great extent, still identical in both countries. However, if one seeks to learn the provisions of Belgian law one cannot mechanically rely upon French authors and French judicial practice; one must rather determine, independently, the interpretation that is prevailing in Belgium itself.

3.4 The Foreign Legal System Must be Studied in its Entirety

Often when studying foreign law one is interested only in a specific issue, for example the financial support the government provides to families with children or the statute of limitation for monetary claims. It occurs

---

[12] See David & Brierley, *Major Legal Systems*, p. 149.

[13] See e.g. Constantinesco, *Rechtsvergleichung*, vol. 2, pp. 216-220.

[14] See sec. 204-a(3) (a) in New York Banking Law, as quoted in 61 *A.J.I.L.* 611 (1967).

that an inexperienced student of foreign law, and even at times an experienced comparatist, obtains the impression that the foreign legal system completely lacks rules on the issue under scrutiny. But this can be due to – and in the majority of cases most probably is due to – that one has looked in "the wrong place" within the foreign legal system, most often because one only has looked in the place where the same issue is dealt with within one's own legal system.[15] This is a dangerous mistake.

To begin with, it may be that the foreign legal system's systematic divisions differ to a significant degree from those which one is accustomed to in one's own legal system. Thus Soviet law, and not so long ago also English law to a certain extent, lacked the – for a Continental jurist fundamental – division of the law into public and private. On the other hand, the Continental legal systems lack the division within English law into "common law" and "equity" (see section 9.3 below). But even those divisions, which on their face are the same, can be defined in various ways in various countries. If one wishes, in an Anglo-American legal system, to find the rules concerning the statute of limitations for monetary claims, one must, surprisingly for a Continental European jurist, normally look into books and collections of judgments concerning procedural law.

Another fact that must not be disregarded is that a foreign lawmaker, even in a country with similar divisions in the legal system as in one's own, may have chosen another method to attain the same or similar objective, and that this perhaps means that the relevant legal rules are found in another part of the legal system. A Swedish jurist interested in the legal regulation in a foreign country on the public financial support to families with many children should not limit his research to welfare-law instruments such as those used in Sweden (child and housing allowances), since a substantial share of the public support in the foreign country is perhaps not paid out in the form of welfare subsidies but rather via the tax law in the form of a tax reduction (a form of support not used in Sweden). In a similar manner, the right of the surviving spouse to share in the division of the property of the deceased spouse is in certain countries primarily based on inheritance law, while in other legal systems the same matter is regulated by matrimonial law. A student of foreign law consequently cannot assume that a particular problem in other legal systems is regulated within the same part of the legal system as in his own law.[16]

The significance of the above is that one must have a look at the foreign legal system in its entirety even when one is only interested in a specific issue. It is not sufficient to investigate only the particular legal field which according to its designation corresponds to the relevant field in one's own legal system. In addi-

---

[15] See Strömholm, *SvJT* 1971, pp. 261-262; Zweigert, 7 *Israel L.R.* 467 (1972), in *Mélanges Maury*, vol. 1, p. 589 and in Rotondi, ed., *Inchieste*, p. 739; Zweigert & Kötz, *Introduction*, p. 35.

[16] See Constantinesco, *Rechtsvergleichung*, vol. 2, pp. 240-247; David, *Traité*, pp. 12-15; Schwarz-Liebermann von Wahlendorf, *Droit*, p. 187. Strömholm, *SvJT* 1971, pp. 261-262 speaks in this connection about "the problem of congruence".

tion, the small part of the foreign legal system being studied is equally influenced by those principles which influence the foreign legal system as a whole,
for instance the hierarchy of the sources of law and the principles of interpretation.[17] This confirms that one should not "clip out" a detail from the foreign law
and study only that, without keeping in mind its interaction with the remaining
parts of the legal system. A different matter is that time and other restraints
make this ambition often difficult or even impossible to fulfill.

3.5 Translation Problems

A jurist involved in the study of foreign law in a foreign
language will at times need the assistance of a dictionary. Ordinary bilingual
dictionaries attempt to translate each word by looking for the directly corresponding word in another language. Many foreign legal terms and phrases, however, lack in fact a directly corresponding translation. For example the English
legal term "trust" has no counterpart in most Continental European languages.
Furthermore, even when there ostensibly is a direct translation, one should not
assume that the meanings are exactly the same.

Legal terms often have the disadvantage that they also exist in everyday
language and frequently with a somewhat different – often less precise – meaning than they have in the legal context. For example, the word "attempt" in
ordinary English usage does not mean exactly the same as it does in English
criminal law. Nor does the word "attempt" in English criminal law necessarily
mean the same as the literal translation of "attempt" in another legal system.

One may question if it is at all possible to translate with just one word even
relatively common legal terms, such as "marriage". For example, marriage in
English law has legal effects which in some respects differ from the legal effects
of marriage in accordance with French law, the conditions for entering into and
dissolving differ, etc.[18] The English "marriage" and the French *mariage* can
be said to mean the same as long as they refer to marriage more as a sociological, biological and/or religious institution than as a legal one. To arrive at an
internationally accepted *legal* definition of marriage is however much more difficult. Defining marriage as a "relationship between one man and one woman,
established in a prescribed manner, to which the law accords particular legal
effects varying between different legal systems" is so vague and general that
the meaning of the definition is quite insipid. It can also rightly be accused of
being too narrow, as it excludes polygamous and same-sex marriages existing in

---

[17] See Constantinesco, *Rechtsvergleichung*, vol. 2, pp. 247-249.

[18] See Kisch in Rotondi, ed., *Inchieste*, p. 411. On legal translation problems in general see de Cruz,
Comparative Law, pp. 220-222; de Groot in Smits, ed., *Elgar Encyclopedia*, pp. 423-433; Jamieson, 44
A.J.C.L. 121-129 (1996); Grossfeld, *Kernfragen*, pp. 118-122; Kjær, *Retfærd* 1998, no. 83, pp. 4-14 and in
Van Hoecke, ed., *Epistemology*, pp. 377-398; Legrand, *Rev.int.dr.comp.* 1996, pp. 310-313; Pfersmann, *Rev.
int.dr.comp.* 2001, pp. 283-286; Sacco, *ZEuP* 2002, pp. 734-735; Vogel, *Juridiska översättningar*.

many countries; on the other hand it is too broad as it also includes heterosexual registered partnerships (existing in e.g. Dutch law) and legally recognized *de facto* cohabitation.

Translation problems can occur even concerning typical legal terms which are not even used in non-legal contexts. An American notary public is, for example, not at all the same figure as a Swedish *notarius publicus* or a German *Notar*.[19] Or similarly, the French *"détention préventive"* does not have the same meaning as preventive detention in England.[20] It occurs that legal terms have different meaning even in countries which have the same official (legal) language. The concept of *"Auftrag"* (roughly translated into English as commission or mandate) in Swiss law does not mean the same as *"Auftrag"* in German law. The Swiss concept includes both remunerated and unremunerated commissions, while the German concept is much narrower and includes only the latter type. Remunerated commissions are denoted in German law in another manner, usually as *"Dienstvertrag"* or *"Werkvertrag"*.[21]

Attempts to create a special borderless comparative legal terminology remain utopian.[22] The best advice one can give the student of foreign law is to make use of specialist bilingual dictionaries for legal terms[23] or law dictionaries where legal terms and concepts are explained in their own language, provided of course that such dictionaries are available. The last-mentioned dictionaries are particularly valuable, as they make it easier to understand the meaning behind the foreign legal terminology, assuming of course that one has sufficient knowledge of the language.

The problems with translation are especially troublesome when one is elaborating a multi-language legal text, for example an instrument of EU law or an international treaty with authentic versions in several different languages.[24]

3.6   Obsolete and Living Law

When one studies foreign law it is of the greatest importance to determine which rules of conduct in the foreign country have the status of a legal rule.[25] The answer naturally depends on how one defines "valid law" and it is therefore important that the comparative jurist begins with defining this for himself. It may often be the case that the definition in the comparatist's own country differs somewhat from the definition used in the foreign country whose law is being studied. For instance, the borderline between moral rules and legal

---

[19]   See e.g. Kahn-Freund, 82 *L.Q.R.* 52-53 (1966); Schlesinger, *Comparative Law*, pp. 622-623.

[20]   See Backe, *TSA* 1968, p. 386.

[21]   See Bogdan, *Travel Agency*, pp. 40-42.

[22]   See Gerber, 46 *A.J.C.L.* 719-737 (1998).

[23]   See Backe, *TSA* 1976, pp. 189-191 and in 1977, pp. 311-312.

[24]   See Gutteridge, *Comparative Law*, pp. 121-122.

[25]   See e.g. Constantinesco, *ZvglRW* 1981, pp. 177-198; Husa, *FJFT* 1997, pp. 412-421.

rules in certain foreign legal cultures can be more vague or be different from what one is accustomed to.

Previously (see section 1.3 above) I have defined legal rules as those norms for human conduct that are maintained by the authority and power of the state. If one accepts this definition, the question arises whether formal declarations of the citizen's political and civil rights in the constitutions of some countries belong at all to these countries' legal systems, since there is no possibility to have them enforced. In some countries, the courts and other authorities do not have the right to invalidate or refuse to apply laws and regulations that are in violation of the formally valid constitution, and the legislation passes laws without any real control of their constitutionality. In the best case, it can be said that in such countries the constitutional provisions constitute a political declaration of intentions but do not fulfil the criteria according to this book's definition of valid law. On the other hand, in some one-party states the ruling political party issues instructions and decrees that are followed by i.a. courts and the police; in spite of the fact that the party is on paper separate from the state, its rules are in reality part of the law there.

In most legal systems it will occur that certain legal rules become obsolete, i.e. despite that they may formally continue to be valid they are no longer applied in practice. At a certain point such legal rules may simply cease to be a part of the "living" legal system. This may be confusing for foreign jurists. For example, a jurist from a country where "life imprisonment" really means imprisonment for the rest of the natural life of the criminal may become somewhat preplexed when he reads that an alien found guilty by a Swedish court has been sentenced to "life imprisonment and to be deported after the sentence has been served". It is often difficult to discover that a rule in a foreign legal system has become obsolete. The fact that a statutory rule is no longer applied in practice is of course not apparent in the text of the statute itself. The lack of recent published judgments applying the rule may be due to other reasons than that it has become obsolete and lost its significance. Because of various reasons, authors in the foreign country may have chosen to refrain from pointing out certain rules as obsolete. For instance, legal scholars living in a totalitarian country seldom dare to explicitly describe how formally applicable guarantees of the rule of law are disregarded by the government.[26]

As the above-mentioned example regarding Swedish life imprisonment shows, when investigating if certain formally valid statutory rules are still living law one should not limit oneself to judicial decisions. It can for instance be that the foreign statute provides for capital punishment (death penalty) for certain crimes, and that the country's courts in practice also issue such verdicts, but that subsequently the sentence is always commuted by the head of state to life imprisonment. The question then arises whether the commuting of the punishment occurs after considering the circumstances in each individual case or because the head of state regards himself compelled to pardon the person

---

[26] Cf. Lando, *Mélanges Tallon*, pp. 143-144; Zweigert, *Mélanges Maury*, vol. 1, p. 588, note 25.

sentenced to death on the basis of an unwritten customary legal rule, which has transformed the death penalty into an obsolete institution.

It is important when studying foreign law to keep in mind the various rules of conduct that have been developed *praeter legem* but function as legal rules.[27] Included here is also the practice of the police and the prosecutors: it can for instance be imagined that a statute requires even private babysitters to declare and pay tax on their income, but in practice that almost never occurs, perhaps due to the fact that is is generally known that according to an unwritten rule this statute is never enforced.

3.7   Social Context and Purpose of the Legal Rules

The legal system is a social phenomenon and expresses only one aspect of the society. It therefore cannot be seen isolated from the same society's other aspects. To be able to understand the legal rules of a foreign country, one should, as far as possible, attempt to understand their "non-legal" (such as the economic, political, ethical, religious and cultural) environment and their social purpose.[28] Only in this way is it possible to understand what role the legal rule in question really has in the society and how it functions in reality. The same problem is well-known among legal historians, since one can hardly correctly understand, for example, the law of the fifteenth century without knowing the economic and political system, and the cultural, religious and ethical values, of that time. Naturally one must distinguish between legal rules whose background and purpose are obvious or easy to understand (for instance traffic rules) and rules whose understanding requires a deeper study of the foreign society.

What has just been said is of special importance when one studies legal rules originating in a different type of society than that which exists in one's own country.[29] One must keep in mind that the same or similar legal rules and legal institutes can play different roles in different societies. The former communist-governed countries of Eastern Europe thus had relatively developed and detailed legislation on, for example, the protection of trademarks, even if this did not fulfil any significant practical purpose as there was no functioning market with competition. They were, however, forced by international conventions, to which they have acceded in order to protect their own trademarks in the world market, to have trademark legislation. Without knowledge of the planned-economy system that existed in these countries, one could easily misunderstand their

---

[27] Cf. Neumeyer in Rotondi, ed., *Inchieste*, pp. 512-515; Reitz, 46 A.J.C.L. 629-630 (1998).

[28] See e.g. Ancel, *Utilité*, p. 93; Blagojević in Rotondi, ed., *Inchieste*, p. 39; Constantinesco, *Rechtsvergleichung*, vol. 2, pp. 201-203 and 252-276; David, *Traité*, pp. 15-25; Glendon, Gordon & Carozza, *Comparative Legal Traditions*, pp. 9-13; Kamba, 23 I.C.L.Q. 513-515 (1974); Müller-Römer, *Recht in Ost und West* 1969, p. 6; Rodière, *Introduction*, pp. 139-141; Savatier, *Problèmes contemporains*, vol. 2, pp. 377-378; Strömholm, *SvJT* 1971, p. 262; Winizky, *Problèmes contemporains*, vol. 2, p. 531.

[29] See e.g. Loeber, *RabelsZ* 1961, p. 218; Szabó, *Act.Jur.Hung.* 1971, pp. 131-141.

trademark legislation's meaning and function. Similar difficulties naturally could also arise in the opposite direction: a jurist from a country with a planned economy, where all industrial and commercial activity was managed in detail by the state, could only with difficulty understand Western competition law without first having obtained a certain basic knowledge on how a market economy works.

But knowledge of economic and social factors beyond the basic social system may too be necessary for the understanding of foreign law. Imagine that a state enacts legislation obligating employers to absorb the costs for language training for newly employed immigrant manpower. It may appear on the surface that this legislation is for the advantage of immigrants, but in reality the intention and the effect of the rule may be to limit immigration by discouraging employers from employing immigrants and thus to reduce the unemployment rate among nationals. A foreign jurist, who is not familiar with the situation in the country (the state of the economy, level of unemployment, immigration policy), can easily gain a wrong picture of the real purpose of the legal rule and its practical effects.

It is also important to know the attitude towards the legal system that prevails among the inhabitants of the foreign country. Thus, Japan, Taiwan and South Korea have taken over a number of important legal rules from for example Germany, but these rules play another role in countries where one traditionally is inclined to resolve disputes by means of mediation and compromise and where it is regarded to be almost shameful to turn to the courts.[30] Important cultural differences in attitudes towards law may exist even among Western countries, for example between the Continental European countries and the countries of common law.[31]

Knowledge concerning the non-legal aspects of the society whose legal system one is studying is of value not only when one wishes to learn how certain legal rules function, but even when one wants to understand how the foreign society manages problems on which legal rules, surprisingly enough, are lacking. It occurred that a foreign labour law specialist became surprised and had some difficulty to comprehend that Sweden does not have any legal rules concerning minimum wages; the understanding of the Swedish situation on that point requires namely knowledge of the high degree of unionization of the Swedish labour force, the strength of the trade unions and the role of collective bargaining agreements. It may also occur that some legal relationships, which in certain countries are the object of detailed regulation by means of legislation, are regulated in other countries by legally recognized customary rules or by standard contract clauses. A task, which in one country is regarded as belonging to national or local government, may in certain other countries be regarded as a private concern and as such not requiring detailed regulation by law. Thus some countries have a national social insurance system regulated in detail by admin-

---

[30] See Noda, *Livre du Centenaire de la Société de législation comparée*, vol. 2, Paris 1971, pp. 161-164.

[31] See e.g. Legrand, 45 *I.C.L.Q.* 52-81 (1996); Kjær, *TfR* 2001, pp. 870-905, with further references.

istrative law, while the same tasks in other countries are taken care of by private insurance companies relying on contracts. Some such contracts may have a special status due to the fact that the state was involved in their formation.[32] This used to be the case in Sweden, where the general contract terms in some consumer contracts were formulated by the organizations of businessmen in cooperation with the Consumer Ombudsman (a state instrumentality protecting the interests of the consumers).

---

[32] See e.g. Kahn-Freund, 82 *L.Q.R.* 87 (1966); Zweigert, 7 *Israel L.R.* 467-468 (1972).

CHAPTER 4

The Comparison

4.1 General Remarks

It has already been pointed out that the mere study of foreign legal systems, no matter how necessary it may be for comparative legal research, by itself falls outside the framework of comparative law. The same applies to parallel presentations of multiple legal systems,[1] even if they normally include certain comparisons, for instance in connection with the translation of legal terms or with the study of whether the parallel texts are in reality concerned with the same matters.

It is the *comparison* that is the essence of comparative law: this means to place comparable elements of two or more legal systems against each other and determine their similarities and differences. Which legal systems and which elements one chooses to compare naturally depends on the purpose of the comparison and on the interests of the comparatist.

The comparison can be bilateral (between two legal systems) or multilateral (between more than two legal systems). It can be a comparison of substantive rules of law or a formal comparison (between the formal characteristics of the legal systems, such as the role of precedents or the manner of interpreting statutes). It can compare laws of societies sharing the same cultural and socio-economic features (intracultural comparison) or societies fundamentally different in these respects (cross-cultural comparison). One can further distinguish between a micro-comparison (between details) and a macro-comparison (between whole legal systems in their entirety or between entire families of legal systems).[2] Of course also in connection with micro-comparison one must compare the details in their proper legal and non-legal setting; it would be less meaningful to compare the naked wording of, for example, two statutory provisions from two different societies without taking account of the differences in their interpretation, factual application, function and effects in their respective countries, as well as their underlying theories and concepts. Some speak in this context about "deep level comparative law".[3]

The value of rule-comparison has been contested by some authors, who consider comparisons based on substantive rules of law to be trivial, of no real significance and a waste of "intellectual horsepower".[4] Thus, the American comparatist John H. Merryman maintains that law cannot be reduced to a system of rules and that the factors that deserve to be studied and compared, if one wants to engage in serious scholarship in comparative law, are rather legal extension (the area of social activity to which the legal system attempts

---

[1] Cf. Zweigert & Kötz, *Introduction*, p. 43, who point out that merely to juxtapose without comment the law of the various jurisdictions is not comparative law: it is just a preliminary step.

[2] See e.g. Lando, *Kort indføring*, pp. 187-188; Rheinstein, *Einführung*, pp. 31-36; Sacco interviewed by Legrand in *Rev.int.dr.comp.* 1995, p. 953; Vicente, *Direito*, pp. 21-22.

[3] See Van Hoecke in Van Hoecke, ed., *Epistemology*, pp. 165-195.

[4] See e.g. Merryman, interviewed by Legrand in 47 *A.J.C.L.* 4, 46 and 63-64 (1999). Cf. also Van Hoecke & Warrington, 47 *I.C.L.Q.* 495 (1998).

or purports to apply), legal penetration (the impact of the legal system on the lives of significant segments of the population), legal culture (the inner logic of the legal system), legal institutions (courts, legislatures, law schools, etc.), legal actors (attorneys, judges, scholars, litigants, etc.), legal processes (judicial and administrative proceedings, legislation, legal education, etc.), secondary rules (rules of jurisdiction and procedure, rules governing the creation of substantive rules, etc.), and legal expense (costs to operate the legal system).[5] Merryman suggests that these categories together describe the whole legal system. In his own words, substantive rules of law "are prominently absent from this list of legal system components"[6].

In fact however, most comparative legal research is rules-oriented and it is a relatively very small group of legal scientists who prefer solely to focus on and compare the general legal and social features of different legal systems or even entire groups of legal systems. There is, of course, nothing wrong with such macro-comparisons, provided they are done well. Both macro-comparisons and rule-oriented comparisons (which often deserve the name micro-comparisons, because they usually focus on a relatively limited legal problem) can be scholarly or trivial depending on their quality, but to generally declare the former to be scientific and the latter to be trivial is nonsensical.[7] The evaluation of the answers provided by each of the two types of comparison must be done in relation to the questions asked at the outset. It seems that rule-comparison is treated with contempt by some macro-comparativists because it does not provide an answer to *their* questions, while they fail to grasp and understand the immense value the same rule-comparison may have for other comparativists who are interested in comparing how two or more legal systems deal with a certain particular problem of substantive law. As pointed out above, rule-comparison does not of course mean mechanically comparing the wording of statutes, but rather comparing the *real* rules, which presupposes the taking into account of most of the factors on Merryman's list.

4.2 The Problem of Comparability

For a comparison to be meaningful, the two objects of the comparison (*comparatum* and *comparandum*) must share some common type of characteristics, which can serve as the common denominator. This common feature, called *tertium comparationis*, is required not only for comparisons of law, but for any comparison in general. A bag of potatoes and a package tour to Paris can, for instance, be compared in terms of price, as both are sold for money. It

---

[5] See e.g. Merryman, interviewed by Legrand in 47 *A.J.C.L.* 63 (1999). A similar list of factors, called "basic elements of a legal culture", is suggested by van Hoecke & Warrington, 47 *I.C.L.Q.* 513-516 (1998).

[6] See Merryman, interviewed by Legrand in 47 *A.J.C.L.* 64 (1999).

[7] See Bogdan, *Festschrift für Erik Jayme*, pp. 1233-1242.

would, on the other hand, be less meaningful to compare them in terms of taste, as the package tour does not have such a feature.

Suppose that one wishes to compare the text of a German statutory provision on marriage with the text of a Swedish statute on the registration of title to real property. The two statutes are fully comparable as far as certain common characteristics are concerned, for instance if one is interested in comparing how the texts of statutes are divided into chapters, sections and subsections in Germany and Sweden. On the other hand, it would hardly be meaningful to compare the substantive contents of the two rules, apart from the simple observation that they concern entirely different matters (such an observation may however be of value in and of itself, in particular when the difference is not manifest).

Within comparative law, one is normally interested in comparing the substantive contents of the legal rules, or more specifically, how the various legal systems regulate a certain situation or problem that arises in both (or all) of the countries involved. Such a comparison requires that the legal rules being compared in fact deal with the same matter. When comparing legal rules from different countries one should consequently strive to compare such rules that regulate the same situations in people's lives.[8] Whether two legal rules, which at first view appear to be comparable, in fact deal with the same problem will often not be apparent until one has begun the comparison. Consequently, one frequently begins with a working hypothesis that they are comparable. The conclusion in itself that the legal rules being compared do or do not concern the same thing will at times require extensive comparative work. To compare rules and institutions bearing the same name (a nominalistic comparison) or occupying the same place in the structure of the two legal systems (a structural comparison[9]) can thus sometimes be useful as a first step for the purpose of determining whether they deal with the same problem and are comparable as to their contents.

It is obvious that the use of an identical or similar term in the legal terminology of the two countries does not guarantee comparability. On the other hand, the legal rules may be comparable even when the differences between the legal terminologies are so great that one purely linguistically has difficulties to recognize the common problem.

A nominalistic comparison, for instance between the meaning of the legal concept of "murder" in an English-speaking country and the legal concept "*le meurtre*" in a French-speaking country can be of terminological value, for exam-

---

[8]   This does not apply to the comparison of legal rules within one and the same legal system, where it often suffices that the compared legal rules refer to problems which in one way or another have analogous characteristics. It may, for example, at times be of value to compare within a single legal system the obligation of parents to support their children with the obligation of children to support their parents. It would be, however, without much meaning to compare the rules in country A on the parents' obligations to support their children with the rules in country B on the children's obligations to support their parents.

[9]   See e.g. Suksi, *FJFT* 1993, p. 266.

ple for elaboration of an English-French and French-English legal dictionary. Such comparison does not, however, necessarily concern the legal rules regarding the same situation or problem. The legal concept "murder" in an English-speaking country certainly covers approximately the same types of acts as the French legal term "*le meurtre*", but significant differences are fully conceivable. The French concept may for instance encompass even some acts that in the law of the English-speaking country involved would qualify as "manslaughter" rather than "murder". If so, then the rules on "murder" and the rules on "*le meurtre*" are only partly comparable with each other, presuming that one is interested in comparing the substantive contents of the rules and not their terminology. Drawing the line between murder and manslaughter can of course be different even between two legal systems using the same language, so that, for example, the rule on murder in one English-speaking country may partly deal with other situations than the rule on murder in another such country.

If one wishes to ascertain the real similarities and differences between the substantive contents of two (or more) legal systems, one must consequently not pay much attention to the names and labels of the legal rules, but should instead consider the real or potential conflict situations that the rules being studied are intended to regulate. The compared legal rules and institutions must be comparable functionally, i.e. they must be intended to deal with the same problem. The theory emanating from the realization of this rather elementary fact, often called "functionalism",[10] defines the common problem as the comparison's *tertium comparationis*.[11] To a certain extent, this necessitates a case-to-case

---

[10] Various authors do, however, understand functionalism in various ways. See e.g. de Cruz, *Comparative Law*, pp. 236-238; Husa, *RabelsZ* 2003, pp. 419-447, in *Rev.int.dr.comp.* 2006, pp. 1099-1105 and in *Maastricht Journal of European and Comparative Law* 2011, pp. 548-553; Jaluzot, *Rev.int.dr.comp.* 2005, pp. 39-43; de Joninck, *RabelsZ* 2010, pp. 251-317; Kaufmann, *E.J.C.L.*, vol. 12.1 (May 2008), pp. 7-8; Michaels in Reimann & Zimmermann, eds, *The Oxford Handbook*, pp. 339-382; Örücü in Örücü & Nelken, eds, *Comparative Law*, pp. 50-53; Peters & Schwenke, 49 *I.C.L.Q.*808-810 (2000); Smits, *Maastricht Journal of European and Comparative Law* 2011, pp. 554-558; Vicente, *Direito*, pp. 43-45; Zweigert & Kötz, *Introduction*, p. 34.

[11] See e.g. Ancel, *Utilité*, pp. 101-102 and in *Mélanges Malmström*, pp. 8-9; Banakas, *Revue hellénique de droit international* 1980, pp. 156-163; Constantinesco, *Rechtsvergleichung*, vol. 2, pp. 68-91; David, *Livre du Centenaire de la Société de législation comparée*, vol. 2, Paris 1971, p. 152; Engström & Wesslau, *Anteckningar*, p. 10; Erbe, *RabelsZ* 1942, p. 196; Glendon, Gordon & Carozza, *Comparative Legal Traditions*, pp. 11-12; Kamba, 23 *I.C.L.Q.* 517 (1974); Knapp, *Rev.roumaine* 1968, pp. 76-78 and in *Velké právní systémy*, pp. 38-39; Kokkini-Iatridou, *NILR* 1986, pp. 157-178; Kramer, *RabelsZ* 1969, pp. 1-16; Lando, *Kort indføring*, pp. 200-202; Michaels in Reimann & Zimmermann, eds, *The Oxford Handbook*, pp. 367-369; Mincke, *ZvglRW* 1984, pp. 323-324; Müller-Römer, *Recht in Ost und West* 1969, pp. 5-6; Örücü in Smits, ed., *Elgar Encyclopedia*, pp. 442-445 and i Örücü & Nelken, eds, *Comparative Law*, p. 48; Reitz, 46 *A.J.C.L.* 620-623 (1998); Samuel in Van Hoecke, ed., *Epistemology*, pp. 38-43; Sandrock, *Sinn und Methode*, pp. 67-68; Schmitthoff, 7 *Cambridge L.J.* 98 (1941); Schwarz-Liebermann von Wahlendorf, *Droit*, p. 206; Siesby, *TfR* 1967, pp. 501-502; Strömholm, *SvJT* 1973, p. 812; Zweigert, 7 *Israel L.R.* 466-467

approach to the comparison.[12] One does not compare general or abstract notions and terms but rather how the compared legal systems regulate the same factual situations in real life, i.e. the same "segments of life". Certain comparativists speak in this connection of "the factual approach".[13]

For two legal rules to be comparable, it is not necessary that they also are intended to achieve the same goals. Consequently abortion legislation in two countries can be compared even when the purpose of the legislation in one country is to limit the population growth and in the other country to promote it. Knowledge of the different purposes of the legal rules being compared is unquestionably important for the understanding of the differences discovered by the comparison. The different purposes of the rules must also be taken into consideration at the comparative evaluations of the solutions used (see Chapters 5 and 6 below).

The very essence of comparability came in the 1990s under attack by some "post-modern" jurists, who claimed that objective and scientific comparative legal research is impossible, attempts to achieve it are naïve and doomed to be futile, and all comparisons are inescapably biased.[14] The central argument of this school, which seems to be an outgrowth of the leftist "critical legal studies" movement that enjoyed considerable influence at certain universities in the USA some years ago[15] but whose appeal now appears to be declining, seems to be that there can be no objectively and neutrally formulated problems that can be used as *tertium comparationis*, as whatever turns a factual situation into a legal problem already contains a value judgment inescapably rooted in the national legal system and thereby in the ethnocentric political (usually Western) ideology of the comparatist, thus legitimizing and fostering Western hegemony and domination. This argument, if taken literally, denies the possibility not only of comparative law research but of any scientific legal research altogether. It is also noteworthy that the proponents of this criticism against mainstream comparative law research have an agenda aimed at deconstructive disruption[16] rather

---

(1972), in *Mélanges Maury*, vol. I, pp. 589-590, in *Festschrift Schmitthoff*, pp. 405-406 and in Rotondi, ed., *Inchieste*, p. 739; Zweigert & Puttfarken, *Act.Jur.Hung.* 1973, pp. 111-112.

[12] See Lando, *Kort indføring*, pp. 203-204.

[13] See e.g. Neumayer i Rotondi, ed., *Inchieste*, pp. 518-521; Schlesinger & Bonassies, *Rev.int.dr.comp.* 1963, pp. 510-511.

[14] See, in particular, Frankenberg, 26 *Harvard International L.J.* 412-455 (1985) and the papers presented at a symposium held in 1996 at the Utah Law School and published in (1997) *Utah L.R.* 255 *et seq.*; de Coninck, *RabelsZ* 2010, pp. 318-350. For a well-balanced criticism of the exaggerations and absurdities of such generalizations, see Peters & Schwenke, 49 *I.C.L.Q.* 800-834 (2000). Cf. also e.g. Demleitner, 46 *A.J.C.L.* 647-655 (1998); Husa, *RabelsZ* 2003, pp. 434-439; Michaels, *RabelsZ* 2010, pp. 351-359; Palmer, 53 *A.J.C.L.* 264-265 (2005); Platsas, *E.J.C.L.*, vol. 12.3 (December 2008); Ponthoreau, *Rev.int. dr.comp.* 2005, pp. 23-26; Reimann, 50 *A.J.C.L.* 681-683 (2002).

[15] See Mattei in Reimann & Zimmermann, eds, *The Oxford Handbook*, pp. 815-836.

[16] See Bucher, *RabelsZ* 2010, p. 275; Mattei in Reimann & Zimmermann, eds, *The Oxford Handbook*, p. 819.

than at offering constructive alternatives[17]. Of course, the comparatist, being human, is not always immune against the influence of his values and beliefs, but this should not make him give up his research and hinder him from doing his best to overcome his preconceptions. Besides, it is not necessarily desirable that the comparatist be neutral in the sense that he places himself outside all the legal systems he compares. For example, there is nothing wrong with a research project focusing on a problem in the comparatist's own legal system and investigating whether corresponding problems arise in other countries and, if so, how they are dealt with there.

4.3 Comparability of Laws of Countries with Different Social Systems

The question of the comparability of legal rules in countries with different social systems (what is meant here with social system is first and foremost the basic socio-economic order of the society, such as a planned economy or market economy) has been much discussed, primarily with regard to the comparability between the socialist law of communist-governed countries and Western (capitalist or bourgeois) law. Due to the collapse of the economic and political system of the communist regimes and their replacement with a market-oriented economy, the issue of that particular comparability has lost most of its immediate relevancy. However, similar questions may reoccur in the future and they may also come up in connection with the comparison between Western law and the law in certain developing countries with a predominantly feudal society. The discussion on the comparability between Western law and socialist law is, in addition, rich in tradition and of such a great general comparative interest that it warrants a few pages in this book.

Certain legal authors in the then socialist countries regarded socialist law to be so different from the law in the Western countries that they were of the opinion that any comparison between the two was impossible or meaningless.[18] They argued that socialist law was a law of a totally new, "higher" quality and with an entirely new, revolutionary class character,[19] and that it was based upon

---

[17] An attempt to provide an alternative to *tertium comparationis*, namely "empirically substantiated behavioral patterns", was made by de Coninck, *RabelsZ* 2010, pp. 344-349, but her suggestions can be said to suffer from the same weaknesses as the functionalism she criticizes, see Michaels, *RabelsZ* 2010, pp. 351-359.

[18] See e.g. Szabó, *Ann.Univ.Budapest.* 1964, pp. 114-115; Tchkhikvadze & Zivs, *Livre du Centenaire de la Société de législation comparée*, vol. 2, p. 596; Zivs, *Act.Jur.Hung.* 1971, p. 177. See also Bobek in Bobek *et al.*, *Komunistické právo*, pp. 405-416 ; Hazard, 79 *Harvard L.R.* 279 (1965-1966), in *Livre du Centenaire de la Société de législation comparée*, vol. 2, Paris 1971, p. 172, and in *Rev.dr.int.dr.comp.* 1979, pp. 292-308. Some Western comparatists have also expressed doubts about the comparability of socialist and Western law, see e.g. Moss, *TfR* 1997, pp. 777-778; Zweigert, *Mélanges Maury*, vol. 1, pp. 585-586.

[19] See e.g. Blągojevič, *Rev.roumaine* 1968, pp. 19-35.

an entirely new economic system and served entirely different class interests than the bourgeois legal systems.[20] It has even been asserted that socialist law was the direct opposite to bourgeois law: *"le type socialiste du droit est la négation et le contraire du type bourgeois"*.[21]

It is very possible that socialist law served other class interests than the Western legal systems. However, one must not confuse the legal norm's legal/political goal (for example to contribute, in one manner or another, to the development of society in a socialist direction) with its function, i.e. the actual problem or situation that the legal norm regulates. It is only the identity as far as the function is concerned that is necessary for considering two legal rules as mutually comparable. If and to the extent the same situations and problems arose and were subject to legal regulation in both the Western countries and the socialist states, one could compare that regulation to discover to what extent it diverged. To take a very simple example, it is hardly possible to deny that traffic regulations served the same function in both societies, and that these therefore to a significant degree could be compared with each other.[22] One does not, however, need to rely upon such an elementary example, as many important segments of life in the socialist countries, at least in Eastern Europe, were not significantly different from the life in the Western countries. This included many such situations which in both societies were subject to legal regulation.[23]

No socialist country has, for example, entirely done away with the use of money as a means of exchange for goods and services. In other words, instead of a direct distribution to citizens of goods and services, the distribution was made with the assistance of money, in a kind of a market.[24] In connection with this, there arose a number of problems which were similar in both the socialist and Western countries, for instance the matter of the seller's responsibility for the quality of product sold to a consumer. Furthermore, even a legal concept so loaded with subjective values as the right of ownership had to a certain extent the same function in both socialist and Western law and consequently was also comparable to the same extent.

In connection with the comparison between legal systems in countries with different social orders there are consequently grounds to distinguish between the legal rules regulating situations that are specific for a particular type of society and the legal rules that regulate situations existing in both types of

---

[20] See e.g. Ionasco, *Rev.roumaine* 1974, p. 49; Knapp, *RabelsZ* 1962-1963, p. 500; Szabó, *Ann.Univ.Budapest.* 1964, p. 115. Cf. Bobek in Bobek *et al.*, *Komunistické právo*, pp. 409-410 ; Constantinesco, *Rev.int. dr.comp.* 1973, pp. 9-12. Cf. also Eörsi, *Comparative Civil Law*, pp. 298-301.

[21] See Szabó, *Ann.Univ.Budapest.* 1964, p. 114.

[22] This was not undisputed though. The Czechoslovak author Luby wrote in the Czechoslovak legal periodical *Právny obzor* 1970, pp. 16-17, that the legal system was a totality and that there were no legal rules which were neutral from a class point of view, not even traffic regulations. Therefore, according to Luby, the socialist and the bourgeois traffic regulations were "in opposition to each other".

[23] See e.g. Friedmann, *Law in a Changing Society*, pp. 23-24.

[24] See e.g. Eörsi in Rotondi, ed., *Inchieste*, pp. 199-203; Markovits, 78 *Yale L.J.* 7-8 (1968-1969); Zweigert & Puttfarken, *Act.Jur.Hung.* 1973, p. 122.

societies.[25] The latter category includes i.a. the majority of the rules pertaining to family law.[26] On the other hand, antitrust laws are limited to countries with a market-oriented economic system, in the same manner as detailed planning regulations are specific to countries with a planned economy. In these cases the comparison is impossible, beyond the observation that the rules lack comparable counterparts in countries with a different economic system. Nevertheless, even such economic legislation may be comparable on a higher level of abstraction, where the comparative task is not to compare legislation on competition or central planning but rather legislation on state interference into the economy (such interference exists in both planned and market economies, albeit through different legal instruments).[27] On such a higher level of abstraction, comparisons are not only possible but even very interesting. They show, for instance, that the socialist legal systems used prohibitions and commands to a considerably larger extent than Western legal systems, which ordinarily prefer to rely on various economic stimulants (taxes, fees, customs duties, interest rates, subsidies, etc.).

It can thus be concluded that legal rules and institutions in practically all countries are mutually comparable, at least in part and to the extent they have to deal with the same or similar problems.[28] The basic features of human and societal behaviour result in some – even though not all – problems being universal.[29]

It deserves, however, to be stressed that comparability does not mean likeness, as the two qualities are often confused even by experienced comparatists. Comparability, as the term is used here, means merely that the compared elements share a feature or property in relation to which they can be compared; it does not imply or predict anything about the degree of similarity the comparative research will ultimately disclose.[30]

---

[25] See e.g. Loeber, *RabelsZ* 1961, p. 226; Zweigert, 7 *Israel L.R.* 471 (1972). Cf. also Drobnig, *RabelsZ* 1984, pp. 239-243; Schwarz-Liebermann von Wahlendorf, *Droit*, pp. 207-208.

[26] So says David, *Livre du Centenaire de la Société de législation comparée*, vol. 2, Paris 1971, p. 155 with certain irony directed towards the dogmatic socialist comparatists that he, during his visit to the socialist countries, did not notice any significant differences between the socialist and the capitalist family life: "*Quand j'ai vu des familles socialistes – car on m'a fait l'honneur et le plaisir de m'inviter dans des familles socialistes – j'avoue qu'à certains moments, je ne me suis pas senti dans un milieu tellement étranger et je n'ai pas observé des comportements qui opposent, d'une manière très nette, la famille socialiste aux familles françaises et dites capitalistes qui me sont plus familières!*"

[27] The problem can be illustrated by the following metaphor: as oranges are not grown in Sweden, it is impossible to make a meaningful comparison between Spanish and Swedish oranges, whereas it may be meaningful to compare Spanish and Swedish fruits (that comparison would include, among other fruits, both Spanish oranges and Swedish apples). Cf. Reitz, 46 *A.J.C.L.* 625-626 (1998); Valcke, 52 *A.J.C.L.* 720 (2004).

[28] See Constantinesco, *Rechtsvergleichung*, vol. 2, p. 128.

[29] Cf. Husa, *RabelsZ* 2003, pp. 434.

[30] See Chapter 8 below.

CHAPTER 5

Explaining Similarities and Differences between Legal Systems

5.1 What Needs to be Explained?

Discoveries of the similarities and differences between the compared legal systems naturally lead to the question "why?" One of the most interesting and most important tasks of comparative law is to attempt to to explain such similarities and differences.[1] While searching for conceivable explanations, one learns which factors influence the structure, development and substantive contents of the legal systems, as it is the similarities and differences between these factors that create the similarities and differences in the field of law.

The similarities and differences between legal systems are two sides of the same coin. A similarity signifies a lack of differences, while a difference is no more than a lack of similarity. Both the similarities and the differences are therefore influenced by the same factors, even if in opposite directions. If for instance the similarities in economic systems are regarded as leading to similarities between legal systems, then the differences in the economic systems must be regarded as contributing to differences in the field of law. Explanations of the similarities and differences are consequently found within the same set of relevant factors, and an objective comparison should look for and try to explain both.

Despite what has just been said, in concrete cases one usually concentrates on only one side of the coin, i.e. explaining either the similarities or the differences. Which approach should be chosen depends upon the aims, values and attitudes of the individual comparatist. This does not mean that a comparatist believing in the similarity of legal systems should focus on similarities and a believer in differences should focus on those. In fact, the opposite is true, as a good scientist assuming a hypothesis should try to falsify it rather than to prove it. If one starts out with the assumption (often an instinctive one) that the legal systems compared are fundamentally similar, then the differences in the actual case need to be explained. If one starts from the opposite point of view, i.e. the legal systems are assumed in principle to be different, it is the discovered similarities that need to be explained. Of course, assumptions (expectations) of the similarities or differences must also be explained, even though one can often presume that the reasons behind the assumptions are evident and therefore do not require extensive explanations. For instance, if one compares the laws of New York with those of New Jersey, one can reasonably assume that the historical, economic, geographic, demographic and other factors which are the basis for the similarities between the two legal systems are so generally known that there is not much point in discussing them and it is more useful to concentrate on explaining the differences.

When comparing two closely related legal systems, such as the law of New York and the law of New Jersey, it is thus usually more interesting to attempt

---

[1]   See Dannemann in Reimann & Zimmermann, eds, *The Oxford Handbook*, pp. 416-417; Reitz, 46 *I.C.L.Q.* 626-627 (1998).

to explain the differences rather than the similarities. If one instead compares the legal rules in two entirely unrelated legal systems in very different societies, it becomes more interesting to explain the similarities. Among related legal systems there may also be reasons to distinguish between the fundamental legal principles and the more detailed rules. Similarities between the fundamental principles can be presumed to exist in related legal systems, for example monogamy within family law or freedom of contract within business law, and it is the differences that require an explanation. Detailed rules, for example the statute of limitations or the range of punishments for a particular crime, can however vary even between closely related legal systems and it can be of interest to explain the reasons why they are identical in a particular case.

Which factors are regarded as being relevant and decisive for the formation of the legal system depends of course to a great extent on the comparatist's own ideological and other opinions. A Marxist with strong materialistic views on the relationship between the legal system and the system of ownership of the means of production is obviously going to be inclined to attribute greater importance to the economic system than would an idealist looking for the origin of the legal rules in human beings' abstract ideals of justice, or an Islamic scholar seeking the roots of legal rules in religious sources. It would naturally be desirable if comparatists could conduct their research without preconceived opinions about the factors forming the legal system, or if they at least were prepared to reconsider their position when it is shown to be unfounded in an actual case. In that manner, comparative law could serve as means of verification for the various theories. The reality is however that the comparatist often has his own preconceived view of the world that he sticks with, for instance by only investigating the factors that according to him can possibly be relevant, and refraining from studying other factors, which perhaps are regarded as relevant by other comparatists.

Nevertheless, the list of relevant factors probably does not differ very much from one comparatist to another; what differs is primarily the relative weight which different comparatists ascribe to the different factors. Nowadays it is generally accepted that it would be unscientific to choose only one factor and say that this, and only this, determines the legal system.[2] The following text deals with some of the factors that are often referred to in comparative law literature as explanations of similarities and differences between legal systems. The factors are not independent of each other but rather must be seen as interrelated. Their influence on the legal system is not mechanical, and it can vary from case to case.

---

[2]   See Constantinesco, *Rechtsvergleichung*, vol. 2, pp. 292-293.

5.2   The Economic System

One does not have to be a Marxist to aknowledge that a legal system is to a very high degree a "super-structure" based on the society's economic system.[3] The legal system is normally developed to serve, among other things, the needs of the economy, and not the other way around. Hardly anyone believes that people discovered the possibility to buy and sell as a consequence of the introduction of the law on sales; the truth is that the law on sales came into being due to a need to regulate and protect those already frequently occurring transactions that we refer to as purchase and sale. Many similarities, for instance in the field of legal rules against restrictive business practices (antitrust law), have frequently economic grounds, in particular the efforts of both countries to introduce rules that have proven to be most efficient from the economic point of view.[4]

Countries with different economic systems thus have, in many regards, different legal rules in the economic field. What is meant here with similarities and differences in the economic system is not only whether they are economies of the same basic type (planned economy, market economy, feudal economy) but also whether the economies of the same type have attained the same degree of development. For example, the need for antitrust legislation does not actually arise until the market economy has led to a certain level of concentration of economic power.

To the extent the economic system influences other areas in the society, such as criminality and family life, it also has an indirect effect within such legal fields as penal law and family law. An interesting question is whether, and if so in which way, the differences in economic systems can explain, entirely or partially, the differences between attitudes concerning the protection of political and civil rights of the citizens and to the rule of law in general. Purely empirically, it can be observed that all countries having a functioning political democracy, as it is normally understood, also have an economic system that is basically market-oriented. A market economy thus appears to constitute a necessary precondition for political and civil rights (even though it is not a sufficient condition on its own, as is evidenced by the numerous market-oriented dictatorships). On the theoretical level, this connection between market economy and political democracy can possibly be explained with three factors.[5] The first factor has to do with the superior efficiency of the market economy: low standards of living have often been the primary reason for the general dissatisfaction that caused the regimes in countries with a planned economy to feel threatened and thereby compelled to limit political and civil rights of the population. It often occurs that a dictatorship is introduced just for the purpose of preventing the transition to a superior and more efficient economic system, since the inferior and

---

[3]   See Tolonen, *FJFT* 1976, pp. 100-107.

[4]   Cf. Faust in Reimann & Zimmermann, eds, *The Oxford Handbook*, pp. 837-865.

[5]   See Bogdan, *SvJT* 1991, pp. 785-786.

inefficient system that the regime wishes to preserve would not survive a free discussion and free elections. The second factor is connected with the fact that a market economy does not give the state total control over the everyday life of its citizens. In a country where the state is the one and only employer, the one and only landlord, and the one and only provider of medical care and education, the citizens are in all respects of their daily life dependent upon the goodwill and benevolence of the regime, which can oppress and punish them in many ways that are not available to the same extent in a market economy. The third factor is that for a market economy to function at all a certain degree of the rule of law is necessary. Experience has shown that the market-economy dictatorships are forced by the economic system to respect, to a considerable degree, the rule of law in such legal fields as commercial and tax law, as lawlessness in these areas would paralyze the economy. This is of course no justification for these regimes' gross violations of human rights in some other areas in the society, but it is of significant importance when democracy is to be established. In the former market-oriented dictatorships, even those that existed for a very long time such as in Spain under Franco, the idea of the rule of law was very much alive; it was rather the lack of it in certain narrow fields that was the exception and therefore could be repaired relatively quickly. In this regard, the situation was worse in countries that have previously had a planned economy for a long period of time, and where therefore the very concept of law as the protector of the individual *vis-à-vis* the state had to be established in the consciousness of the people.

5.3   The Political System and Ideology

The legal system is influenced to a high degree by the country's political system, especially in matters of constitutional law, criminal law and administrative law. To say that these fields of law look different, or in any case function differently, in a dictatorship than in a democracy, is hardly anything new.[6] As has been pointed out in the previous section, the political system is however influenced in turn by other factors, such as the country's economic structure.

There is a strong connection between a country's economic and political system on the one hand and the prevailing ideology on the other. Normally a particular economic and political system is followed by a particular type of ideology, but significant ideological differences can be found even between countries with the same or similar economic and political system. Even these relatively minor ideological differences can influence the legal system. Despite all their similarities, Switzerland and Sweden for example do not share the same views about the need for social equality and the responsibility of the state for the welfare of each individual member of the society, which is reflected in for instance the social welfare and tax law. Differences between the prevailing opinions in two countries on the position of women influence not only family law,

---

[6]   See e.g. Friedmann, *Law in a Changing Society*, pp. 22-23.

but also many other fields, for instance labour law, tax law and penal law. The fact that all such ideological differences have their own explanations, among them the history of the country, is another story.

5.4 Religion

The population's religious attitudes and beliefs can play an important role for the legal system, especially within family law but also in other areas, such as penal law. For example, a predominantly Christian country would have some difficulty to accept polygamy, while in a Moslem country the opposite position is not unusual. A religious ban on the consumption of alcohol can lead to a state prohibition of alcohol, but it can also in certain instances constitute the explanation of a more liberal attitude to certain soft drugs. Religious rules (for instance from the Koran in Islamic countries, or from the Old Testament in Israel) have often directly obtained the status of a law or in another manner have been incorporated into the legal system.[7]

5.5 History and Geography

The legal system is formed under the strong influence of the country's historical development. The fundamental features of a country's constitutional structure, for instance whether it is a republic or a monarchy, can usually be explained by reference to historical factors. The historical colonial background of most of the third world countries, but also of some developed countries including the United States, has left deep traces in their legal systems. In these countries it is in fact the historical inheritance from colonial times that determines which "legal family" the country's legal system belongs to, even if the legal rules received from the colonial power have often been changed and adapted to local requirements. The former colonies have inherited from their colonial masters not only concrete legal rules but more significantly the fundamental basic attitudes towards the legal system, the hierarchy of its sources of law, and the legal terminology and concepts.[8]

The physical conditions existing in a country, primarily the geography, climate and natural resources, exert a noticeable influence on the country's legal system. The risk of earthquakes influences the legal rules concerning construction of buildings, the climate influences the rules on the control of food, the discovery of oil fields creates a need for legislation on oil exploration, etc.[9] The

---

[7] See e.g. Arminjon, Nolde & Wolff, *Traité*, vol. 1, pp. 63-79; Berman in Reimann & Zimmermann, eds, *The Oxford Handbook*, pp. 739-751.

[8] See e.g. Elias, *ZfRV* 1966, pp. 45-56; Modéer, *JT* 1999-2000, pp. 82-86.

[9] See e.g. Erbe, *RabelsZ* 1942, p. 225, note 153; Grossfeld, *The strength*, pp. 75-84. Rodière, *Introduction*, p. 8 asks: "*Imagine-t-on par exemple, que le régime de l'eau puisse être le même et doive jamais être le même dans un pays d'oasis ou en Suède?*".

fact that the maximum lease on farm land according to the law of Vanuatu in the South Pacific is 75 years is not an arbitrary figure; it is rather due to the fact that 75 years is the average economic lifespan of a coconut tree. This is a factor which naturally does not need to be taken into consideration in countries where coconut trees are not grown.

Certain comparatists go much further than this and assert that geographic factors indirectly influence almost all fields of law, i.a. by means of influencing the mentality of the population. For instance, the "fatalistic" attitude allegedly prevalent in certain Asian countries has been said to result from the frequent earthquakes, floods and other natural disasters.[10]

5.6 Demographic Factors

Humankind consists of numerous ethnic groups. As the different groups frequently have different historical backgrounds, live in countries with different geographic conditions and profess different religions, it is hardly surprising that they often live with legal systems that differ to a relatively high degree from each other. One may ask, however, whether some of the differences can be explained solely or at least to a significant extent by the genetic differences between people belonging to different ethnic groups.[11] Long time ago there have in fact been comparatists who regarded the population's "race" as the most important factor affecting the formation of the legal system.[12] Nevertheless, the influence of genetics on the legal system is entirely unproven. Particular biological differences between populations in different countries can in certain cases influence the law, but such differences often arise even between populations of the same or closely related ethnicity and can, rather than by genetics, normally be explained by such factors as access to food, climate, religion, etc. Among the relevant demographic differences, one can mention differences in the average life expectancy, which can influence i.a. the rules on retirement pensions, and differences in the birth rate, which may influence the laws concerning abortion or public financial incentives to have children.

It is obvious that some biological factors exert an important influence upon the legal system, but these are as a rule factors common for all humankind. For example, humans build families that are more permanent and stable than most "families" in the animal kingdom. This has led to the development of legal institutions which exist, although in different forms, in practically all human societies, for instance marriage. The ultimate cause is said to be biological: a human child needs the assistance of both parents for many years before it can take care of itself.[13]

---

[10] See e.g. Wahl, *Rev.int.dr.comp.* 1973, pp. 261-276.

[11] See Constantinesco, *Rechtsvergleichung*, vol. 1, p. 262.

[12] See e.g. Picard, *Clunet* 1901, pp. 417-423.

[13] An interesting description, even from a legal point of view, of humans as biological creatures is found in Morris, *The Naked Ape*, New York 1967.

According to some comparatists, significant importance should be given even to such demographic factors as differences in the "national temperament" of various ethnic groups.[14] At a discussion on the harmonization of taxes within Western Europe, one of the participants asserted that indirect taxes must play a larger role in southern Europe than in Europe's northern parts, due to the fact that the "temperament" of the people of southern Europe is incompatible with the filing of tax returns and paying income tax!

5.7   Co-Influence of Other Means of Control

The purpose of legal rules is to regulate human conduct in certain situations. Law is, however, not the only instrument that can be used to influence human behaviour and it can be imagined that the same purpose which in one country is achieved by means of legal regulation, is achieved in another country in another manner, i.e. through other control mechanisms (see section 3.7 above). For instance, collective bargaining agreements may take the place of labour law legislation, or a well-developed system of private retirement insurance may serve needs that elsewhere are met by statutory state pension plans. To be able to explain the reason why two countries' legal rules in a particular field of law differ from each other, one must sometimes investigate the situation outside of the legal system to find possible non-legal means of control that conceivably replace or complement the legal regulation.

5.8   Accidental and Unknown Factors

A structure of such a degree of complexity as a legal system can never be explained in every detail with only a limited list of relevant factors. Even if all of the factors discussed so far were extremely alike in two countries, with all probability there would exist many differences between their laws. There is much room for different incidental and fortuitous factors leading to similarities or differences between legal systems. The particular personal preferences of an important person with great authority and power can significantly influence the legal system: it has been said that Napoleon Bonaparte's own family situation was the reason for the design of certain family-law rules in France when the French Civil Code was adopted during his reign (see section 11.2 below). At times new statutes or amendments have been adopted as a direct consequence of a scandal or another event that evidenced the need of a legislative change; even if the latent need of such legal regulation may also exist in other countries, these lack a "trigger" that would set the legislative machinery into action. Certain statutes bear the traces of having been enacted during

---

[14] See e.g. Herzog, *Rev.int.dr.comp.* 1957, p. 340.

a time of unusually high inflation or a recession, despite that they were not intended to be of a temporary character.

These and many other similar incidental factors can, at times, contribute to the explanation why the legal rules in two countries are similar or different on a particular point. But there will surely always be similarities and differences, which a comparatist despite all efforts will not be able to explain. Even in these cases the similarities and differences naturally do have their causes, but they remain unknown. The comparatist should not expect that he can explain everything. He should normally concentrate on finding explanations to the most important and most interesting similarities and differences. To attempt to explain each detail would either be impossible or would require so much time, energy and other resources that it would not be in any reasonable proportion to the practical and scientific value of such an explanation.

CHAPTER 6

Comparative Evaluation of the Compared Solutions

After having compared two or more legal systems, and after having studied their similarities and differences concerning a particular issue, it is often difficult to avoid the question which of the compared solutions is the best or better one. Such a comparative evaluation is of course not necessary after each comparison, but it is of great value, particularly if one intends to use the results of the study for suggesting changes in the law (suggestions *de lege ferenda*). Under which conditions is it possible and meaningful to make a comparative evaluation of the different solutions that the compared legal systems have arrived at?[1]

To begin with, one must keep in mind that the adoption of good legal rules is not an end in itself, but rather only one of the instruments used to attain desirable effects in the society, in other words for the purpose of attaining a good and/or better society. How a good society should look like and which effects upon the society are desirable is something on which there will be divided opinions. Jurists do not have a greater right to influence this choice than any other citizens. To decide whether one should limit, or stimulate, an increase in population, or whether the economy should be built upon a planned- or market-oriented foundation is not the objective of the comparative study of the law,[2] even though comparative legal research can provide those making the decisions with certain concrete information on the alternatives and in that manner make it possible for them to choose a position based upon knowledge and not entirely upon intuition. The comparatist can of course regard a particular solution as being more appropriate or more just than another, but the understanding of what is appropriate and just varies often not only from country to country but even between different persons within the same community.

Each comparative evaluation must therefore be made in relation to a certain subjective set of values (value judgments). This does not mean, however, that the evaluations are meaningless, but one must be conscious of the fact that the set of values one applies is perhaps not shared by others. To follow one's own set of values is fully acceptable if, for instance, the purpose is to utilize the experience of foreign countries within one's own country: the comparatist naturally chooses to propose the solution that he himself regards to be the best. Greater regard to foreign values must be taken into account for instance when suggesting a unification of laws intended to result in an adoption of uniform rules by a large number of states. In other words, one can legitimately determine what is best for oneself, but should be careful not to apply one's own values to determine what is best for others. This is always to be kept in mind when studying foreign legal solutions with a critical eye.

---

[1]   See e.g. Constantinesco, *Rechtsvergleichung*, vol. 2, pp. 323-325; Jeschek, *Entwicklung*, p. 43; Kokkini-Iatridou, *NILR* 1986, pp. 189-193; Lando, *Mélanges Tallon*, pp. 147-148; Michaels in Reimann & Zimmermann, eds, *The Oxford Handbook*, pp. 373-376 and 378-380; Zweigert, *Mélanges Maury*, vol. 1, pp. 595-596, in 7 *Israel L.R.* 473-474 (1972) and in *Festschrift Schmitthoff*, pp. 403-420; Zweigert & Kötz, *Introduction*, pp. 46-47; Zweigert & Puttfarken, *Act.Jur.Hung.* 1973, pp. 113-119 and 126-129.

[2]   Cf. Zweigert, 7 *Israel L.R.* 474 (1972) and in *Festschrift Schmitthoff*, pp. 414-418; Zweigert & Puttfarken, *Act.Jur.Hung.* 1973, p. 129.

It would be naïve to believe that there are uncontroversial and universally acceptable political or other criteria for the evaluation of legal rules and legal systems, even though some values, such as those expressed in the universal human rights instruments, may of course be more widely accepted than other values. This is particularly conspicuous in public law. One of the possible criteria proposed for evaluations within public law is the legal rules' "degree of humaneness".[3] Such a criterion would perhaps be accepted by everybody, but it can be interpreted in so many different ways that unanimity would only be illusory. A more interesting scheme of evaluation criteria, measuring less the substantive content of a particular legal system than its efficiency, has been proposed by McWhinney.[4] Among these criteria, which have been adapted for the comparison of public-law rules, there is for instance the criterion that the use of the power of the state should occur in proportion to its purposes and that the power should be distributed to those instances and levels of government where it can be used with the greatest possible convenience and efficiency.

As has been pointed out above, a meaningful comparison between legal rules in different countries presupposes that the rules to be compared have a common function, i.e. that they regulate the same situations and problems (see section 4.2 above). Comparative evaluations additionally require that the rules have the same legal/political purpose, i.e. that they aim at influencing the regulated situation in the same direction. When comparing for instance the rules concerning abortion in two different countries, it is impossible to say which of the rules is better from a legal point of view if they have entirely opposite objectives: one desires to reduce the population explosion while the other desires to increase the birth rate. It is a common mistake among comparatists that they unconsciously assume that the goals of a foreign law are substantially the same as the objectives of the corresponding rule in the comparatist's own country. Due to this assumption, they criticize the foreign legal rules for not leading to results that these rules in fact are not at all intended to attain.

If one knows for certain or can reasonably assume that the objectives of the two legal systems are in fact identical, a comparative evaluation can be of great value but remains a difficult task. One complication is that the same legal rule can serve many different purposes and consequently may be a compromise between many sometimes mutually incompatible interests. Another complication is that the law-making authorities in different countries can use different legal instruments to attain the same goals. Three countries, all desiring to slow down the population explosion, may for example choose three different methods (or their combinations). Country A chooses perhaps to introduce unrestricted abortion paid for by the government, country B withdraws the existing subsidies to families with more than one child, and country C raises the minimum age for the entry into marriage from eighteen to twenty years. It is apparent that in making the comparative evaluation one should not limit oneself to studying a

---

[3] See Del Vecchio, *ZvglRW* 1962, p. 12.

[4] See McWhinney, *Essays Yntema*, pp. 29-41.

certain isolated measure but must also keep in mind its interrelationship with other legal instruments and even such methods other than law that can be used to influence the population (for instance an information campaign promoting the use of contraceptives, or publicizing the possibility to obtain an abortion).[5] This is one of the reasons why it is usually difficult to rank the laws of various countries using quantified criteria (such as points) for determining the place of an individual country on a list such as "top 30 countries with laws facilitating doing business".[6] A further complication is that a legal instrument that functions satisfactorily in one country can be entirely without any effect in another society, for instance in countries with another economic system or with another predominant religion or morality. It is improbable to be of any practical value to raise the minimum age for marrying if the intention is to reduce the population growth in a country where premarital relationships and extramarital children are socially accepted among the population. All this must be taken into account before one can proclaim a particular legal instrument or solution to be better than another and recommend that it be "transplanted" to other countries.

Comparative evaluations of various national legal solutions must not be confused with the mostly excessively simplistic and often impossible comparative evaluations of whole legal cultures, for example discussions whether Anglo-American common law is better for economic growth than Continental European law[7] or whether Western law as such is superior to other types of legal systems.[8]

---

[5] Cf. Zweigert & Puttfarken, Act.Jur.Hung. 1973, p. 113.

[6] Cf. e.g. Siems, RabelsZ 2008, pp. 354-390.

[7] About the "legal origins thesis", arguing just that, see e.g. Grosswald Curran, 57 A.J.C.L. 863-876 (2009); Michaels, 57 A.J.C.L. 765-795 (2009); Reitz, 57 A.J.C.L. 847-862 (2009).

[8] See Hondius, Essays Spruit, pp. 337-342.

CHAPTER 7

Grouping of Legal Systems into Families of Law

Among the hundreds of existing legal systems, certain legal systems display obvious and substantial similarity to each other. These similarities are normally due to the same or very similar types of societies, common or very similar historic developments, common religion and other common aspects. Knowledge of the similarities between the legal systems makes it much easier to study foreign law. The same introductory course can, for instance, be used to present English, Australian, Canadian and New Zealand law. But even apart from its practical value, the "legal genealogy", i.e. the grouping of legal systems of the world into various families of law, appeals to the comparative legal scholar's sense for order and classification, just as a botanist obtains satisfaction from classifying plants and discovering the relationships between them.

One can, of course, speak about relationships on different levels. Most legal systems in the world have certain common characteristics (see Chapter 8 below) and to a visitor from another planet all legal systems on Earth would most probably appear to constitute a single "family of law". A division of legal systems into families can, furthermore, be followed by subdivisions into various levels of subfamilies, etc.[1] Comparatists in the former socialist countries used to ordinarily speak of only two families of law, the socialist and the "bourgeois", and regarded differences between for instance Anglo-American common law and Continental European law as a secondary subdivision within the frame-work of the bourgeois "family".[2] On the other hand, some jurists in the Western countries were of the opinion that the two main families of law were the Anglo-American and the Continental European, and that the latter even encompassed the socialist legal systems.[3] It is also possible to divide legal systems into religious and secular; both Western and socialist legal systems belong to the latter group while the family of religious laws can be subdivided into Islamic law, Jewish law, etc.

The main problem, when dividing the legal systems into families of law, is to find an appropriate criterion for the division. Is primary consideration to be given to the substantive contents of the legal rules, so that legal systems will be regarded as belonging to the same family if their substantive legal rules are similar? Or should one place more emphasis on the formal characteristics of each legal system, such as the hierarchy of the sources of law, the legal concepts, and legal terminology? Should the economic system be decisive, or perhaps the general attitude towards the role of the law in the society?

Previously, many comparatists attempted to identify a single criterion for the division of legal systems into families, for instance the economic system or

---

[1]   See e.g. Heiss, *ZvglRW* 2001, pp. 412-414.

[2]   See e.g. Eörsi, *Comparative Private Law*, pp. 22 and 61, in *Rev.int.dr.comp.* 1967, pp. 408-412, in *Fest-schrift Zepos*, vol. 2, p. 89 and in Rotondi, ed., *Inchieste*, pp. 181-209; Rozmaryn in Rotondi, ed., *Inchieste*, pp. 586-587; Štefanovič, *Porovnávanie*, p. 93; Szabó, *Ann.Univ.Budapest.* 1964, pp. 111-112; Zlatescu, *Rev. roumaine* 1976, pp. 245-246.

[3]   See e.g. Ehrenzweig in a book review in 58 *California L.R.* 1005-1010 (1970); Quigley, 37 *AJ.C.L.* 781-808 (1989).

historical origins.[4] Nowadays, however, most consider that a meaningful division should be based on several different criteria.[5] Some authors still speak of a single criterion, but a closer look will reveal that this is in reality a conglomerate of many factors. Accordingly, Zweigert and Kötz write that one should group the legal systems on the basis of their "style", but the style must, in their view, be determined taking into consideration many aspects, namely the legal system's historical origin and development, the prevailing way of legal thinking, the characteristic legal institutes (for example, trust or estoppel in the Anglo-American legal systems), the hierarchy and interpretation of the sources of law, and the legal systems' ideology (for example, in the former socialist countries).[6] On the basis of this "style", they divide legal systems into Romanistic, Germanic, Anglo-American, Nordic, Far-Eastern and religious families of law. Among the more recent proposals, one may mention the division on the basis of "legal culture" into African, Asian, Islamic and Western law, as suggested by van Hoecke and Warrington;[7] Glenn's division on the basis of "legal traditions"[8] into chthonic,[9] Talmudic, civil-law, Islamic, common-law, Hindu and Asian law, Moura Vicente's division on the basis of the idea (concept) of law into Romano-Germanic law, common law, Moslem, Hindu and Chinese law,[10] and the proposal of Mattei dividing legal systems on the basis of "patterns of law" into professional, political and traditional.[11] Among the Nordic comparatists, attempts to classify legal systems have been made by e.g. Lando,[12] Sundberg[13] and Malmström[14].

　　Probably the most widely known division has been used by David, who proposed two equally decisive criteria for the division. The first criterion is of a

---

[4]　For a critical overview of the different proposals see e.g. Husa, *Juridiska fakultetens i Uppsala* årsbok 2011, pp. 35-39, in *Rev.int.dr.comp.* 2004, pp. 11-38 and in Smits, ed., *Elgar Encyclopedia*, pp. 382-392; Schnitzer, *Vergleichende Rechtslehre*, vol. 1, pp. 133-142; Arminjon, Nolde & Wolff, *Traité*, vol. 1, pp. 42-47. See also Malmström, *Festskrift Nial*, pp. 381-403.

[5]　See e.g. Grzybowski in Rotondi, ed., *Inchieste*, p. 334; Husa, *Juridiska fakultetens i Uppsala* årsbok 2011, pp. 32-33; Lando, *Juristen* 1965, p. 49 and in *Kort indføring*, p. 211; Malmström, *Festskrift Nial*, p. 383; Moura Vicente, *Direito*, pp. 58-91; Zweigert, *Essays Yntema*, p. 46.

[6]　See Zweigert, *Essays Yntema*, pp. 46-54; Zweigert & Kötz, *Introduction*, pp. 63-73. Similarly de Cruz, *Comparative Law*, pp. 38-43.

[7]　Se Van Hoecke & Warrington, 47 *I.C.L.Q.* 532-536 (1998). Cf. also Cotterrell in Reimann & Zimmermann, eds, *The Oxford Handbook*, pp. 709-737, speaking about "European legal culture".

[8]　See Glenn, *Legal Traditions* and in *Rev.int.dr.comp.* 2003, pp. 263-278, as well as the criticism by Wijffels, *Rev.dr.int.dr.comp.* 2008, pp. 238-252.

[9]　Glenn describes this "chthonic law" as the law of peoples who live ecological lives in or in close harmony with the earth, see Glenn, *Legal Traditions*, pp. 59-60.

[10]　See Moura Vicente, *Direito*, pp. 473-474.

[11]　See Mattei, 45 *A.J.C.L.* 19-43 (1997).

[12]　See Lando, *Kort indføring*, pp. 208-212 and in *Juristen* 1965, pp. 47-48.

[13]　See Sundberg, 13 *Sc.St.L.* 185-205 (1969).

[14]　See Malmström, *Festskrift Nial*, pp. 401-403.

"technical" nature: one should ask whether a jurist educated in a particular legal system is able without great difficulty to work within another legal system. If the answer is in the negative, it must be concluded that the two legal systems most probably do not belong to the same family. This criterion is however insufficient in and of itself, according to David, as two legal systems despite their similarities in legal technique and terminology cannot be regarded as belonging to the same family of law if they are based on opposite philosophical, political and economic principles and strive to create entirely different types of societies. These two criteria (the technical and the ideological), according to David, should be used cumulatively, not separately,[15] and result in a division into Romano-Germanic systems (also called Continental European or civil-law systems), socialist systems, common law, and "other" systems (this last-mentioned residual family consisted mainly of religious and traditional law).[16]

The division of legal systems into families of law is not an end in and of itself. It is conducted for a particular purpose or particular purposes and a division appropriate for one purpose may not necessarily be useful in another connection.[17] The division's primary objective is normally (albeit not always) pedagogical, i.e. to facilitate studies of foreign law, particularly on the introductory level, by providing students and others with a quick introduction into and overview over the bewildering multitude of legal systems existing in the world today. Such "pre-understanding"[18] of legal systems enables the comparatist to proceed with greater ease to the study of and comparison between more specific legal rules and solutions.[19] In order to be able to work with a foreign legal system it is not necessary to learn the substantive contents of its rules. The rules change often and can relatively quickly be found by a jurist who is familiar with the particular foreign legal system and its way of reasoning and sources of law. The same can be said of the comparatist's own legal system: it is certainly not the primary task of university legal education to teach students the substantive contents of the law, as such knowledge will become outdated within a few years and to a large extent worthless. Well-educated jurists are expected to work in their profession for many decades after graduating from a law school, because they are able to quickly find and learn new legal rules. For this purpose, they should have at their command the fundamental knowledge of those principles of the legal system that do not change even when the actual substantive contents of the law changes, such as the design, structure and sources of the law, interpretation, legal reasoning, fundamental legal concepts, etc. It is this type of knowledge that a student of foreign law should also primarily work to acquire. Consequently, the division of legal systems for pedagogical purposes should

---

[15] See David & Brierley, *Major Legal Systems*, pp. 20-21.

[16] See David & Brierley, *Major Legal Systems*, pp. 22-31. Cf. also David, *Traité*, pp. 215-393; Ancel, *Utilité*, p. 68; Malmström, *Festskrift Nial*, pp. 401-403.

[17] See e.g. Malmström, *Festskrift Nial*, pp. 382 and 391-392; Schlesinger, *Comparative Law*, p. 252.

[18] See Husa, *Retfaerd* 2001, no. 4, p. 21.

[19] See e.g. Heiss, *ZvglRW* 2001, p. 398; Kötz, *ZEuP* 1998, p. 504.

focus on these general features rather than follow similarities in their substantive contents,[20] even though similarities between the general features are often accompanied by similarities of contents. In this regard, David's first, "technical" criterion stands out as being especially appropriate (see above). One can at the same time question whether his second criterion is in reality entitled to an independent existence, since a jurist can hardly work, without encountering great difficulties, with a foreign legal system based on philosophical, political and economic principles, and striving to develop a type of society, that he finds strange and difficult to understand.

Generally speaking, it must be stressed that most divisions of legal systems into families of law serve as a very basic and blunt pedagogical instrument, which should be used primarily to provide beginners with a quick overview over the legal systems in the world.[21] Lando has spoken in this context of a "legal world atlas"[22] and Wigmore has in fact produced "a world-map of present-day legal systems"[23]. In connection with more advanced and detailed studies, the pedagogical divisions should only be used with great care and with necessary caveats.[24] Significant differences can unexpectedly appear even between legal systems belonging to the same legal family and it can even happen that one and the same legal system in different fields of law belongs to different families, for example the law of many former British colonies can be regarded as belonging to the common-law family as far as commercial law is concerned, while their family and land law are based on entirely different legal traditions with roots in religious or local customary law. Pointing out such complications and difficulties should not, however, be interpreted as a criticism against or a devaluation of all classification work and its results. It has rightly been said that it is easy to criticize the classification attempts that have been made by others, while it is much more difficult to come up with something better in their place.[25]

Most comparatists, despite that they use various criteria for the classification of legal systems, have developed divisions (systems of families of law), which to a significant degree are similar to each other.[26] The divisions are, nevertheless, not given once and for all. The once important family of socialist law has become almost extinct or reduced to insignificance, as almost all socialist legal systems have reverted to the Continental family,[27] while the Continental and

---

[20] See e.g. Göranson, *Festskrift Agell*, p. 198: Heiss, *ZvglRW* 2001, pp. 401-402.

[21] See Lando, *Kort indføring*, p. 208.

[22] See Lando, *Erhvervsøkonomisk tidsskrift* 1963, pp. 153-163 and in *FJFT* 1966, p. 266.

[23] See Wigmore, *A panorama*, vol. 3, pp. 1133-1146.

[24] See Husa, *Retfærd* 2001, no. 4, pp. 20-23; Malmström, *Festskrift Sundberg*, p. 285.

[25] See Malmström, *Festskrift Sundberg*, p. 285 and in *Festskrift Nial*, p. 381. Cf. Zajtay, *RabelsZ* 1973, p. 216.

[26] An overview of a number of older proposals can be found, for example, in Malmström, *Festskrift Nial*, pp. 384-403.

[27] See de Cruz, *Comparative Law*, pp. 193-199; Scholler, *ZvglRW* 2002, pp. 381-382; Knapp, *Základy*, pp. 52-53 and 58. It is still possible to observe certain specific common features of the "post-socialist" legal systems, such as the ideological burden of the older generation of jurists reflected in their attitude to

common-law families may one day in the future merge into a common family of Western law (*"droit occidental"*),[28] especially in Europe under the influence of the European integration process[29]. The harmonization of law of the EU Member States is, in fact, achieved not only through EU legislation but also through the pressure of economic forces in the free common market, where no Member State can afford to impose much more stringent legal requirements on the economic actors than the other Member States, because the business community can "vote with their feet" and transfer their activities to the more advantageous laws of another Member State[30] (this type of harmonization has been derogatorily called "race to the bottom"[31]).

It is submitted that the pedagogically oriented classification method of David (see above) is normally the optimal one, even though today probably it would not lead to the same results as several decades ago. A jurist desiring to obtain an almost comprehensive overview over the legal systems existing in the world today should study the basic features of Anglo-American, French, German, Chinese and Islamic law. It is true that this choice can be criticized for paying more attention to Western legal cultures than to the other legal traditions,[32] but

---

the rule of law, as well as the objective fact that these countries are subjectively perceived, both by others and by themselves, as a special group. Cf. e.g. Castellucci, *E.J.C.L.*, vol. 12.1 (May 2008), p. 11.

[28] See David, *Essays Yntema*, pp. 56-64; Gordley, *ZEuP* 1993, pp. 498-518; Markesinis in Markesinis, ed., *The Gradual Convergence*, pp. 30-32 and in 110 *L.Q.R.* 607-628 (1994). On the other hand, Legrand, 45 *I.C.L.Q.* 52-81 (1996) and in 60 *M.L.R.* 53-63 (1997) asserts that continental and and common law have different "mentalities" to such a degree that they cannot converge. See also de Cruz, *Comparative Law*, pp. 499-504 and 514-517; Kötz, *ZEuP* 1998, pp. 497-504; Merryman, *The Loneliness*, pp. 17-49; Sefton-Green, *Rev.int.dr.comp.* 2002, pp. 85-95; Tontti, *Retfærd* 2001, no. 94, pp. 40-54.

[29] See Berger, *ZEuP* 2001, pp. 4-29; Modéer, *JT* 1999-2000, p. 72; Smits, *Maastricht Journal of European and Comparative Law* 1998, pp. 328-340, in Örücü & Nelken, eds, *Comparative Law*, pp. 219-240, and in Van Hoecke, ed., *Epistemology*, pp. 229-245; and cf. Bussani, 8 *Eur.Rev.Priv.L.* 85-99 (2000); van Gerven, 9 *Eur.Rev.Priv.L.* 485-503 (2001). To treat the law of the European Union, which is not a comprehensive legal system in the usual sense of the word, as being on the same level as e.g. common law or Continental law (see e.g. de Cruz, *Comparative Law*) seems incorrect, even though comparisons between EU rules and national rules can of course be meaningful and interesting, for example in the field of competition law. EU law should rather be seen as an integral part of the legal systems of the Member States. See Dehousse, 42 *A.J.C.L.* 761-781 (1994); van Gerven in Harding & Örücü, eds, *Comparative Law*, pp. 155-178.

[30] Cf. the *Centros* judgment of the Court of Justice of the European Communities, Case C-212/97, where the freedom of establishment within the EU forced Denmark to allow an English company to do business in Denmark in spite of the fact that it did not do any business in England and had been founded in England solely for the purpose of avoiding stringent requirement of Danish company law. The judgment has led to a mitigation of the Danish rules. About the "free movement of legal rules" and "competition between legal systems", cf. also Ogus in in Örücü & Nelken, eds, *Comparative Law*, pp. 155-167 and Smits, *Maastricht Journal of European and Comparative Law* 1998, pp. 337-340.

[31] See Birkmose, *Maastricht Journal of European and Comparative Law* 2006, pp. 35-80.

[32] See e.g. Glenn in Reimann & Zimmermann, eds, *The Oxford Handbook*, pp. 434-436; Mattei, 45 *A.J.C.L.* 10-12 (1997).

this is justifiable from a pedagogical point of view[33]. The majority of the law students and jurists need, because of purely practical reasons, to know more about the main Western legal systems than about the laws of the "chthonic" peoples. Most of the legal systems in the third world are to a substantial extent based on the law of their former colonial master, so that studies of for example English and French law open the door to studies of the law of many non-Western countries. A classification that is optimal for pedagogical purposes may, of course, be inconsistent and wrong for other than pedagogical purposes, where the pedagogical division may resemble a division of cars into cabriolets, German cars and green cars.

The Nordic legal systems in Denmark, Finland, Iceland, Norway and Sweden are ordinarily classified as belonging to the Continental European family of law. There are, however, exceptions, for instance Zweigert and Kötz discuss Nordic law as an independent group.[34] Malmström treated Nordic law as an independent family within the Western law, which he divided into Continental, Latin American, Nordic and common-law families.[35] Sundberg however has no doubts that Scandinavian law belongs to the Continental group, while Strömholm and Gomard seem to have some doubts in this respect.[36] It is impossible to determine with scientific precision which of these authors is right, as the relationships between legal systems are not rooted in any biological reality, but instead often exist primarily in the eyes of the beholder and depend on i.a. the degree of detail of the division. For the needs of an average beginner, Nordic law can certainly be placed in the Continental family in spite of it having certain special features such as that the Nordic legal systems usually are more pragmatically oriented than German and French law (Zweigert and Kötz speak of the Nordic legal systems' "refreshing lack of dogma"[37]), that they lack codifications similar to the German *Bürgerliches Gesetzbuch* or the French *Code civil*, and that they are not influenced by Roman law to the same degree as French and German law[38].

---

[33] See Heiss, *ZvglRW* 2001, pp. 399-400.

[34] See Zweigert & Kötz, *Introduction*, pp. 276-285, especially p. 277. See also Eörsi, *Comparative Civil Law*, pp. 135-145, who considers Nordic law as a special group within the capitalist (bourgois) type of legal systems, and Sola Cañizares, *Iniciación*, pp. 175-176, who places Nordic law in an independent group within the large family of "Western law" (*"sistemas occidentales"*). Arminjon, Nolde & Wolff, *Traité*, vol. 1, p. 50 write: *"Le droit scandinave n'est ni romain, ni français, ni germanique dans ses origines et son évolution"*; they treat Scandinavian law as an independent group, equal to French, Germanic, English, Russian, Moslem and Hindu law.

[35] See Malmström, *Festskrift Nial*, pp. 401-403.

[36] See Sundberg, 13 *Sc.St.L.* 179-205 (1969); Strömholm, *Publications of the Turku Law School*, no. 1/1994, pp. 13-14; Gomard, 5 *Sc.St.L.* 27-38 (1961).

[37] See Zweigert & Kötz, *Introduction*, p. 41. See also e.g. Lando, *Juristen* 1965, p. 48 and in *Kort indføring*, p. 209. There are divided opinions on whether such a difference actually exists.

[38] See e.g. Pihlajamäki in *Juridiska fakulteten i Uppsala årsbok 2011*, pp. 85-94; Zweigert & Kötz, *Introduction*, pp. 284-285.

There are a large number of legal systems that are difficult to place into the basic categories used in legal literature. The pedagogical divisions are made for the purpose of obtaining an overview, which makes it difficult to take nuances and special features into consideration. Among the special cases, the legal systems that historically represent a mixture of legal traditions from two or more different families of law can be mentioned,[39] for example, the legal systems in Québec and Louisiana (French and English/American roots),[40] or South Africa (Roman-Dutch and English roots)[41]. As has been mentioned previously, the legal systems in many developing countries represent a mixture of traditional local law, religious law, and law imported during or even after the colonial period from the former colonial power.[42] Palmer suggests that mixed systems outnumber all other kinds in the world and represent diversified blends with unlimited possible recombinations.[43] The study of the experiences of the existing mixtures of French and common-law traditions is useful in view of the European integration process, which at its start in 1950s was deeply rooted in Continental legal culture but must, after the UK and Ireland became members, also deal with common-law thinking, both by being affected by it and by, in turn, influencing the thinking of English and Irish jurists.[44]

It deserves to be repeated that classifications of legal systems for pedagogical purposes do not hinder other classifications for other purposes. For example, a comparative research project investigating whether and how small legal systems, weak in terms of economic and personal resources, manage to develop through legal imports may be well-served by dividing legal systems into groups depending on their grade of weakness. It is equally possible and legitimate to group legal systems on the basis of their approach to a specific problem of substantive

---

[39] See e.g. Heiss, *ZvglRW* 2001, pp. 408-410; Palmer in Smits, ed., *Elgar Encyclopedia*, pp. 467-475; Örücü in in Örücü & Nelken, eds, *Comparative Law*, pp. 169-187; du Plessis in Reimann & Zimmermann, eds, *The Oxford Handbook*, pp. 477-512; Moura Vicente, *Direito*, pp. 479-515; a number of papers in Örücü, Attwooll & Coyle, eds, *Studies*. In a wider sense, practically all legal systems can be said to be mixed, as they all are exposed to foreign influences in one way or another, see Örücü in the same volume, pp. 342 and 351.

[40] See e.g. Beaulieu, *Rev.int.dr.comp.* 1961, pp. 300-306; Dainow, 14 *A.J.C.L.* 68-97 (1965-1966) and in *Rev. int.dr.comp.* 1954, pp. 19-38; David, *Traité*, pp. 305-307; Zweigert & Kötz, *Introduction*, sid. 116-118.

[41] See e.g. David, *Traité*, pp. 310-311; Zweigert & Kötz, *Introduction*, pp. 231-235.

[42] See e.g. Elias, *ZfRV* 1966, pp. 45-56; Reyntjens, *Rev.dr.int.dr.comp.* 1991, pp. 41-50.

[43] See Palmer, *E.J.C.L.*, vol. 12.1 (May 2008), pp. 5 and 16, who in an appendix to his article lists and exemplifies several existing different mixtures, such as mixed systems of civil and common law (e.g. Québec), civil and customary law (e.g. Ethiopia), civil and Muslim law (e.g. Morocco), civil, common and customary law (e.g. Vanuatu), common and Muslim law (e.g. Pakistan), common and customary law (e.g. Malawi), common, Muslim and customary law (e.g. Malaysia), common, Muslim and civil law (e.g. Iran), and Talmudic, civil and common law (Israel). Cf. also Örücü in Van Hoecke, ed., *Epistemology*, p. 375.

[44] See e.g. Castellucci, *E.J.C.L.*, vol. 12.1 (May 2008), p. 10; Palmer, *E.J.C.L.*, vol. 12.1 (May 2008), pp. 21-22; Smits, *E.J.C.L.*, vol. 12.1 (May 2008).

law.[45] A comparative research project on dissolution of marriage may, for example, be well served by a grouping of legal systems reflecting how easy or difficult they make it to obtain a divorce. A classification focusing on procedural law may differ from that focusing on substantive legal regulation.[46] Any classification can be justified if it serves its specific purpose and no classification can claim being the only correct one.[47]

---

[45] On the methods used at such selections, see e.g. Lando, *TfR* 1998, pp. 392-394; Oderkerk, *NILR* 2001, pp. 293-318.

[46] See Koch, *ZEuP* 2007, pp. 735-753.

[47] See David & Brierley, *Major Legal Systems*, p. 21; Palmer, *E.J.C.L.*, vol. 12.1 (May 2008), p. 3; Zweigert & Kötz, *Introduction*, p. 73.

CHAPTER 8

The Common Core of Legal Systems and the Presumption of Similarity

It is a well-known fact that the substantive contents of legal rules of different countries is often very similar. Even people who have not studied law at all travel abroad and engage in legal transactions such as shopping, renting cars and hotel rooms, travelling by public transportation, etc. Although little thought is given to them, these are actually relatively complicated types of contracts. Tourists travelling abroad get by because they simply more or less instinctively assume that the above-mentioned contracts are made and function in the same way as equivalent contracts in their own country. In a similar manner, a foreign visitor may, even without studying the local law, presume that certain types of behaviour, such as theft and murder, should be avoided because they are illegal. These and similar assumptions are based on pure common sense, which tells us that many legal rules in foreign countries must reasonably be similar to the legal rules in our own country. This concerns however the substantive contents of the legal rules and not their formal characteristics: a Swedish and an English legal rule can of course have the same meaning and effect even if the Swedish rule is based on a legislative enactment while the English rule is based upon a judicial precedent.

For a tourist it is sufficient, most of the time, to make common-sense assumptions on the similarity of the legal systems. A qualified comparative legal study cannot, on the other hand, be built on mere assumptions; it requires factual knowledge. This also applies when one wishes to ascertain whether there is a common core to the legal systems; French scholars sometimes prefer to speak of a common "trunk" (*tronc commun*).

The first question one must ask oneself is whether the search is for the common core of all legal systems or for rules common for a limited group of countries, for instance legal systems belonging to the same family of law,[1] legal systems in countries belonging to the same international organization (e.g. the EU),[2] or legal systems in countries engaged in drafting an international convention. Discussions about the legal systems' common core pertain, however, normally to the legal principles that are common for all or almost all legal systems. The issue is treated most often in connection with Article 38 of the Statute of the International Court of Justice, according to which "the general principles of law recognized by civilized nations" are one of the sources of public international law (see section 2.6 above). This formulation might be interpreted to require that a principle, in order to qualify, must be known and recognized in all countries of the world (it can nowadays be difficult to assert that some nations are not civilized enough in the meaning of the provision). Such an interpretation would, however, be manifestly unreasonable. There is hardly any rule in existence, which in reality is recognized by all legal systems without excep-

---

[1]   See e.g. Hazard, *Communists and Their Law*.

[2]   Cf. e.g. the reference to "the general principles common to the laws of the Member States" in the second paragraph of Article 340 in the Treaty on the Functioning of the European Union. On the common core of the private law of EU Member States, see Bussani & Mattei, *Rev.int.dr.comp.* 2000, pp. 29-48. Cf. also Lando & Beale, eds, *Principles of European Contract Law*, parts I and II, Kluwer 2000.

.VERPOOL JOHN MOORES UNIVERSIT
LEARNING SERVICES

tion. Furthermore, it would be practically impossible to investigate and properly understand in each particular case all of the world's legal systems. In the legal literature, the provision is normally understood as to mean that the principle under scrutiny must be recognized by "all or almost all" legal systems, but there are public international law scholars who are satisfied with it being recognized in "the most important legal systems in the world" or by "a reasonable number of civilized peoples".[3] It is suggested that the best and most appropriate manner of ascertaining the relevant principles is, however, to make use of the division of legal systems into families of law (see Chapter 7 above). If a particular legal principle is well represented in each family of law, it can be reasonably regarded as belonging to the common core in the meaning of Article 38.[4] It is clear however that the division of legal systems for this purpose should differ from the methods of grouping which are used for purely pedagogical purposes; this especially applies to some often disregarded non-Western legal systems (e.g. the African, Talmudic and Hindu legal traditions),[5] which would need to have more attention paid to them and be subjected to more detailed subdivisions.

To attempt to ascertain all of the rules and principles belonging to the common core would be an enormous task. The question is therefore normally not posed so that one looks for legal principles belonging to the common core, but rather the comparatist investigates the status of a certain legal principle he happens to be interested in. Some alternate routes have been suggested in the literature, which might be used instead of actual studies of the existing legal systems. According to one suggestion, the common core could be determined by the use of logic and a *reductio ad absurdum*, i.e. by showing that certain legal principles are quite simply absolutely necessary in every developed legal system.[6] One might for instance argue that the prohibition against the use of private violence for the purpose of revenge must exist in every society that has attained a certain degree of development; the rule that an individual must not take the law into his own hands belongs, according to this theory, consequently to the common core of civilized legal systems and it is unnecessary to determine whether this is in fact the case by means of comparative investigations and studies. This approach may be tempting, but it is hardly acceptable. To begin with, there are more exceptions to the rule than one might expect (the prohibition against the use of private violence is, in any case, only to a limited extent transposable to public international law, where a developed and efficient collective enforcement system is still lacking). Secondly, such a speculative method would often result in that the jurist looking for a common core would elevate rules from his own law, since to most jurists the legal system they have been educated

---

[3] See references in Bogdan, *NordTIR* 1977, p. 46.

[4] See Bogdan, *NordTIR* 1977, p. 46.

[5] See e.g. Glenn, *Legal Traditions*, pp. 58-124 and 273-302; Knapp, *Velké právní systémy*, pp. 202-205; Vicente, *Direito*, pp. 415-483.

[6] See e.g. O'Connel, *International Law*, ed. 2, vol. 1, London 1970, p. 11.

in appears to be self-evident and reasonable, almost as a kind of natural law.[7] The International Court of Justice compensates to some extent for similar effects by being composed of jurists representing all principal legal cultures of the world.

As has already been noted, there are significant similarities between the existing legal systems as far as the substantive contents of the legal rules are concerned, in particular within private law.[8] This often applies also to legal systems which do not belong to the same family of law. The German-American comparatist Max Rheinstein estimated that approximately 80 percent of private-law cases would reach the same result regardless of whether they arose and were decided in the USA, Canada, France, Argentina or Japan.[9] Certain comparatists have attempted to explain the similarities by asserting that all existing legal systems on Earth, in one manner or another, originate from the same "original law" (*"Urrecht"*, *"protodroit"*),[10] but the more likely explanation is that the now prevailing similarities are due to the present-day similarities between peoples' way of life in different countries: it is possible to speak about a "natural convergence" of legal systems.[11] Many factors, for example the ongoing economic integration (such as the EU), modern technology (in particular in the information field), the cross-border cultural influence of the mass media (including news, discussions and entertainment related to legal matters) and international development aid in the field of law play a role in this globalization process. Concerning the Western legal systems in general, there is usually no reason why their substantive contents should be substantially different from each other, even though this does not apply to the same degree in, for instance, public law

---

[7]   A well-known example of this phenomenon is the arbitral award in the matter of *Petroleum Development Ltd.* v. *The Sheikh of Abu Dhabi*, rendered in 1951 by the English arbitrator Lord Asquit of Bishopstone. The law of Abu Dhabi was applicable to the dispute, but it lacked the necessary legal rules on the point. The arbitrator filled in the lacuna with English law, with the justification that English rules "are in my view so firmly grounded in reason, as to form part of this broad body of jurisprudence – this modern law of nature" (18 *International Law Reports* 149).

[8]   Traditionally, most comparative investigations are concerned with questions which according to Continental European terminology belong to private law. Comparative law can of course be used even within public law, however cautiousness is called for there to a higher degree than in connection with private-law comparisons. Public law is more politicized than private law, which affects i.a. the comparability and the comparative evaluation of the national legal rules. See Bell in Harding & Örücü, eds, *Comparative Law*, pp. 235-247; Bernhardt, *ZaöRV* 1964, pp. 431-452; Halász in Szabó & Péteri, eds, *A Socialist Approach*, pp. 163-182; Harding in Harding & Örücü, eds, *Comparative Law*, pp. 249-266; Kaiser, *ZaöRV* 1964, pp. 391-404; Strebel, *ZaöRV* 1964, pp. 405-430; Zweigert & Puttfarken, *Act.Jur.Hung.* 1973, p. 122; six papers in *Livre du Centenaire de la Société de législation comparée*, vol. 1, Paris 1969, pp. 165-255. Concerning comparative criminal law, see Herzog, *Rev.int.dr.comp.* 1957, pp. 338-352; Jeschek, *Entwicklung*.

[9]   See Rheinstein in Rotondi, ed., *Inchieste*, p. 553.

[10] See Noda, *Recueil Ancel*, vol. 1, pp. 23-41.

[11] Cf. e.g. de Cruz, *Comparative Law*, pp. 513-514.

as it does in commercial law. The Western countries have the same economic system, a largely common history, closely related religious beliefs, and other similar common characteristics (see Chapter 5 above). It is therefore not surprising that their legal systems often arrive at identical or at least similar solutions, even if they sometimes do so taking different paths to get there.

In some parts of private law, the similarities in the substantive contents of the legal rules are so significant that some authors have found it possible to formulate a *praesumptio similitudinis*, i.e. a rebuttable presumption that the legal rules are normally similar in their contents.[12] This presumption has at times been recommended as a valuable pedagogical tool in studies of not too exotic foreign private law. If the comparison between the legal systems shows that their solutions are identical or similar, this can be considered as a confirmation that one *probably* has understood and compared them in a correct manner. If the comparatist, on the other hand, has discovered substantial differences between the compared legal systems, this should be considered as a warning that he *may* have made a mistake and that he should re-check the results carefully.

In connection with *praesumptio similitudinis* one can also speak of the so-called compensation phenomenon (some prefer to speak about the law of substitution, *loi de substitution*[13]), which means that substantial differences between the legal systems on a certain point are often (albeit far from always) compensated for by means of other differences on other points, so that the differences cancel each other out wholly or partially. This phenomenon underscores again the importance of the principle that a foreign legal system should be considered in its entirety (see section 3.4 above). Discovery of important differences on a certain point should stimulate the comparatist to investigate the conceivable compensation possibilities before he expresses himself on the actual differences between the contents of the compared legal systems.[14]

The comparatists pointing out the similarity of legal systems have been criticized for being biased: "If you set out to find differences, you will find them. If you set out to find similarities, you will find them".[15] It has even been hinted that the inclination of some comparatists to look for and find similarities rather than differences had something to do with their background as refugees from Nazi Germany and was a reaction to the Nazi regime's exclusionary discrimination

---

[12] See e.g. Jenks, *The Common Law*, p. 106; Zweigert, *Rev.int.dr.comp.* 1966, pp. 5-18 and in Rotondi, ed., *Inchieste*, pp. 737-758; Zweigert & Kötz, *Introduction*, p. 40. See also de Cruz, *Comparative Law*, p. 239; Del Vecchio, *ZvglRW* 1962, pp. 6-8 and Schwarz-Liebermann von Wahlendorf, *Droit*, pp. 139-145. The existence of such a presumption is, however, highly controversial, see Husa, *RabelsZ* 2003, p. 419-443; Grosswald Curran, 45 A.J.C.L. 43-92 (1998); Gessner, *RabelsZ* 1972, p. 235; Göranson, *Festskrift Agell*, pp. 198-199; Legrand, *Maastricht Journal of European and Comparative Law* 1997, pp. 123-124 and in Legrand & Munday, eds, *Comparative Legal Studies*, pp. 240-311; Michaels in Reimann & Zimmermann, eds, *The Oxford Handbook*, pp. 369-372; Moura Vicente, *Direito*, pp. 43-45.

[13] See Rodière, *Introduction*, pp. 53-59.

[14] See, for example, several examples given by Sacco, 49 A.J.C.L. 181-188 (2001).

[15] Merryman, as quoted by Legrand, 47 A.J.C.L. 42 (1999).

justified by the purported "otherness" of the excluded.[16] The *praesumptio simili-tudinis* should, however, be seen a practical tool, based on empirical experience, rather than as an ideological instrument.[17]

The alleged preference for similarities rather than differences is by some critics seen as a legitimate reason for criticizing the fundamental functional approach to the issue of comparability (see section 4.1 above), even though the two issues are totally separate: the functional approach is designed to discover and analyze differences as well as similarities and does not, *per se*, favor one more than the other.[18]

---

[16] See e.g. Grosswald Curran, 46 *A.J.C.L.* 666 (1998).

[17] See e.g. Platsas, *E.J.C.L.*, vol. 12.3 (December 2008), p. 15.

[18] See e.g. de Coninck, *RabelsZ* 2010, pp. 325-326 and 329-332; Glenn in Smits, ed., *Elgar Encyclopedia*, p. 63; Husa, *RabelsZ* 2003, pp. 424-425; Michaels in Reimann & Zimmermann, eds, *The Oxford Handbook*, pp. 371-372; Platsas, *E.J.C.L.*, vol. 12.3 (December 2008), pp. 15-16.

PART II

The Most Important Legal Systems

CHAPTER 9

English Law

9.1 Introduction

It has been estimated that approximately one-third of all humankind lives in countries with a legal system based to a significant degree upon English law (English law meaning here the law of England and Wales). This is not a bad mark for a legal system, which started out from only a part of an island (Scotland has an independent legal system of its own) on the fringe of Europe, and which for an outside observer appears at times to be a bit comical due to its outer attributes, such as the wigs of the judges and advocates, along with their continued insistence on the use of many archaic phrases and ceremonies which appear to be meaningless and outdated from a practical point of view.

The success of the English legal system throughout the world is largely due to the colonial expansion of the British Empire, but its continued presence there would hardly have been possible if this law had not proven itself to be extraordinarily flexible and practical. One should thus not be misled by the English legal system's apparently medieval features; it is in fact a modern legal system of very high quality.

One of the distinguishing characteristics of English law is, nevertheless, its undeniable strong connection with the past. These historical ties are due in great part to its uninterrupted legal continuity. Since 1066, the year of the Norman conquest of England when the Saxon forces were defeated at Hastings, English law has not been subject to radical and sudden upheavals (such as those that occurred during the revolutions in France or Russia). Nor has it undergone a large-scale reception of foreign law or major codifications. In the central parts of the legal system one can still rely upon statutes and precedents from the Middle Ages. Even more important is that the very way of functioning of English law is still built upon traditions developed during the Medieval period. This means that in order to comprehend the present-day English legal system, a certain fundamental knowledge of its historical development is necessary.

9.2 Common Law

Even though England was an integrated part of the Roman Empire for four centuries, there does not appear to be any trace of this in the form of some significant influence of Roman law. The Latin terms, which not infrequently appear in present-day English legal terminology, were mostly introduced during the Middle Ages or later, without any direct connection with the application of Roman law as such. After the decline of the Roman Empire, England was divided into several small kingdoms whose legal systems consisted of different more-or-less local rules of largely Germanic origin. The England of that time can be divided roughly into three major regions applying three somewhat different systems of law: Wessex law (in the South and West), Mercian law (Midlands) and the Nordic-influenced Dane law (North and East).

The Norman conquest after the battle of Hastings in 1066 did not automatically result in a change in the prevailing law. The conquerors refrained from forcing their own Norman customary law on the population; they devoted instead substantial energy to building up a strong centralized administration for the whole country that became unified under the English Crown. The constitutional division of powers was an unknown concept at that time, and the legislative, executive and judicial powers were all concentrated in the King and his advisors, who formed the royal council, *Curia Regis*. By the twelfth century, this council had branched into a number of institutions including the Royal Courts in Westminster (now part of London), which administered justice in the name of the King in such matters as the right to land, collection of taxes, and punishment for serious criminal offences. Very soon there were three courts, which to some degree had overlapping jurisdiction: the Court of Exchequer, Court of King's Bench and Court of Common Pleas. Various local courts continued to exist, but the jurisdiction of the Royal Courts was expanded successively and they eventually replaced the traditional courts, primarily due to the fact that the Royal Courts were more modern and more efficient, and were consequently preferred by plaintiffs. The royal judges were "itinerant justices", who travelled around in the country to hear cases, but they also retained their permanent winter residence in London. In the beginning, the judges applied the various local customary laws, despite the fact that they worked in the Norman variant of the French language of the time. This old legal French, today termed "Law French", continued to be the official legal language until the seventeenth century and much of it is found even in modern legal English, for instance in words such as law, court, judge, attorney, jury, tort or venue, which are, however, as is the case with Latin terms, pronounced in the English manner.

With their travels, the royal judges became acquainted with the various local customary laws, the advantages and disadvantages of which they most likely compared and discussed among themselves when they spent the winter months in London. Gradually this led to the situation where the royal judges more and more frequently applied the same legal rules throughout the entire country; the "common" law (*comune ley* in Law French) was born. This new legal system seems to have been substantially established already by the middle of the thirteenth century, when the most important early work on English law was written – *De legibus et consuetudinibus Angliae* by Henricus de Bracton (the first known work was written as early as in the twelfth century by Glanvil). Certain local customary rules have survived, however, and can in fact be relevant even today, provided that they can be shown to have existed from time immemorial, the so-called "immemorial custom". In the typically English pragmatic manner, in 1275 time immemorial was defined by statute to mean that a local customary law fulfils that requirement if it can be traced back to 1189 (the year of King Richard I's accession to the throne).

Common law was thus not created by means of legislation but by the courts using their judicial decisions as precedents. The principle developed very quickly that earlier judicial decisions, made in a similar case, should be followed, i.e. that precedents should be respected (the principle of *stare deci-sis*). This principle was not regarded as formally binding in the beginning, but gradually became so between the seventeenth and the beginning of the nine-teenth century. When a legislated rule does not exist, this principle constitutes a prerequisite of any legal system wishing to preserve a certain degree of predicta-bility and respect for the rule of law.

The principle of *stare decisis*, which even today is the backbone of English law, has never been laid down by legislation. It has been developed by the practice of the courts themselves, which may even decide to modify it. Thus, the House of Lords, which at the time was the highest court in England, declared in 1966 that it changed its approach towards its own precedents and considered itself no longer formally bound by them.

At the time of its inception, common law was with all probability a very flex-ible legal system, but it quickly rigidified, not only due to the *stare decisis* princi-ple but also because of – and perhaps primarily because of – the introduction of the system of "forms of action", also called "writs".

To have his claim heard by one of the Royal Courts was not, in the begin-ning, the plaintiff's right but was seen rather as a privilege, requiring special permission. The reason for this was that the Royal Courts were originally intended to deal only with matters of interest to the Crown and did not aspire to acquire general jurisdiction and entirely replace the then existing court system. A person who wished to file a case at the Royal Courts had to turn to the King's secretariat (Chancery), which among other tasks functioned as the administrative office of the Royal Courts. For the payment of a fee, the plaintiff could obtain from the Chancery a document – a "writ" – which in the name of the King ordered the defendant to comply with the demands of the plaintiff or subject himself to a trial and the resulting judgment. The document speci-fied the legal ground alleged by the plaintiff for his case and was valid only for that particular ground. In the beginning, an individual inquiry and deci-sion was made in each individual case before the issuance of a writ. As time passed, a number of established writs were developed, such as the writ of debt for a demand for repayment of money, writ of detinue for the owner's demand for compensation for unlawful retention of his property, or writ of trespass for claims concerning injurious acts, and so on. The established writs gradually became standardized to such a degree that they resembled today's standard forms, with only some basic information such as the names of the parties having to be filled in. They began to be issued automatically, without an indi-vidual hearing, with the plaintiff merely paying a set fee. By creating a particu-lar type of writ the Royal Chancery was in fact acknowledging or approving the existence of a certain type of legitimate claim, so that one can almost speak of a kind of royal legislation. Each potential plaintiff's chances of a successful outcome of the case depended upon whether there was an appropriate writ, and if not, whether the Royal Chancery was willing to create one; in this manner the writ system constituted the outer framework or the outer limit for the entire substantive common law, which was sometimes expressed with the words "no writ, no right". The Chancery's writ-creating activity was consequently an important aspect of the power of the King. It was strongly objected to, especially by the nobility, and the Chancery was successively compelled to use a great deal of restraint. The nobility achieved an almost total prohibition on the creation of new writs in the Provisions of Oxford of 1258, but in accordance with the Statute of Westminster II of 1285, the Chancery (in reality its head, the Lord Chancellor) again obtained certain possibilities to create new types of writs, even if only in cases which were similar to the already accepted ones (writs *in consimilii casu*). The development of the law was gradually taken over by the courts, which began to allow "actions on the case" in situations which were regarded as being analogous to a writ already in existence (in this manner, the writ of assumpsit, which constitutes the basis for the English law of contracts, was derived from the action for non-contractual damages). The writ system continued to exist substantially unchanged until the middle of the nineteenth century when it was abolished in 1852, but certain parts survived until 1875.[1] The purpose of abolishing the writ system was primarily to simplify the judicial proceedings, not to change the substantive law. The fact that a certain claim was not encompassed within any of the old writs no longer constituted a procedural obstacle to the lawsuit after these reforms, but the plaintiff's chances of winning the case continued to be poor due to the lack of precedent to support the alleged substantive grounds for the plaintiff's claim. The number of established writs varied over the centuries between approximately 50 and 80, as some became obsolete and some new ones were created depending upon the legal and other developments in the society.

The writ system was only one of the external expressions of a typical characteristic of English law, namely the dominat role of procedural rules. It was of less importance whether an individual had the substantive law on his side than whether he, according to the various complicated procedural rules, had the possibility to enforce his rights. As an example of the exaggerated importance of procedure, each writ had its own unique set of procedural rules (concerning evidence, the use of a jury, possibilities of obtaining a default judgment, etc.). Having to choose between the available writs meant that the plaintiff was forced at the beginning of the lawsuit to decide irrevocably the manner of proceeding; if he did not choose the correct writ, the case was dismissed, perhaps after several years of litigation, and he had to start all over again from the beginning. There existed, on the other hand, a substantial overlap between some of the various writs, and the well-informed plaintiff's choice of writ sometimes depended upon tactical grounds such as when the writ of trover, which gave the plaintiff the right to a jury trial, was chosen instead of the writ of detine, for which there was no such right.

---

[1] A different type of writ, which still survives and has been adopted in may other legal systems, is the writ of *habeas corpus*, by which a person deprived of liberty can have the legality of the imprisonment promptly heard by a court.

The dominant role of procedure is also one of the reasons why English lawyers have only shown a limited interest in the Roman law's sophisticated substantive private law. They regarded their primary task as managing the procedure and avoiding all its traps, while the substantive issue in dispute was turned over to the jury. Of course English law nowadays contains many highly developed and sophisticated substantive legal rules, but even today the procedure-oriented way of thinking shows up in many different ways.

Many questions, which in Continental European countries would be considered to be issues of substantive law, are traditionally regarded as procedural matters in England, for example the expiry of debts due to time limitation or set-off. While the parties in Continental European countries can usually rely on any relevant evidence, issues regarding the admissibility of evidence attract much attention in the legal systems of the common-law countries, often with complex rules on what evidence is allowed and what is prohibited. For example, regardless of how relevant and trustworthy it may be in a particular case, evidence about out-of-court statements of persons who due to their absence are not available for cross-examination ("hearsay") is normally not allowed, even though there are exceptions. The interest of finding and proving the truth frequently comes into conflict with the rigid rules of evidence. It is said that these rules have been developed taking into consideration the jury system, since members of the jury, having no legal education or judicial experience, were thought to be easily manipulated. At the same time, it was assumed that the jury could reach a just decision with the help of common sense even without the burden of substantive legal rules, provided that the procedural rules have been properly followed.

An English characteristic that resulted from the traditional writ system is that the English jurists, in their division of the law into legal fields, did not accept, for a long time, the distinction, fundamental for a Continental European jurist, between public law and private law. All writs were issued in the name of the King, and even a dispute between individuals was understood to be, even if only symbolically, a conflict between the Crown and the defendant. The aversion against the distinction between *jus publicum* and *jus privatum* is, however, also connected to the political power struggles of the seventeenth century, when this distinction for some reason was regarded as an expression of the royalists' desire to keep the monarch above the law.

The English division of the law into legal fields follows to a certain degree even today the former distinctions between the various writs, which, despite their being formally abolished more than a century ago, continue by tradition to influence the legal concepts of English jurists. When referring to contracts, an English jurist is consequently referring to the legal relationships that used to be sanctioned by the writ of assumpsit. This means that, for instance, the entrusting (depositing) of property for safe-keeping or the giving of a gift, both of which were protected by other writs, are not considered to be of a contractual nature. The English law's divisions have been criticized from a Continental

European point of view because they do not reflect the fundamental connections and relationships between different areas of legal problems. The English classification of law is not especially logical or consistent, but rather splinters the legal system into a number of small divisions which frequently partly overlap each other.

The rigid common-law system was not suitable for the requirements of international trade. In this field, a customary law called *lex mercatoria* prevailed during the Middle Ages in practically all of Europe. In the English ports special courts were established, often consisting of the mayor together with an English and a foreign merchant, which applied this "law merchant". In the eighteenth century, law merchant was integrated into common law and the special courts were replaced by the Royal Court, using however a jury consisting of merchants. The principle of *stare decisis* began to be followed even in this field of law, which resulted in that English commercial law became more "English", but the roots of the substantive legal rules even today can often be traced back to the old trans-boundary *lex mercatoria*.

Due to the rigid writ system, the development of common law became seriously impeded, as the existing rules ceased to keep up with the developments in society and no longer conformed with the values and prevailing legal consciousness of the times. In the typical English manner, the problem was not dealt with by changing the existing rules, but rather by developing, at the end of the fifteenth century, a parallel system known as "equity".

9.3 Equity

Equity (from the French *équité*, i.e. justice or fairness) has its roots in the position of the King as the ultimate "fountain of justice": justice was administered in the Royal Courts in the name of the King. The Lord Chancellor, who in today's terminology might be characterized as the director of the King's secretariat (the Chancery), was until the beginning of the sixteenth century normally a Catholic priest, often a bishop. In his capacity as the King's secretary, the Lord Chancellor received and presented to the King petitions from parties who begged the King "to do what is right for the love of God and in the way of charity", when the Royal Courts according to existing common law could not decide a case in a just manner (which often was due to the shortcoming of the procedural rules, for instance the unavailability of a suitable writ or the impossibility to render a judgment of specific performance). In the capacity of the King's confessor and spiritual advisor, the Lord Chancellor also had the task to guide the King's conscience in these cases. Gradually the King assigned the various matters entirely to the Lord Chancellor to deal with. At the end of the fifteenth century a special court was created for this purpose, the Court of Chancery, with the Lord Chancellor as the judge. Shortly thereafter, the office of the Lord Chancellor ceased to be occupied by a priest and began to be held by a jurist (today the Lord Chancellor has no judicial functions any more; he serves in the government as the Minister of Justice and is appointed primarily out of political considerations).

Originally the application of these "rules of equity" was to a high degree dependent upon the sense of justice of the particular King or the Lord Chancellor holding the office at the time. The Lord Chancellor, being a Catholic priest, was influenced by canon law and to some lesser extent also Roman law. As early as in the sixteenth century however, the precedents from the Court of Chancery started to create an independent and complex set of rules called equity, which gradually became as rigid as common law itself. A characteristic element of equity was and still is that it is not as fixated on procedural rules as common law is, and that it places greater weight on the substantive law issues. In the seventeenth century the "legal" character of equity was strengthened by means of the introduction of a possibility to appeal decisions of the Court of Chancery to the House of Lords, but the development of equity into a complex set of established rules was not completed until the beginning of the nineteenth century.

The principle that the courts should be independent of the authority of the King was not especially developed in England of the Middle Ages, as the King and the Lord Chancellor did not mind involving themselves, upon the request of one of the parties, in the administration of justice in order to prevent inequitable results of the application of common law, even if this amounted to interfering with what was a lawful exercise of the other party's rights under common law. What is interesting, however, is that the court of equity did not interfere by means of requiring the common-law court to decide the case in a certain manner or by means of reversing the unjust decision: one of the main principles of equity was that it did not go against the existing common law. On the contrary, the principle was *"equitas sequitur legem"* (equity follows the law). By 1616 it became accepted however that if a conflict arose between the two systems of rules, equity prevailed, but this occurred not by means of equity invalidating the common-law rule in question, but rather by the court of equity issuing an injunction whereby, for instance, a party who in a common-law court had filed a legally well-founded but unjust case was forbidden to continue with proceedings or to have the unjust judgment enforced. The party formally retained his rights, but if he violated the equity injunction he risked being fined or even imprisoned for showing contempt of the court (such civil contempt of court must be distinguished from criminal contempt of court consisting of, for example, disrupting the court proceedings or offending the court).

Equity still constitutes only an incomplete complement to common law. At every legal inquiry an English lawyer must, in the absence of legislation, first determine the common-law rules, and afterwards ask how those rules might be affected by equity. Consequently, one cannot in principle separate the two systems from each other on the basis of the legal relationships they regulate, as any question of law can be a question for equity as well, depending more upon historical developments than on some logical principles. It can, however, be said that equity has its greatest importance within private law, while its influence on criminal law is insignificant.

A typical characteristic of equity is that it operates by means of prohibitions and orders addressed to the parties (equitable remedies) rather than by deciding who owns a certain asset or who ows money to whom. This is often expressed with the phrase "equity acts *in personam*" and means, in practice, that the instruments used to exert pressure on the parties are various types of orders (injunctions) under penalty of fine (subpoena). Certain orders contain prohibitions (negative orders or prohibitive injunctions), allowing equity to prevent injurious conduct. Other orders are positive, ordering the person to whom they are directed to perform some particular act (positive orders or mandatory injunctions): in this way equity created, for instance, the possibility to demand specific performance, such as delivery of unlawfully held personal property (under common law, the defendant could choose to pay compensation instead of delivering the property). Another example of the weakness of common law was that it did not recognize the effects upon the debtor of the transfer of a claim; this deficiency was remedied by equity in that the assignor could be compelled by the court to authorize the assignee to collect the debt in the name of the assignor. An assignee did not obtain the right to collect the debt in his own name until 1875.

One of the differences between law and equity that continued through the centuries was that they were applied by different courts, with different procedural rules and at times even using different languages (common-law courts continued for a long time to use Law French, while equity courts relatively early went over from Latin to English). Equity courts did not, for instance, use a jury. On the other hand, even with equity it was of decisive importance that the plaintiff formulated his demand correctly and submitted it to the proper court. In some cases the plaintiff was even compelled to institute two different proceedings before two different courts, such as when he, because of the defendant's non-fulfillment of a contractual promise, wanted to demand both damages and specific performance. Since 1875, when the Judicature Act of 1873 entered into force, both sets of rules are applied by all types of courts. This does not mean, nevertheless, that the differences in the English legal system between law and equity have lost all their practical significance, even if there has been a certain terminological confusion between the two (the term "law" nowadays often covers the whole legal system, for instance when one speaks about English law as opposed to foreign law, while in certain other contexts it refers only to that part of the judge-made rules which has not at one time been developed by equity courts). The 1875 reform was not intended to merge substantive common law and equity, but only to simplify the judicial proceedings. The rules of equity must even today be interpreted and applied in accordance with a number of general principles of equity, which have been developed over the centuries, and which do not always have a counterpart in common law. The principle "he who comes to equity must come with clean hands" means for instance that the party who is relying upon an equity rule must not himself have acted in an improper manner. Such a principle is not found in common law. Furthermore, equity does not help a procrastinating party: "delay defeats equity". This means that even today it can be of decisive significance whether a certain claim is based "at law" or "in equity", even if today the borderline between the two does not always correspond to their historical delimitations.

Equity's perhaps most important contribution to the development of the English legal system has been the creation of the institute of the "trust". In the same way as many other creative legal inventions, this seems also to have arisen as a means of avoiding various kinds of taxes and duties, in this case the special duty, which during the Middle Ages was paid in connection with the inheritance of real property. To avoid this obligation, the owner[2] assigned, while he was still alive, the property to a trusted relative or friend (the trustee), who after the owner's demise transferred it to the decedent's heirs. In this way the acquisition of the property by the heirs was not treated as an inheritance. During the period of time between the two conveyances the trustee was, according to common law, the full owner of the property, which he formally had the right to retain or dispose of (in relationship to creditors his title of ownership, however, was not full as the property for instance could not be taken by his creditors to pay his debts). If the trustee violated the confidence of the person who established the trust (the settlor), the heir (in this connection called *cestui que trust* or the beneficiary) could get no help from common law, but he could seek and obtain assistance from equity. The respect for common law meant that equity did not deny or annul the trustee's ownership rights, but instead compelled him by means of an injunction to use and dispose of the property in accordance with the terms of the trust (as an expression of the respect for common law, the beneficiary was not, however, said to have a right, but only an "equitable interest"). If the trustee sold the property in violation of his obligations, the sale was regarded in principle as being valid, but he then became the trustee for the amount of money received from the sale; in certain circumstances (for instance if the purchaser acted in bad faith or if the property was sold for an amount below market value) the purchaser also became a trustee, with all of the accompanying obligations. Even today the trust is used in a great number of different situations where, for some reason, it is necessary to distinguish between legal ownership and equitable (beneficiary) ownership, i.e. where property is held by someone for the account of somebody else. In many such cases where one in the Continental countries uses some form of an administrator, English law uses a trustee, such as in connection with the distribution of estates, bankruptcy or guardianship. It is sometimes said that the trust institution is as frequent and indispensable in English legal life as afternoon tea is in the everyday life of the English people.

---

[2] A somewhat simplified terminology is used here. According to English law, all land formally belongs to the Crown and the individual can only obtain one of the different types of the right of usage, such as a freehold or lease.

Another example of the interrelationship between common law and equity is the institute of equitable estoppel, which can be illustrated as follows. According to common law, in order for a contract to be binding, there must be valid "consideration", i.e. each party must have obtained something (or at least a promise of something) in return. A naked promise is not binding by itself. This requirement of consideration is connected to the historical fact that the contractual writ of assumpsit has been developed from the claim for non-contractual damage and therefore presumes that the plaintiff who sues the defendant for a violation of the contract has suffered a real loss. The consideration does not have to be commensurate or substantial, but it must constitute an advantage for the party receiving it or a disadvantage for the party tendering it. In certain cases, where one party has promised the other party to relinquish certain rights, the promise has been upheld with the help of equity despite the lack of consideration, as the other party had acted in reliance upon the promise. Despite that the promise was not binding according to common law, equity prevented the person making the promise to go back on his word and claim the relinquished right from the other party.[3]

9.4 Interpretation of Precedents

Precedents play a very significant role in both common-law and Continental legal systems and some of the principles of interpretation of judicial decisions are the same in both families of law. In the English legal system, where precedents can be formally binding on future cases, additional problems can arise as to where to draw the line between binding and non-binding precedents, and between the binding and non-binding parts of a precedent. Of course, even non-binding precedents and non-binding judicial statements can have significant persuasive authority depending upon the position and reputation of the judge, but the question of what is actually binding is in many cases of decisive importance.

Which courts can create binding precedents is closely related to the structure of the judiciary and will be discussed in section 9.5 below; this section deals instead with the determination of which statements made in a judicial decision should be regarded as being binding in future cases. An additional problem, which will not be dealt with here, is that with hundreds of thousands of published judgments, the finding of relevant precedents presupposes the availability of efficient search instruments. Many of these are provided by commercial publishers and other companies and nowadays involve the use of computers.

While a Continental jurist normally starts by a search for a relevant generally formulated statutory legal rule, and by means of deduction (i.e. inference from a general rule to a particular situation) makes conclusions concerning the actual case at hand, an English lawyer must start with the actual issue and compare

---

[3] See e.g. *Central London Property Trust Ltd.* v. *High Trees House Ltd.*, [1947] K.B. 130.

it with the same or similar legal issues that have been dealt with by courts in previously decided cases, and from these relevant precedents find the binding legal rule by means of induction (i.e. the inference of a general rule from particular cases).

It is openly admitted in England that English courts create and change law by their decisions, but in their judgments English judges tend to pretend to the greatest extent possible that in the particular case at hand they have done no more than "discovered" the legal rules that had already existed, hidden in previously decided precedents. Even when one studies well-known precedents which very clearly have changed the law (the so-called leading cases), one seldom finds that the court openly admits having done so. Most such decisions pretend that they are derived from already existing rules and refer to previous judgments to prove it. It is possible that this fiction has the purpose of legitimizing the judgment, since the application of new judge-made rules means, normally, that they are given a certain retroactive effect, in any case if one looks at it from the point of view of the losing party, which has presumably acted relying upon the prevailing legal rules and reacts negatively to the fact that the court has chosen to use his case for the purpose of changing those rules at a disadvantage to him. Only in some very special situations is it possible to overrule a precedent prospectively, i.e. to follow the precedent in the case at hand but at the same time declare it to be overruled for the purpose of future decisions.[4]

The principle of *stare decisis* can be summarized in a simplified way to mean that two cases dealing with the same issue on the basis of substantially the same relevant facts shall be decided in the same way. But how does one decide, when comparing an actual case with similar previously decided cases, which facts are or should be treated as relevant? That the plaintiffs in both cases are named Smith can hardly be a relevant similarity, but where shall one draw the line? Should one, when interpreting a precedent, only take into consideration the facts that the court has relied on explicitly in its reasons for the judgment?

The fundamental line when interpreting English precedents is between the *ratio decidendi* (also called "the holding" or just "ratio") and the *obiter dictum* (in plural *obiter dicta*). The *ratio decidendi*, which is binding, is the legal rule with which the court decided the case, i.e. the legal rule which in view of the circumstances of the case was necessary for the decision. *Obiter dictum*, on the other hand, is a pronouncement "in passing" or "by the way", which was not necessary for the decision and therefore is not binding in future cases (it can however at times have significant persuasive authority, depending primarily on the status of the court and the reputation of the judge rendering the decision). The reason why *obiter dicta* are not binding is primarily the fact that they were made without the judge having to test them and consider their actual consequences in a real case. This means that they most probably were not thought through to the same extent as the *ratio decidendi* was.

---

4   See *Re Spectrum Plus Ltd. (in liquidation)* [2005] 2 A.C. 680 (House of Lords).

To draw the line between *ratio decidendi* and *obiter dicta* can sometimes be an easy task, particularly when in the previous case the judge, conscious of his role as the creator of law, has clearly indicated that his statement was *obiter*, for instance by saying that "I want to add that I would have found the contract to be invalid if the facts had been such-and-such". The purpose of such conscious but formally superfluous *obiter* statements can be, for example, that the judge desires to explain and illustrate his reasoning with various examples or distinguish the issues arising in the case from other similar issues. It often occurs, however, that the judge himself is not aware that he has made statements going beyond what the case before him actually required. In these cases, it is not the judge making the precedent who draws the line, but judges in subsequent cases, practicing lawyers, legal scholars, law students and others who due to some reason are interested in doing so. The problem can best be illustrated with the assistance of a very simplified fictitious example.

Suppose that a person was bitten by his neighbor's dog and that a court ordered the owner of the dog to pay compensation, with the reasoning that an owner of a domestic animal has strict responsibility if the animal injures someone. Many years later, another person is injured by his neighbor's boa-constrictor and the question arises whether the earlier decision is a binding precedent for the new case (which most likely will be asserted by the lawyer of the injured person) or not (which of course will be the position of the owner of the boa). On its face, it is clear that the injurious incident which occurred with the boa is covered by the statement made in the reasoning of the court in the first case. The lawyer for the owner of the boa will now, however, attempt to convince the judge hearing the case that the previous judicial decision should be considered binding only pertaining to dogs, because boa-constrictors are so different in relevant respects from dogs (for example, dogs can be trained and disciplined while boas cannot) that the same rule does not necessarily apply to both types of animals. The court in the previous case of course had no reason to make statements concerning boas. It only needed to take position on injuries caused by dogs, and to the extent the judge did make a wider statement concerning all kinds of domestic animals, that statement should be regarded as a non-binding *obiter dictum*. Whether this reasoning, submitted by the lawyer for the owner of the boa, would be successful, can be left unstated; the purpose of the example is to show how one, by means of finding and pointing out relevant differences between the present case and the precedent, i.e. by "distinguishing", can avoid the binding effect of a precedent, despite the fact that it contains statements, which according to their wording clearly cover even the newly arisen situation.

It can, on the other hand, also be imagined, even if it rarely occurs, that the judgment's value as precedent extends beyond the judge's own words. If the judge in a decision, for instance, held that the parents had the right to take their son out of a private boarding school before the end of term, in spite of a contract they had made with that school, that decision should probably be regarded as binding precedent also on the same issue concerning daughters, as the gender of the child was not relevant to the decision (the situation would however change if the reasoning in the precedent attributed importance to the gender of the child or if one was successful in convincing the judge in the subsequent case, concerning a girl, that the gender of the child should be recognized as being relevant in that context).

Distinguishing cases is regarded among English jurists as an art rather than an exact science or a simple craft or trade. The task is to discover such differences that are relevant, or may possibly be regarded as being relevant by the court. To return to the above-mentioned example concerning the responsibility of the owner for injuries caused by his domestic animal, it cannot be excluded that relevant differences exist even when both cases concern a dogbite. That the dog in the case referred to as precedent was black, while in the case now before the court the dog is white, is hardly a relevant difference, no more than that one dog bit on a Monday and the other bit on a Wednesday. It is, however, not so sure than one can brush aside such differences as that the injury in one case occurred in the home of the dog owner, while the other occurred in a public place, or that one of the dogs was big and belonged to a race known to be aggressive while the other was a small poodle. There is consequently a significant amount of leeway to limit the binding effect of a precedent by means of distinguishing (restrictive distinguishing).

It can thus be said that the *ratio decidendi* of a decision is not set once and for all. Several decades or even hundreds of years after the judgment has been rendered, the progress of scientific knowledge or changed values in the society can result in that one begins to attach greater importance to certain circumstances, which previously were considered to be irrelevant. An English court consequently contributes to the continuing developments of the law not only by means of taking a position on issues that have not previously been decided by a court (cases of first impression), or by means of overruling earlier precedents; the same occurs also by means of distinguishing. English judges are known for their reluctance to change the law by means of explicitly overruling an accepted precedent, this even in the cases where they have the authority to do so (an overruling must not be confused with a reversal, where a higher court, acting upon appeal, overturned or changed the lower court's decision in the same dispute). If an English judge disapproves of a particular precedent he prefers whenever possible to avoid it by distinguishing the case before him from the facts of the precedent, so that almost any difference in the details is considered to be sufficient. Certain older decisions, which were at one time very important precedents, have in this manner lost practically all weight without any court ever expressly declaring them to be obsolete (such precedents have facetiously been called "very distinguished cases"). This is connected with the previously mentioned reluctance of the English courts to explicitly create new legal rules and their preference for "discovering" rules that are already in existence, hidden in the great treasure of precedents. An English judge is quite willing to state in general terms that he and his colleagues have a law-creating function, but he ordinarily will not openly say that he has exercised it in a particular judicial decision. In the wealth of precedents a judge can often find support for almost any position.

If the judge has used several independent alternative justifications to arrive at the decision, each reasoning is usually regarded as constituting a separate *ratio decidendi*, but it sometimes occurs that the jurist interpreting the decision, who perhaps desires to avoid some of the justifications, asserts that all except one are *obiter dicta*. Especially great difficulties to formulate the *ratio decidendi* of a case can arise where it was decided by a court with more than one judge, since different judges may have arrived at the same decision but with different reasons. The effort to determine the *ratio decidendi* can be further complicated by the fact that even the dissenting opinions are published and studied, and can have a certain weight. It may, for instance, happen that the borderline between two fundamentally different understandings of the legal issue is other than the borderline between the majority and the minority, such as when a judge belonging to the majority shares the dissenting judge's view of the law but votes for another result because he is of the opinion that certain facts have not been proven. The value as precedent of such plurality decisions is uncertain, even though they of course resolve the particular dispute that has caused the case to reach the court in the first place.

9.5 The Judiciary

Similar to other countries of the world, England also has through the centuries undergone many changes in the structure of its judicial system. Considering the role of precedent and legal continuity, the previously existing English judicial systems are of interest not only to legal historians, but may be of practical importance even today since older precedents may be still binding depending upon the position of the court that rendered them. Fortunately, the English judiciary has been relatively stable during the last 137 years, at least regarding the courts whose decisions may be cited as binding precedent. Citations to judgments rendered prior to 1875 have become more and more rare, which is the main reason why this presentation will be limited to the present system. Another reason is that the previous judicial structures were rather complex.

Not all English courts are regarded as law-creating ones. It is only the higher courts that have such a position, and it is only these courts that have their decisions systematically published (reported). The publication of the most important decisions takes place in the semi-official Law Reports (consisting of several series, mainly for the various courts), but there are also several private reports (for example, the All England Reports), some of them specializing in a particular field of law (for example, the Lloyd's List Law Reports reporting commercial cases, many of which have not been reported in the Law Reports). As could be expected, many decisions can be found in electronic databases, operated by private publishers, or on the official websites of certain courts.

The English judicial system is even today relatively complicated, due not any more to the number of different courts, but rather to the large number of special rules and exceptions concerning the choice of proper trial and appellate court for some types of cases. The composition of the courts and the various judicial titles also vary greatly. The following presentation is therefore a simplified summary. Nor is there room here to describe the special English judicial jargon, including the obligatory polite ceremonial phrases and mannerisms used by judges and lawyers when addressing each other, etc.

Judicial System in England (Simplified Diagram)

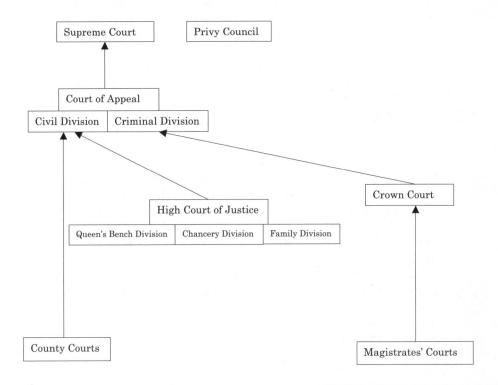

The Court of Justice of the European Union in Luxemburg and the European Court of Human Rights in Strasbourg function in matters of EU law and the European Human Rights Convention as the highest judicial instances for the Member/Contracting States including the United Kingdom, but their role is too special to be dealt with here.

The ordinary citizen will usually come into contact with one of the more than 200 county courts, which hear as the first instance the majority of civil cases. The name of these courts is somewhat misleading as the territorial jurisdiction of the county courts does not coincide with the administrative division of the country into counties. The judges in these courts, who are called Circuit Judges, are appointed from among barristers or solicitors who have had a minimum of seven years of practical experience. Prosecutions for less serious criminal offences are normally, in about 98 percent of the cases, dealt with in the first instance by one of the almost one thousand magistrates' courts, which also hear certain special types of civil cases pertaining to family law matters. In the larger cities, the magistrates' courts consist of professional judges who are trained lawyers (Stipendiary Magistrates), but in the countryside the magistrates are often unpaid Justices of the Peace who may have no legal background at all. In the latter case, the court clerks in the magistrates' courts have significant importance and influence, as they are normally qualified lawyers. The procedures in the county courts and the magistrates' courts are relatively informal and simple, and there is no jury. Decisions in county courts and magistrates' courts have no value as precedent.

The judgments rendered by the High Court of Justice, on the other hand, have precedential value, despite the fact that even these are mostly (but not always) first-instance decisions, albeit normally in more important cases. Until 1971, cases before the High Court of Justice were always heard in London, but nowadays it may also "sit" in other places in England and Wales. It is, however, still formally a single court, even though consisting of three divisions, called the Chancery Division, Queen's Bench Division (King's Bench Division when England has a male monarch) and Family Division. The last-mentioned division was established in 1970, when it replaced the Probate, Divorce and Admiralty Division. As the name of this former division implies, it was concerned with inheritance, marriage and maritime cases, which led to it somewhat jokingly being called the "3W Division" (wills, wives and wrecks). The three divisions have, to a certain extent, overlapping jurisdiction, but the cases are routinely divided so that the Family Division deals with family-law disputes, the Queen's Bench Division deals with most common-law cases (i.e. cases which prior to 1875 were heard by the common-law courts), and cases that rely primarily upon equity tend to be heard by the Chancery Division. These differences have resulted in that some barristers tend to specialize and only work in one of the divisions. The largest division by far is the Queen's Bench Division, which even encompasses an Admiralty Court for maritime cases and a Commercial Court for commercial law cases. The Queen's Bench Division also has jurisdiction over certain criminal law matters.

Nowadays the High Court of Justice makes use of a jury only in very special cases. There are more than 100 judges on the High Court (they are called "puisne judges"), but aside from a few exceptions, each case is in principle decided by one single judge. The precedents from the High Court bind the magistrates' and county courts but are not binding upon other High Court judges, even though they ordinarily treat each other's judgments with great

respect. The judgments from the High Court of course are not binding precedent in higher courts, but that does not mean that their decisions do not have
any persuasive authority there. Besides, the higher instances are reluctant to
change an existing rule, especially if it has been accepted for a long period of
time and individuals and companies have come to rely upon it. It does occur that
even the highest instances will refer to and rely upon a High Court judgment for
support, even though they obviously do not regard themselves as being bound
by it. Only about ten percent of all High Court decisions are published, and the
value of the unpublished decisions is naturally somewhat doubtful.

Formally on the same level as the High Court of Justice is, since 1971, the
Crown Court, which hears appeals from magistrates' courts. It is also the
trial court for more serious criminal matters, i.e. cases concerning indictable
offences, where a twelve-person jury will decide the guilt or innocence of the
accused. In practice however, jury is used relatively seldom, as many defendants
plead guilty or do not make use of their right to demand a jury trial. Crown
Court judgments are not regarded as having value as precedent, which is probably connected with the fact that they are not systematically published. The
Crown Court is formally one court, but its many judges work throughout the
country. The Crown Court in London is officially called the Central Criminal
Court, but it is more commonly known as "the Old Bailey" and is one of the
city's popular tourist attractions.

Next above the High Court and the Crown Court is the Court of Appeal,
whose task, as the name implies, is to hear the appeals directed against judgments rendered by the above-mentioned lower courts. It consists of two divisions: a Civil Division for civil matters and a Criminal Divisions for criminal
matters. The judgments of the Court of Appeal, at least those 25 percent of them
which are published, are binding precedent on all lower courts and, apart from
certain exceptions, even upon the Court of Appeal itself, so that normally it may
not diverge from its earlier decisions, provided of course that they have not been
overruled by the Supreme Court or by means of legislation. Frequently the Court
of Appeal succeeds in increasing its freedom of action by means of sophisticated distinguishing (se section 9.4 above). The Court of Appeal consists of 37
judges who hold the title Lord (or Lady) Justice of Appeal. They sit usually as a
three-member panel, but five-member panels are used in some cases. The Civil
Division is headed by the Master of the Rolls and the Criminal Division by the
Lord Chief Justice.

The highest court instance is the Supreme Court, which in 2009 replaced,
as far as its judicial functions were concerned, the House of Lords, i.e. the
upper house of Parliament. According to an unwritten constitutional rule,
well-established since 1844, the hereditary lords did not take part in the delib-
erations when the House of Lords functioned as a court; the participation was
reserved to the professional "Law Lords", i.e. the twelve well-respected jurists
who, if not already a peer, had been elevated to a peerage and remunerated just
for the purpose of judicial work. In 2009, even this symbolic bond to the House

of Lords was broken, but the principal functions and manner of operating did not undergo a substantial change. The number of Supreme Court judges who participate in each individual case varies, most often five but never less than three. For the Supreme Court to consider a case, a leave to appeal is required, which can be granted not only by the Supreme Court itself but also by the Court of Appeal. Leave to appeal is, however, ordinarily granted only in cases where a question of law of general interest has arisen, so that the number of Supreme Court judgments is only about 100 per year. The precedents of the Supreme Court and of the House of Lords, of which approximately three-quarters are published, are binding upon all lower courts and, because of the desire to preserve stability, only very rarely are overruled by the Supreme Court itself. In practice the Supreme Court normally functions as a court of cassation, i.e. it limits itself to uphold or reverse the appealed decision without replacing it with its own final judgment; in the case of reversal, the case is usually sent back to a lower instance court which is however obliged to follow the Supreme Court's view on the relevant point of law.

The Supreme Court also constitutes the highest instance of the judiciary of Scotland and Northern Ireland (for Scotland only in civil cases). Appeals against judgments issued in Scotland or Northern Ireland are of course heard apply-ing Scots law or the law of Northern Ireland, but in cases where the rules being interpreted and applied are identical with the rules in England, for instance legislation which is applicable for the entire United Kingdom, these decisions will have a value as binding precedent also in England.

The fact that the Court of Appeal is bound by its own precedents had led to a procedural finesse called "leap-frogging": civil cases, where the outcome depends upon such a precedent being followed or overruled, may, since 1969, in certain situations be appealed directly from the High Court to the Supreme Court (before 2009 the House of Lords), since a detour via the Court of Appeal would be meaningless under the circumstances.

A bit apart from the actual English judiciary, but to a high degree similar to a court, stands the Judicial Committee of the Privy Council, which is formally a mere advisory body to the monarch. The Privy Council is composed of some of England's and the British Commonwealth's most respected jurists including the judges of the Supreme Court. It hears appeals from i.a. the courts in the Channel Islands and the Isle of Man, the few remaining British colonies (e.g. Gibraltar), plus some of the now independent sovereign common-law countries, which continue to acknowledge the Privy Council as their court of last resort, for example some small island countries overseas. The Privy Council consequently more often than not applies law which is not English in the strict meaning of the word, but as the legal systems in question are normally based upon English law, the differences are most often insignificant or even non-existent. Even though the decisions of the Privy Council are not formally binding as precedent, their statements will be treated with great respect and have substantial persua-sive authority, primarily due to the fact the the Privy Council mainly consists of high English judges. This is also the reason for the Privy Council decisions being published in the same reports series as the judgments of the Supreme Court. A Privy Council judgment is normally regarded as constituting a binding precedent in the legal system where the case arose from. Formally however, the decision of a Privy Council is not a judgment at all, but rather a mere piece of "advice", albeit this advice is always followed. Until 1960s, dissenting opinions were not published, as it was deemed that good advice should not consist of contradicting opinions.

In addition to the courts of general jurisdiction that have just been described, England also has a significant number of special courts usually called "tribunals", such as the Employment Appeal Tribunal for labour disputes, the Competition Appeal Tribunal for anti-trust cases, and several quasi-judicial organs within the administration. Decisions of many of the administrative tribunals are subject to appeal on a point of law to the Upper Tribunal (created in 2007), with a further appeal possible in some cases to the Civil Division of the Court of Appeal.

The English judicial procedure's most conspicuous traditional characteristic is the passive role of the judge. The conduct of the proceedings was in principle the responsibility of the parties themselves, i.e. their lawyers. This was referred to as the "adversary principle" in civil cases and the "accusatory principle" in criminal cases. The primary role of the judge during the trial was to make sure that the procedural rules were followed, although it might occasionally occur that the judge took a more active role, depending very much on the personality and disposition of the particular judge.

The procedure in civil cases underwent however a radical reform (the so-called Woolf Reform) in 1999 in order to make the procedure simpler and more efficient. The new Civil Procedure Rules divided civil disputes into three categories (tracks): small claims track, fast track and multi-track. The division depends primarily on the disputed value and the complexity of the case. The new rules give the judge a significantly more active role, even though it is still not comparable to the "inquisitorial" *modus operandi* of the Continental judges. The reform has also brought about a number of terminological changes, but the familiarity with the old terminology remains important, i.a. because it contin-ues to be used in many other common-law countries. A typical civil procedure can be briefly described as follows. The proceedings are started by the claimant (formerly plaintiff) using a claim form (formerly summons), which is served on the defendant. The defendant must answer within a certain period of time whether he intends to contest the claimant's demands or not. If he chooses to contest, there is an exchange of documents called statements of case (formerly pleadings), where the parties summarize and present their respective versions of relevant facts. By means of the statements the need for particular evidence is clarified. The actual obtaining of the evidence is conducted by the parties themselves (their lawyers), who with the assistance of the court can compel the opposing party to answer, under oath, certain questions (interrogatories) and to disclose the contents of and produce certain documents (disclosure, formerly discovery). Juries are not ordinarily used in civil cases any more. At the beginning of the trial, the claimant presents his case and then calls his witnesses. Each witness is questioned by the claimant's lawyer, and then cross-examined by the lawyer of the defendant. After this cross-examination, the purpose of which is to reduce to the furthest extent possible the value for the claimant of the testimony provided by the witness, the claimant has the right to re-examine his witness to attempt to restore such value. When the claimant is finished with the calling of his witnesses and the presentation of his evidence, he "rests" and the defendant may ask ("move") that the judge without further proceedings dismiss the case on the ground that the evidence presented by the claimant, even if not refuted, is insufficient to support the Claimant's cause of action. If the judge does not dismiss the case, the trial continues with the defendant calling his witnesses, who are questioned one after the other by the defendant's lawyer, cross-examined by the claimant's lawyer, re-examined, etc. The defendant concludes with a closing address, followed by the claimant's closing address. The judge renders his judgment either immediately, or after a certain period of consideration (reserved judgment).

9.6 Interpretation of Statutes

It would be a serious mistake to believe that English law is dominated entirely by precedents. Written statutes have always played an important role, and they nowadays clearly prevail in the fields of law where English law is subordinate to the law of the European Union. The most important written legal rules are the statutes enacted by Parliament (Acts of Parliament), but there are also a large number of secondary legislation called Statutory Instruments, such as Orders in Council, Rules, Orders, plus various local ordinances called by-laws.

The United Kingdom does not have a written Constitution and no court may question the validity of an Act of Parliament.[5] This doctrine of the legislative supremacy of the Parliament has been created by the courts themselves and is not stipulated by statute.

Acts of Parliament are published by Her Majesty's Stationery Office and are also available electronically on the Internet.[6]

Even concerning legislation, the continuity of law and historical bonds to the past are very strong. Statutes do not become invalid merely due to their age; after World War II some traitors were prosecuted and sentenced according to the Treason Act of 1351. A number of old statutes have however become obsolete and ceased to be enforced even long before they were formally repealed. This was the fate of, for instance, the Sunday Observance Act of 1677 that upon religious

---

5 See *British Railways Board* v. *Pickin* [1974] A.C. 765 (House of Lords).

6 See <www.legislation.hmso.gov.uk>.

grounds prohibited and criminalized certain public assemblies on Sundays and was not formally repealed until 1969. Since 1965 England has a permanent commission, the Law Commission, which has the task of constantly keeping an eye on the legal system and if necessary proposing new legislation. The work of this five-member commission has resulted in several reforms. Not only legal practitioners but also legal scholars are represented on the commission, which considering the relatively weak status of legal science in the English legal system, is not a matter of course.

If there is a conflict between legislation and a judicial precedent, the precedent must give way to the statute. The judge is bound by applicable statutes and cannot refuse to apply them just because he does not agree with them. In the English lawyers' view however, legislation constitutes a kind of outside inter-ference in the "normal" law, i.e. the judge-made common law and equity. The English judges are known to attempt, whenever possible, to interpret the statu-tory rules restrictively. An English judge once summarized his view by saying that legislation normally changes the law for the worse and that it is the court's task to minimize the damage by presuming, whenever there is the slightest doubt, that common law has not been changed. The skeptical attitude of English judges to legislated legal rules is largely due to their conviction that legislation, in comparison with judicial precedents, is a substandard method of creating legal norms, "a trespass by unauthorised laymen on the province of the lawyers". Legislation, even if so extensive as the great German and French codifications, seems to the English jurist as incomparably poorer than the tens of thousands of existing precedents. Precedents in addition have a pronounced practical charac-ter, since they concern questions that have in fact arisen in real life, rather than theoretical speculations concerning situations that might conceivably arise in the future. The disadvantages of precedent-based, judge-made law, such as the difficulty to get an overview of the legal rules, are seen by the English lawyers sometimes even as an advantage, not the least from an egoistic professional point of view.

One means to achieve a restrictive application of statutes has been to inter-pret the text of the statute strictly according to the literal meaning of its word-ing (the so-called literal rule). Such practice has resulted in that Parliament as a counter-measure has been compelled to formulate the legislation in a very detailed manner so as to make an excessively restrictive application difficult (see section 3.3 above). In the larger statutory texts, interpretation is made easier by the inclusion, at the beginning of the statute, of "interpretation sections" providing detailed definitions of the various terms used in the enactment. In addition, a special Interpretation Act contains certain basic principles of interpretation to be used for all statutes, for instance that words importing the masculine gender are presumed to include the feminine, i.e. "he" also includes "she" unless otherwise stated. When interpreting the text of statutes, it should be kept in mind that many statutes are merely an enactment of law that has previously been established by precedents (codification acts), or a restatement in a more organized manner of the contents of previously existing legislated rules (consolidation acts). In this way important parts of the English commercial law became enacted by the end of the nineteenth and beginning of the twentieth century, such as the Bills of Exchange Act, Partnership Act, Sale of Goods Act and the Marine Insurance Act. In connection with the interpretation of such statutes it is regarded as acceptable to seek direction from judicial decisions, which preceded and constituted the basis for the codification; however, this is not allowed if the text of the statute is clear and unambiguous.

Another characteristic of the English interpretation of statutes is that legisla-tive history is normally not referred to, even though in 1993 this principle was somewhat softened by a precedent from the House of Lords permitting, excep-tionally, reference to clear statements by a Minister, or other promotor of the Bill, in legislative materials, when wording of a statute is ambiguous, obscure or leads to an absurdity.[7] In the English legal literature one notices that prepara-tory legislative materials are a foreign element; it is no coincidence that English authors frequently prefer the French designation *travaux préparatoires*. The reason for this negative attitude towards legislative history is said to be that the wording of the statute cannot be regarded as an expression of the intentions of any particular person or group but rather should be seen as a depersonalized text which has its own linguistic meaning independent of its background. An English judge has summarized this with the following words:[8]

> In the construction of all written instruments including statutes, what the court is concerned to ascertain is, not what the promulgators of the instruments meant to say, but the meaning of what they have said.

The above-mentioned restrictive interpretation of the text of statutes (the literal rule) is however not entirely without exceptions, which have been developed and can be found in the judicial decisions from the courts. Thus, it is accepted that a court is free to diverge from the text of the statute in order to avoid obvious absurdities (the so-called golden rule). The court can also consider the negative phenomenon in the society which the statute in question was intended to correct or mitigate. This is called the "mischief rule", and has been derived from a 1584 precedent (*Heydon's case*). It allows the judge to take into consideration the legis-lative history, however only for the purpose of determining what the legislation was intended to achieve and not to find what it intended to say and how it should be interpreted. The limits for these rather unclear unwritten principles of inter-pretation depend very much on the personality of the individual judge.

Among the other established English principles of statutory interpretation, the rule of *ejusdem generis* deserves to be mentioned. According to this rule, references to for example "dogs, cats and other animals" do not include lions or whales, as "other animals" are presumed to refer only to household animals of

---

[7] *Pepper* v. *Hart* [1993] A.C. 593 (H.L.).

[8] Lord Simon in *Farrell* v. *Alexander*, [1977] A.C. 59, on p. 81.

the same type as dogs and cats. Another principle of interpretation of statutes is *expressio unius est exclusio alterius*, meaning that a reference to, for instance, boa-constrictors justified an *e contrario* conclusion that the rule does not apply to vipers.

An important difference between the English and the Continental approach to the interpretation of statutes is the role of the court decisions regarding the statute under scrutiny. It does not take long before the text of a new statute has been interpreted and applied by the courts, and these decisions, having become binding precedents, are in the practical legal life the real source of law rather than the text of the statute itself. As the principle of *stare decisis* also applies to decisions interpreting the text of statutes, the statutory rule is soon converted into a judge-made rule, so that English jurists can continue to use their traditional common-law working methods even in areas that are seemingly covered by comprehensive legislation.

The membership of the United Kingdom in the European Union (and previously in the European Community) resulted in the need for English courts to interpret and apply European rules, which are not always formulated in the manner that has been traditionally used in England. As the European rules must be understood in the same way in all Member States, the English courts had to realize that they, in these cases, cannot retain their usual English principles of interpretation. The well-known English judge Lord Denning pronounced the following clever words concerning interpretation of the EC Treaty:[9]

> It would be absurd that the courts of England should interpret it differently from the courts of France, or Holland, or Germany [...]. We must, therefore, put on one side our traditional rules of interpretation. We have for years tended to stick too closely to the letter – to the literal interpretation of the words. We ought, in interpreting this Convention, to adopt the European method [...]. In interpreting the Treaty of Rome (which is part of our law) we must certainly adopt the new approach. Just as in Rome, you should do as Rome does. So in the European Community, you should do as the European Court does.

9.7   Legal Education and the Legal Profession

Continental jurists often become surprised when they learn that England lacks a judicial career as it is known in its traditional meaning. A young English lawyer cannot enter the judiciary directly after his legal education; judges are instead appointed from experienced and respected practicing lawyers. To be appointed a judge, especially in the higher courts that create the law, is an honour that requires that the lawyer has practiced law for many years, ensuring indirectly that he has attained a mature age and is sufficiently wealthy (or else he probably would not accept the reduction in income that he

---

9   See *Buchanan & Co. v. Babco Forwarding & Shipping Ltd.*, [1977] Q.B. 208, on pp. 213-214.

suffers when he exchanges his lucrative law practice for the salary of a judge). It is therefore not surprising that English judges are regarded as being one of the more conservative groups in society, which is perhaps not without relevance for their judicial law-making. An English judge tends to have a strong personality and writes his judicial decisions in the first person using "I" and a very personal style.

Practicing lawyers in England and Wales are traditionally divided into two categories, namely barristers (about 12,000) and solicitors (more than 100,000). The difference between the two can be traced back to the Middle Ages, but there have been proposals to abolish the distinction, regarded by many as being outdated, and combine both groups in a unified profession (such amalgamated legal profession is nowadays found in most other common-law countries). As a step in that direction, reforms were introduced with the enactment of the Courts and Legal Services Act 1990, which reduced the differences between the two categories, for example by allowing barristers to advertise and giving solicitors increased capacity to appear before higher courts. In 2007, a new Legal Services Act created a Legal Services Board with the task of regulating the legal profession and removing obsolete restrictions hampering competition. However, due to the conservativism of the English legal profession, the traditional differences between barristers and solicitors have so far remained to a large extent in practice. Progress is being made though; for example, there are today thousands of solicitors authorized to represent clients in higher courts (such solicitors use the title of "solicitor advocate").

A solicitor traditionally works with the same tasks as a lawyer does in most countries, except for conducting the trial itself. He assists his clients with legal advice, helps them to draft contracts and wills, manages estates, negotiates on behalf of his clients, etc. Solicitors used to have a monopoly on providing assistance with the transfer of real property (conveyancing), but on the other hand they did not have the authority to represent their clients before the higher courts, where the clients were required to make use of the services of a bewigged barrister wearing a robe (the wearing of wigs is no longer common in civil cases though).The primary task of a barrister is advocacy, i.e. to appear before the courts. Traditionally, a client does not contact a barrister directly, but rather retains a solicitor who in turn retains ("briefs") a barrister. In fact, it has been regarded as unethical for a barrister to consult with the client outside of the presence of the client's solicitor, which means that the client must retain (and pay) at least two lawyers. This duplication is usually defended by saying that a barrister should not be so engaged in a controversy that he cannot see and present his client's case in an objective and convincing manner. The barrister's profession is regarded as a vocation in the service of justice, which is reflected i.a. in that a barrister by tradition does not have a legally enforceable right to claim his fee and that he, apart from special situations, cannot reject any client (on the other hand, until 2002 he did not normally have any legal liability for negligence in the performance of his tasks). A barrister does not negotiate for his fee; this is taken care of by his "clerk", who is a kind of over-secretary usually working for several barristers for a share in their fees. His negotiating ability is very important, as he must strike the balance between demanding too little and thereby losing income, and demanding too much and losing the client.

A barrister works in his "chambers", often sharing office facilities with other barristers but from the legal point of view normally as a sole practitioner. The establishment of professional companies is, on the other other hand, common practice among solicitors; even if many such firms are relatively small, the largest London solicitor firms consist of more than a hundred solicitors. In the larger firms one should distinguish between "partners" (who are the owners of the firm and share in its profits) and solicitors who are only employees.

A successful senior barrister can apply to the Lord Chancellor to be appointed Queen's Counsel (or of course King's Counsel if the reigning monarch is male), which authorizes him to place the title Q.C. (or K.C.) after his name, to wear a gown made of silk (it is said that the barrister "takes silk") and to decline clients he does not wish to represent. It may also increase his chances of a judicial appointment. A Queen's Counsel is costly and is retained only in particularly important cases. Until recently he could not represent his client before the court without having an ordinary barrister (a so-called "junior") by his side, which increased the number of lawyers per client to at least three. The system has not distinguished itself by cheapness, which led Charles Dickens to exclaim that "the one great principle of English law is to make business for itself".

An academic law degree (usually Bachelor of Laws, LL.B.) has tradition-ally not been a formal requirement to enter the legal profession. An aspiring barrister instead learned the trade by means of working as a "pupil" for an experienced barrister, while aspiring solicitors "served their articles" with an experienced solicitor. Nowadays a university degree is required, but not neces-sarily in law (almost all new barristers and solicitors have, nevertheless, a law degree, which requires a three-year university legal education). A law degree does not replace the requirement that the prospective lawyer take certain special courses organized by the profession, successfully pass the special barrister or solicitor examination, and during a set period of time practice as a pupil or serve his articles. A law degree obviously makes it easier to pass the exams, but it is still possible to meet practicing lawyers or even judges who have never studied at a law faculty. This is perhaps the principal reason for the English courts' scep-ticism towards making use of the opinions of legal scholars. If a part wants to influence the court's interpretation of a legal rule, he does not ordinarily submit a legal opinion from a professor of law or other legal scholar, but rather from a respected Queen's Counsel. In fact, in the not too distant past, it was considered improper to cite to a scholarly legal work at all as long as the author was still alive.

A newly established barrister is said to have been "called to the bar", which means that he now has the right to appear before the courts (what is meant by "bar" is the railing that separates the judge from the parties and their lawyers). As one of the remaining relics of the guild system, every barrister must be a member of one of the four barrister's associations called Inns of Court (Lincoln's Inn, Gray's Inn, Inner Temple or Middle Temple), where one of the conditions for admission until the 1990's was that he must have participated in a certain number of dinners. The Inns were originally also a kind of educational institution, a task which is now fulfilled by the Inns of Court School of Law.

In addition to the Inns of Court, barristers have a General Council of the Bar (Bar Council), which among other matters deals, through its Bar Standards Board, with education and disciplinary affairs. Corresponding matters concerning solicitors are dealt with by their Law Society and the Solicitors Regulation Authority.

9.8 Geographic Spread of English Law

As has been mentioned above, approximately one-third of all mankind lives in countries with a legal system which to a significant extent is based upon English law. This might seem surprising, as the common law, with its hundreds of volumes of cases, at least before the advent of the new means of communication such as the Internet, could be considered to travel less easily than codified law, summarized in a few handy volumes of statutes.

Naturally, the explanation of the geographical success of the common law is most often historical and connected with the British colonial expansion. Even though the British settlers originated from Scotland and Ireland as well as England, they were considered to take with them the English law and equity, which therefore constituted the nucleus of the legal system of the colonies. A distinction must in that connection be made between the territories that lacked a developed legal system prior to the arrival of the British (for example North America, Australia and New Zealand) and such British colonial acquisitions that already had a well-established legal system (for instance French law in Québec, Dutch-Roman law in South Africa, Islamic or Hindu law in India, and developed customary law of certain tribes in Africa). In the first-named territories, it was natural that English law came to dominate the legal system that was established to fill what was perceived as a legal vacuum. In the latter group, the British did not have any ambition to force English law upon the local population, in any case not in the field of private law. In territories where a different European legal culture had been introduced before the British takeover, such as Québec and South Africa, that culture has largely survived until today (see section 11.5 below). Non-European legal cultures have shown less resistance to the English influence, especially in the field of commercial affairs, where English law most often soon replaced the local law, while for example family and succession law often remained regulated by local rules. As the local law was administered by British judges, it at times received a certain English flavor, particularly as the judges were authorized to disregard those rules and legal concepts, which from the British point of view were considered to be "repugnant to justice and morality". In some instances the British went so far as to codify the local law; for instance in India one could find British codifications of both Hindu and Moslem law on marriage.

The English law, which in one way or another became applicable in the colonies, was not always identical with the English law in England. To begin with, the reception of English law was regarded to have occurred by a particular cut-off date, determined in the document granting the colony in question the right to establish its own courts, and it was uncertain what weight should be given to, for example, an English judicial decision rendered after that date. The English rules in the colonies were additionally subjected to local legislative changes. English legislation was regarded as being applicable outside of England only if it was intended to have such "general application" and only to the extent that it was appropriate taking into consideration the local conditions, which gave judges a great deal of latitude. A formulation commonly used in the cut-off document was that

> the substance of common law, the doctrine of equity and the statutes of general application in force in England are to be applied but so far only as the circumstances of the territory and its inhabitants and the limits of Her Majesty's jurisdiction permit, and subject to such qualifications as local circumstances may render necessary.

The classic example of a local adaptation is provided by the rules in the American colonies concerning the liability of the owner of livestock for damage caused by his animals in the garden of another. The traditional English rule was that the owner of livestock was obligated to prevent such damage, for instance by means of keeping his animals within an enclosed area. That rule did not work very well in the then sparsely populated American colonies, where it was much more appropriate to allow livestock to graze freely and to enclose the gardens instead. The English rule was therefore quickly replaced.

When the former British colonies gained independence, they virtually always retained most of the legal system which they had become familiar with during the colonial rule. An Eastern-European comparatist has, with some dissatisfaction, stated that[10]

> [i]t is typical of English law that it was not chosen voluntarily by any other country but wherever it was once introduced no country could rid itself of it.

This applies not only to the territories where the population is predominantly of British origin, such as New Zealand or English-speaking Canada, but also to the regions which after the departure of the British were almost entirely populated

---

[10] See Eörsi, *Comparative Civil Law*, p. 196.

by indigenous peoples or other non-Europeans. Not only were the substantive contents of the legal rules largely retained, but also the external forms of the machinery of the law. It is, for instance, not uncommon that when paying a visit to a court in the now independent but formerly British territories in Africa, one meets judges and lawyers wearing wigs of the English type. In most of these former British colonies English is usually the official language of the law, at least in the higher courts. In reality English law has a very strong position in the cities of these countries, while the people in the countryside often follow local rules, which are not infrequently based on the prevailing religion.

The fact that Britain during a very long period of time was the world's leading commercial and seafaring nation has contributed to the spread of English law even beyond the former British colonial empire. In certain fields English law has become a kind of universal *lex mercatoria*. Throughout the world, for instance, insurance companies use cargo clauses elaborated by the Institute of London Underwriters that include references to English law. This is done even when none of the parties are from England and the situation has otherwise nothing to do with England. Certain English legal institutions have, due to special reasons, been adopted by countries without any other legal or political connection to England. For example, Liechtenstein introduced in 1926 a form of the trust, primarily to be able to offer Anglo-American investors an investment form with which they were familiar.

The most important common-law country outside of England is without any doubt the United States, whose legal system, due to the country's great economic and political importance, deserves to be dealt with separately, i.e. not as a mere appendix to English law.

CHAPTER 10

American Law

10.1 Federalism

The thirteen mutually independent colonies of British North America that originally formed the United States naturally adopted English law. The official British position was that English law followed with the colonists, however only to the extent appropriate for the local circumstances. The bond of continuity to the English law (both common law and equity), as this law was before the American Revolution, has never been entirely severed. Therefore, English judicial decisions from the pre-revolutionary times can even today be referred to in American courts as binding precedent. The states have varying rules concerning the cut-off date, ranging from 1607 to 1776; even later English cases can be referred to, but these have only persuasive authority, i.e. they are not binding upon the court. The influence of English law was significant even under the fist decades subsequent to the Revolution, but the ideology of the new American society led to the elimination of some of the English law's conservative and feudal features.

The demands of modern times have compelled similar subsequent reforms in the United States, as they have in England, for example the abolition of the writ system and the merging of common law and equity as far as procedures are concerned. In the federal judiciary, uniform procedural rules for law and equity were not introduced until 1938 (in a few states special courts of equity still exist, and in a few others the courts follow different procedural rules depending upon whether the case is "in equity" or "at law"). The English legal tradition remains strongest within private law. It is much weaker within public law, as the British system of government was not particularly popular with the settlers, who to a large extent immigrated to North America due to conflicts or dissatisfaction with the British social order. In the field of criminal law the old common-law crimes have become almost completely replaced by written penal statutes.

When studying American law one must always keep in mind that in reality one is dealing with more than fifty closely related, but far from identical, legal systems. The United States is a federation composed of "states", which have never assented to a general unification of their laws. On the contrary, it is a system where the states, at least in theory, have retained all authority which has not been expressly transferred through the federal Constitution to the federal organs. In certain fields both the state and federal authorities have jurisdiction; in the case of such concurrent jurisdiction federal law takes precedence over state law. The individual states have retained and developed their own legal rules in the fields of, for example, the central parts of contract law, corporation law, penal law, family law, inheritance law, property law, torts, and conflict of laws (private international law). However maritime law, bankruptcy, and patent law, for example, are governed primarily by federal rules. The states have retained some subsidiary authority to regulate in these fields as well, but only if and to the extent the federal organs have not made use of their authority and left certain matters unregulated.

With the admission of new states, and the addition of territories such as the federal capital District of Columbia (Washington D.C.), Puerto Rico, Guam, American Samoa and American Virgin Islands, the number of different legal systems within the United States increased. With the exception of Louisiana, where French law has left an imprint, i.a. in the form of a French-inspired Civil Code, the legal systems of the states are almost entirely built upon common-law traditions and they are in this and other ways very closely related with each other.[1] Together with the federal law, which of course applies in the whole country, these similarities make it possible to speak of "American law", but the differences between the law in the various states should not be disregarded. They are often used by sharp lawyers looking for the state whose law would be most favorable to their client. For example, many businessmen find it advantageous to register their corporations in the state of Delaware because of its corporation law, and many couples looking for a quick divorce make use of the liberal divorce laws in the state of Nevada.

In the fields of law reserved to the states, there is not, nor can there be, any federal law. Concerning legislation this is rather self-evident, although the federal government may suggest to the states that they adopt particular legislation and may even entice them to do so using financial incentives. The rule of independence of the states applies even in the absence of state legislation. According to the well-known decision of the U.S. Supreme Court in the case of *Erie Railroad Company* v. *Tompkins*,[2] every state has its own common law, which must also be respected and applied by the federal courts (see section 10.3 below). There is thus no federal common law within the fields of law that are within the sole jurisdiction of the states. This however does not prevent the state courts from taking into consideration judicial decisions from courts in other states, thereby developing legal rules that in reality are substantially the same in all states. Federal common law is, on the other hand, conceivable in the fields that lack legislated provisions and fall within the areas of competency of the federal organs.

As there are significant differences between the laws in the various states, conflict of laws rules are of great importance. The American courts use, to a large extent, the same conflict rules for international situations as for conflicts between the laws of the states, but the conflict rules have been developed primarily with the choice of law between states in mind. The conflict rules are ordinarily not codified but rather constitute a part of state common law and they are often significantly different from state to state. On the other hand, the U.S. Constitution provides that the states in principle shall recognize and enforce each other's judicial decisions (the so-called "full faith and credit clause" in Article IV(1)). Such recognition must, however, be distinguished from the use

---

[1]   In the states which at one time had been part of the Spanish colonial empire one can still find some remaining elements of the influence of Spanish law. Furthermore, the Spanish legal tradition remains very strong in the territory of Puerto Rico.

[2]   304 U.S. 64 (1938).

of a judicial decision as a precedent; state judicial decisions never have binding effect as a precedent in a court of another state, even though they can enjoy
considerable persuasive authority there.

The federal competency to regulate has gradually grown, primarily by
means of an expansive interpretation of the U.S. Constitution. For example, the
Constitution's "commerce clause" in Article I(8) grants to the U.S. Congress the
right "to regulate commerce with foreign nations, and among the several states,
and with the Indian tribes", but the Congress has shown a propensity to regulate
even trade within state borders, usually referring to that even such regulation
indirectly affects commerce between the states. This expansive interpretation of
the commerce clause has been found acceptable by the U.S. Supreme Court.[3]

Violations of federal penal statutes, which of course must not go beyond
the competency granted to the federal legislator by the Constitution, constitute
federal crimes. For example, stealing a car is a crime under state law, but if the
thief takes the stolen car from one state to another he additionally commits a
federal crime (transportation of stolen property across state lines), and he can
be prosecuted and sentenced in the federal courts for this and serve time in a
federal prison. Certain crimes, such as kidnapping, are considered to fall within
the federal competency because they usually have a cross-border dimension; by
making them federal crimes it was made possible to involve immediately federal
authorities, such as the FBI, without having to wait for any indication in each
particular case that the kidnapped person has been moved to another state or
abroad.

An important contribution to the relatively high degree of uniformity of
American law is made by the states themselves and their courts. In the drafting
of state legislation, the laws of other states are ordinarily taken into consideration, and a state normally does not adopt rules that are at great variance with the
rules commonly applicable in most other states, unless there are special grounds
to do so. The state judiciary is not at all bound to follow precedents from courts
in other states, but relevant decisions from other states are commonly cited
and taken into consideration. Another manner of achieving uniformity in law
is the voluntary enactment by each state legislature of "model codes". A special
institution, The National Conference of Commissioners on Uniform State Law,
has since the end of the nineteenth century developed more than one hundred
such uniform model statutes, which have been adopted by the states to varying
degrees. The most successful and important uniform law is without doubt the
Uniform Commercial Code (UCC) of 1951 (with later amendments), which has
been adopted by all fifty states (however in Louisiana not in its entirety) and
covers extensive parts of business law, including contracts for the sale of goods,
rental of personal property, bonds, bills of exchange, checks, different types of
security rights and bills of lading.

A Continental European jurist, accustomed to working with codified law,
may find it practical to make use of the Restatements of the Law, published by a

---

[3]   See e.g. *Wickard, Secretary of Agriculture* v. *Filburn*, 317 U.S. 111 (1942).

private body called the American Law Institute, founded in 1923 by several different organizations including the American Bar Association. Each Restatement
has the ambition to provide, in the form of fictitious codified and commented
provisions, an accurate and concise text that restates the currently valid American law in a particular field. Among the most useful of the Restatements are
those on Contracts, Torts, and Conflict of Laws. Each work is authored by an
appointed Reporter, who is a recognized legal scholar, working with the assistance of a group of advisors. The task is to render a description of the existing
law, but in the situation where the law is unclear or to a significant degree
varies from state to state, the Reporter's views as to what the law should be may
be expressed in the text, which prior to its publication must be approved by
the American Law Institute. The Restatements enjoy considerable persuasive
authority and offer an excellent insight into American law, but they are naturally
not a binding source of law and necessarily contain simplifications required for
the representation of fifty legal systems as a single set of rules. This means that
a foreign jurist who is in need of information on the law in a particular state
should not assume that the Restatement's rule necessarily coincides with the
law of that state.

10.2 Constitutional Litigation

As written binding legal texts, the federal Constitution and the
Constitutions of the states may appear to be a foreign element in a common-
law country, especially if compared with the United Kingdom which does not
have a written Constitution at all but rather still relies, even in this area, on its
common-law method.

In practice, the U.S. Constitution from 1787, which consists of seven relatively extensive Articles plus 27 subsequent Amendments, is to a large extent
only seemingly codified law. This particularly applies to the provisions protecting the civil rights of the individual in the first ten Amendments from 1791,
commonly referred to as the Bill of Rights, the wording of which has long been
buried under a large number of judicial interpretations, primarily from the U.S.
Supreme Court. These decisions are binding upon all state as well as federal
courts and other authorities. Taken together, they provide the real constitutional
rules, to which the provisions written in the Constitution only constitute a kind
of background, just as a white canvas is the necessary, but rather uninteresting,
underlay to an artist's painting. In other words, "the Constitution is what the
judges say it is".

The U.S. Constitution is not only formally, but also in fact, the central core of
the legal system in the United States. It is not a toothless political declaration of
intentions, but rather consists of highly practical legal rules frequently referred
to by the courts. Every American jurist, regardless of whether he specializes in
criminal law, family law, business law, or tax law must keep the Constitution in

mind. A state or federal statute or a municipal ordinance that conflicts with the Constitution can be challenged and refused application. The violation of a provision in the Constitution is frequently related to the violation of a civil right, but it is also possible that the statute under scrutiny is considered to be incompatible with the constitutional division of powers between the legislative, executive and judicial authorities, or with the division of powers between the federal organs and the states. Concerning civil rights, the First Amendment which guarantees the freedom of speech and religion, and the Fifth and Fourteenth Amendments providing for equal protection and due process of law, are particularly often invoked in constitutional litigation.

The right of judicial review of the constitutionality of legislation, although not explicitly stated in the Constitution itself, was firmly established in 1803 in the famous U.S. Supreme Court case of *Marbury* v. *Madison*.[4] Such review is not reserved for any special constitutional court or the U.S. Supreme Court, but can also be carried out by all federal as well as state courts. The lower courts, however, are bound by the precedents of the higher courts with jurisdiction over them, this especially in the situation where the U.S. Supreme Court has issued an opinion on the same question. Ordinarily, the direct effect of a decision that a statute is unconstitutional is limited to the refusal to apply it in the particular case, as the review of the constitutionality takes place within an actual lawsuit and not in a general abstract form, but the decision will also constitute a binding precedent.

One of the characteristic, but not quite uncontroversial, features of constitutional litigation in the USA is that the Supreme Court is inclined to develop and change the interpretation of the rules in the Constitution in keeping with the economic, political, ethical and other developments in the society. The U.S. Constitution is therefore often characterized as a "living document". It sometimes occurs that the provisions in the Constitution are interpreted and applied in a manner that was clearly not foreseen when the provision was written. For example, in *Brown* v. *Board of Education of Topeka*,[5] the U.S. Supreme Court declared in 1954 that the system of separate schools for white and black children violated the Constitution, even though it may be presumed that the authors of the Constitution did not contemplate this issue and may even have had a different opinion. In a similar manner, constitutional rules are considered to take a position even on issues that did not exist at all at the time of their adoption, such as the new reproductive technologies or electronic wiretapping. All this is possible due to the great flexibility emanating from the dual function of the courts, both applying and creating the law.

In addition to the U.S. Constitution, every state has its own state Constitution, which is often based on, and in any case must not conflict with, the federal Constitution.

---

4   1 Cranch 137 (1803).

5   347 U.S. 483 (1954).

10.3 The Judiciary

In the United States there are both federal and state courts. The state judicial system varies somewhat from state to state, but it usually consists of trial courts, most commonly called district courts or county courts (however the trial courts in the state of New York are surprisingly enough called "Supreme Court"), intermediate courts for appeals, and a state Supreme Court as the final instance (in New York called the "Court of Appeals"). In addition, there are usually small claims courts, family courts, juvenile or youth courts, traffic courts, justice of the peace courts for minor offences, etc. In many states, judges on some levels are elected by the citizens for a set term, which means that they are not entirely independent of political support and cannot totally disregard public opinion. In other states, it is the governor who appoints judges but the appointment requires usually a confirmation by the state legislature.

The vast majority of both civil and commercial cases, more than 90 percent, are dealt with solely in state courts. The decisions of the state Supreme Courts are in principle final, but can be appealed to the U.S. Supreme Court if they concern a question involving federal law. Such a situation arises, for example, where the appellant asserts that the state rule on which the decision rests violates the U.S. Constitution, or where the state Supreme Court has refused to apply a statute that it found to be in conflict with the federal Constitution.

The federal court system consists of just under one hundred U.S. District Courts (at least one in every state, where the cases are ordinarily heard by a single judge), thirteen U.S. Courts of Appeals (where the cases are heard by a bench of three judges, except in some important cases where the court sits in plenary session), and the U.S. Supreme Court in Washington D.C. Of the thirteen U.S. Courts of Appeals, eleven cover a particular geographical region called a circuit (for instance, the 5th Circuit includes the states of Mississippi, Louisiana and Texas). The U.S. Court of Appeals for the 12th Circuit hears appeals from the U.S. District Court of the District of Columbia. A thirteenth federal Court of Appeals, the U.S. Court of Appeals for the Federal Circuit, was established in 1982 to hear appeals directed against decisions rendered by certain special courts or semi-judicial bodies, such as the U.S. Court of Federal Claims (which deals with claims against the United States), the Patent and Trademark Office, and the Court of International Trade (dealing primarily with customs cases).

Judicial System in the USA (Simplified Diagram)

Federal Courts   **State Courts**

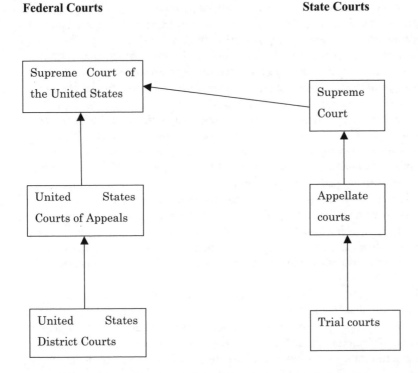

The most important decisions, which receive substantial coverage in the mass media and influence the life of the whole nation, are naturally those rendered by the U.S. Supreme Court. This court consists of a Chief Justice and eight Associate Justices, all of whom participate in every case. The U.S. Supreme Court functions as a court of first instance in a very few special cases, for example it has exclusive jurisdiction over disputes between two states and has non-exclusive jurisdiction in cases filed by a foreign ambassador. Normally, however, it deals with appeals, of which there are over 10,000 per year. To limit its workload, the Court may, without giving any grounds, refuse to hear the case (i.e. deny a writ of certiorari), for example if the case is of no general legal interest. The number of Supreme Court decisions where certiorari is granted is only about 75 to 80 per year. In certain situations, however, the Supreme Court is obliged to hear the appeal, such as in cases where a federal Court of Appeals has refused to apply a state statute on the ground that it is in conflict with the federal Constitution. The Supreme Court ordinarily does not concern itself with questions of fact, but rather only with questions of law.

Justices of the U.S. Supreme Court are appointed by the President for life subject to confirmation by the Senate (the upper house of the U.S. Congress, the lower house being the House of Representatives). This is an illustration of the cherished control mechanism in the Constitution, "checks and balances" between the legislative, executive and judicial powers.

Judges of U.S. District Courts and U.S. Courts of Appeals are also appointed for life by the President with the confirmation of the Senate, but it is the appointments to the Supreme Court that naturally are regarded as politically important and therefore attract great attention. The President who during his time in office gets the opportunity to appoint several new Justices to the Supreme Court, can thereby influence the development of law in the USA for many years after he leaves office; the Justices are appointed for life and it has been somewhat facetiously said that a proper Supreme Court Justice never resigns and only rarely dies. The experience has, however, been that the Justices are fiercely independent and do not always follow the same political course as expected by the President who appointed them.

It is very common that decisions from the U.S. Supreme Court, and from the other American courts composed of more than one judge, are not unanimous or that the judges have reached the same conclusion but with different judicial reasoning. In such cases the judge will write is own concurring or dissenting opinion, which is published and carefully studied along with the majority opinion.

The jurisdiction of the federal and state courts in civil cases may overlap each other, which frequently provides the plaintiff with the possibility to choose. The most common ground for jurisdiction of the federal courts in civil cases is "diversity jurisdiction", based upon that the parties are not residents of the same state *and* the value of the amount in dispute exceeds a set minimum (at present 75,000 USD, which is raised from time to time in order to adapt to inflation). The original philosophy behind the diversity jurisdiction was the fear that the state courts might be partial to their own defendants, to the disadvantage of the plaintiff coming from another state. In diversity cases the federal jurisdiction is never exclusive. In accordance with the U.S. Supreme Court's precedents, the federal courts in these cases must in principle apply the state substantive law including the conflict of laws rules of the state where the federal first instance court sits (the procedure rules it uses however will be the federal procedural law).[6] One may also turn to the federal courts in cases concerning the application of the federal Constitution, other federal legislation or international conventions ("federal question jurisdiction"). In some of these cases, for instance bankruptcy, patent, antitrust and admiralty cases, the federal courts have exclusive jurisdiction, while the plaintiff in certain other cases may choose between a federal or a state forum. If a plaintiff, in a case where both the federal and the state courts have jurisdiction, files the case in a state court in a state other than the defendant's own, the defendant has the right to request that the case be transferred to a federal court. Concerning criminal prosecutions, the federal

---

[6] *Erie Railroad Co.* v. *Tompkins*, 304 U.S. 64 (1938); *Klaxon Co.* v. *Stentor Electric Manufacturing Co., Inc.*, 313 U.S. 487 (1941).

courts have exclusive jurisdiction concerning federal crimes, i.e. prosecution for violations of federal criminal legislation.

In both state and federal trial courts, the use of a jury, whose primary task is to decide questions of fact, is very common. The English jury tradition has survived in the USA to a considerably higher degree than in England itself. For criminal prosecutions in all courts, and civil cases in federal courts, the right to a trial by jury is guaranteed by the Sixth and Seventh Amendments to the U.S. Constitution. Similar guarantees are found in most state Constitutions. A jury trial is however not obligatory if it is not requested by any of the parties, in which case the judge will decide not only the questions of law but also the questions of fact. The constitutional right to a jury in civil cases applies only for suits at common law and not for equity cases, e.g. not in cases where the plaintiff demands specific performance or an injunction against the defendant. Even in the USA it is thus important to distinguish between the two types of rules.

The binding role of precedent is somewhat different in the USA than in the English legal system. To begin with, an American court is never bound by its own precedents. There are, in fact, divided opinions on the question of whether the *stare dicisis* rule is compulsory at all or only followed by tradition. No matter which view is more correct, there is no doubt that the decisions of the superior courts are in fact followed, even if the attitude to precedents in a country with an unbelievably high number of judicial decisions naturally must be somewhat selective.

The state courts follow the procedural rules of their state, while federal courts apply federal procedural rules. Generally speaking, an American civil trial is similar to English trials before the Woolf Reform (se section 9.5 above). An originally English procedural institution which has become popular in the USA is "class action" litigation, where a plaintiff files a lawsuit not only on his own behalf but also for a number of unidentified persons who have suffered the same loss or damage. Such class may consist, for example, of all buyers/users of a certain defective product who have incurred an economic loss or other inconvenience, all persons suffering from certain environmental damage, or all persons who have been overcharged systematically by the defendant company. Despite that the named plaintiff has not obtained the direct consent or a power of attorney to represent the other members of the class, the judgment becomes binding on all who have not explicitly opted out of the lawsuit, and if the action is successful all members of the class will be entitled to compensation. In this way it becomes economically plausible to sue even for relatively insignificant claims, which otherwise would not be raised at all due to practical considerations.

Concerning criminal trials, "plea bargaining" deserves special mention. This refers to negotiations and an agreement between the prosecutor and the person accused (represented by his attorney), whereby the prosecution agrees to reduce the charges to a less serious offense and/or recommend to the judge that a more lenient sentence be imposed, provided that the accused pleads guilty. It has been

estimated that plea bargaining occurs in over 90 percent of all serious criminal cases in the USA. This could be interpreted as undignified haggling with
justice, but on the other hand it constitutes a way of surviving for the overloaded
judicial system (if the defendant pleads guilty there is normally no need for a
jury trial). Taking into consideration that the statutory penalties in American
penal law are more severe, as a rule, than the punishments for similar crimes
in other developed Western countries, it is not unreasonable to suspect that they
intentionally contain a certain leeway for the purposes of plea bargaining.

10.4 Legal Education and the Legal Profession

The number of legal professionals in the United States is
estimated to be almost one million, which makes the USA the country with the
highest density of lawyers in the entire world: approximately half of all lawyers in the world work in the USA! Lawyers and the law in general play a very
important role, even if not always a positive one, in the American society, and
not least in politics. The social position of lawyers and their income are relatively
good and this entices many of the country's most talented to the profession –
and many others. This, however, has not always been the case. The early settlers,
who frequently had negative experiences with the English legal system, did not
have a high regard for lawyers and the law in general. For example, Virginia
prohibited in 1645 all "mercenary attorneys". The developments in society, however, caused rapid changes and very quickly made qualified legal professionals
a necessity. Of the 56 signers of the American Declaration of Independence in
1776, 27 were lawyers and among the 55 delegates to the Federal Convention in
1787, the 31 lawyers constituted a majority. A large number of American presidents have had a background in law.

In contrast to England, but resembling the European Continent, there is
a well-established tradition in the USA that lawyers are educated in academic
law schools. The first American law school was founded as early as 1774 in
Connecticut. There are approximately 200 law schools in the USA, and most of
them are a part of a state or private university. There are no federal law schools.
The law school education is a three-year graduate program, which requires a
previous college degree (e.g. Bachelor of Arts, B.A.). The basic law degree is
nowadays called Juris Doctor (J.D.). Scientific degrees in law, which require
a written dissertation, are additionally offered by certain law schools, and are
called Doctor of the Science of Law (J.S.D. or S.J.D.). The quality and status vary
greatly between the different law schools. Most law schools are accredited by
the American Bar Association (A.B.A.), which requires that the school complies
with certain minimal quality requirements. The top tier of law schools are
also accredited by the Association of American Law Schools, which sets higher
standards than the A.B.A. There are, on the other hand, a number of private
non-accredited schools that may have impressive names but are of dubious qual-

ity, something a foreign jurist should keep in mind when establishing contact with American lawyers.

Some law schools have students almost exclusively from their own state and focus on the education for legal work within that state. The more important and prestigious law schools (e.g. Harvard, Yale, Columbia, Princeton and Stanford) have a different profile and rather than teaching the law of one state they prepare their students for a legal career in any state in the USA or even in any common-law jurisdiction. Between these top schools, which recruit students from throughout the USA and from abroad, there is a strong competition for quality and prestige. There is also fierce competition between the aspiring students wishing to enter the best law schools, which receive many dozens of applications for each available place. In comparison with the legal education in most other countries, American legal education is more practically orientated, with such exercises as "moot court" and detailed analyses of judicial decisions in the form of a dialogue between the professor and the students (the so-called Socratic method), necessitating that the students have studied the decision in advance and are prepared to explain and evaluate it.[7] Compared to many other countries, the US legal education offers the student a much larger freedom of choice, with relatively few required courses and a large selection of elective courses and opportunities for practical experience. Many of the professors have been legal practitioners, while only relatively few have written a legal dissertation. The best schools are, however, eager to recruit respected legal authors and scholars, as these raise the profile of the school and improve its ability to attract the best students and private donations.

As in England, there is no judicial career path. Judges are appointed from among experienced lawyers (in certain states some are elected to the bench). There is no barrister/solicitor distinction; a practicing lawyer is called an "attorney-at-law" on his stationery, but just plain "lawyer" in everyday speech. Admission to the legal profession is regulated by each state independently, with their varying rules concerning matters such as residency, but there is the common requirement of a law degree (with some minor exceptions), and passing the state bar examination. Membership in the state bar association is normally compulsory (integrated bar). Membership in the bar of one state applies only to that particular state, but there are a number of reciprocity arrangements, which make it possible after some years of legal practice in one's own state to seek permission to practice also in another state. To appear before a federal court requires admission to the federal bar, which is a mere formality for a member of the state bar association. There is no requirement that one be a citizen of the United States to become a member of the bar.

Most American lawyers work as sole practitioners, or in small groups of a few lawyers, but in the big cities there are some very large law firms, some consisting of hundreds of lawyers. Members of the firm, who share ownership, are called "partners", while the younger employee lawyers are called "associates".

---

7   An interesting comparative evaluation of legal education in the USA and Western Europe is found in
    Merryman, *The Loneliness*, pp. 53-74.

In certain types of cases, especially when representing plaintiffs in personal injury litigation, American lawyers most often work on a contingent fee basis, i.e. the amount the lawyer will receive for his services is calculated as a percentage of the judgment or settlement payment. The percentage can vary, usually between 25 percent and 50 percent, with approximately 35 percent as average. This method of remunerating lawyers is regarded as being incompatible with good professional ethics in many other legal systems, but is defended by American lawyers by reference to the fact that public legal aid is generally not available for such cases in the USA and that the contingent fee system allows even a plaintiff with very limited financial resources to retain a good lawyer and succeed in obtaining compensation for his injury. The defendant's lawyer is normally paid by the hour. Larger enterprises sometimes employ their own in-house counsel, or pay an outside law firm a retainer, i.e. a fixed monthly fee. Together with the rather peculiar American procedural principle on costs, according to which the winning party normally is not entitled to compensation for its legal expenses from the losing party (the "American rule"), the contingent fee system has contributed to make the USA perhaps the most litigious society in the world, since the filing of a lawsuit frequently does not imply any economic risk to the plaintiff. The American lawyers are, furthermore, well-known for actively recruiting clients, especially in personal injury cases (some less ethical forms of this pursuit are commonly known as "ambulance chasing"). Even in criminal prosecutions the defendant is in principle responsible for his own legal costs, regardless of whether he is acquitted or found guilty, so that even unfounded criminal charges can lead to his economic ruin. There is, however, the possibility to obtain the services of a public defender, who is paid out of public funds, for defendants who cannot afford to pay for their own defence, and successful law firms are expected to do some charitable legal work *"pro bono"*, i.e. free of charge.

10.5   Geographic Spread of American Law

The United States has never been engaged in colonial expansion in the classical sense, but certain territories outside of the USA, which due to different reasons have for a long period of time been under American control, have today a legal system strongly influenced by American law, for instance the Philippines. The former enemy states that the USA has temporarily occupied, such as Germany and Japan, have adopted or had imposed on them a democratic form of government, competition (antitrust) law, etc., to a large extent inspired by the American model. These fields of American law have also had a strong influence in Latin America. Additionally, some countries have adopted important parts of American law due to their special historical ties, for instance Liberia which was founded by African-Americans who had been freed from slavery in the USA.

The significant worldwide influence of American law is largely due, however, to another factor. The position of the USA as the leading military and economic power after World War II has made American law interesting to jurists throughout the world, especially as the position of English as the dominant world language has made American law relatively accessible. Numerous young jurists from countries around the world attend postgraduate master programs at US law schools. Since the USA has for a long time been and continues to be seen as the leading country in the field of commerce, it is not surprising that many modern business legal concepts originated and even obtained their names from the USA, for instance leasing, franchising and factoring. The cultural impact of the numerous American courtroom movies, watched all over the globe, on the general public's perceptions and expectations of law is not quite negligible either.

CHAPTER II

French Law

II.I Historical Background

Up until the French Revolution (1789), France lacked a uniform legal system, at least in the field of private (civil) law.[1] The country consisted basically of two main areas, separated by a line along the Loire river, which went approximately between Geneva and the Atlantic coast at La Rochelle. The somewhat smaller southern part (*pays de droit écrit*) had a codified law, based on the Roman-law tradition (i.a. *Lex romana Wisigothorum*), while in the northern three-fifths of the country (*pays de coutumes*) a number of different privately recorded customary legal rules of predominantly Germanic origin applied. Some of the customary legal rules were applicable over a wide area (about 60 *coutumes générales*), but for the most part they were only of local significance (about 300 *coutumes locales*). Voltaire's comment, that someone travelling through France was forced to change laws as often as he changed horses, was not entirely without grounds. There was some legislation, even in the field of private law, which covered the entire country, for example an *ordonnance* of 1735 on wills, but this was a relatively rare exception.

The most well-known customary law was that of Paris (*Coutume de Paris*), which due to the fact that it was the law of the country's capital and that privately published compilations of it existed as early as in 1510, was considered to follow with the French settlers to the colonies, regardless of what part of France the settlers originated from. Another important customary law was that of Normandy (privately compiled in *Grand coutumier de la Normandie*), which continues to this day to constitute the foundation of the legal system on the Channel Islands of Guernsey and Jersey; at the time of the Norman Conquest of England these islands belonged to Normandy but they have remained faithful to the English Crown even after England lost Normandy itself in 1204. The customary law of Brittany, *Très ancienne coutume de Bretagne*, which differed from the others due to the fact that it had Celtic rather than Germanic roots, is also worth mentioning. The only good thing that this feudalistic legal fragmentation of France brought with it was that the French legal scholars of the time (in particular the so-called French school, represented among others by Dumoulin and d'Argentré) became distinguished in the field of conflict of laws, as the choice of law was an everyday concern of the French courts and lawyers.

The divided pre-revolutionary French law (*ancien droit*) constituted a serious hindrance to the industrialization, trade and general economic development. This was unacceptable to the commercially-minded bourgeois class that came into power in the Revolution of 1789. The first years after the Revolution could, however, be characterized as a time of political turmoil and even general chaos; the focus of legal development was therefore mainly on certain constitutional reforms. When the situation stabilized under Napoleon Bonaparte's control,

---

[1]   It should be mentioned that even today in France there are certain special regional characteristics in the law, for example some remnants of German law (as it was prior to the first World War) in Alsace-Lorraine.

extensive efforts were devoted to the establishment of a civil code. In 1800, Napoleon, who was then the Republic's First Consul, appointed a codification commission consisting of four experienced jurists, who with the assistance of a number of other experts presented after only four months' work the first draft for a new civil code. After some revisions of the draft, the Code (*Code civil des Français*, C.c.) was adopted in 1804, and soon became commonly known as the Napoleon Code (*Code Napoléon*).

The *Code Napoléon* is far from being the only great legal work produced during the reign of Napoleon, even if it is without doubt the best known and most important. The Code of Civil Procedure (*Code de procédure civile* of 1806, C.P.C.), the Commercial Code (*Code de commerce* of 1807, C.com.), the Penal Code (*Code pénal* of 1810, C.P.) and the Code of Criminal Procedure (*Code de l'instruction criminelle* of 1808) together with the Civil Code constituted the basis of post-revolutionary French law. The Napoleonic codifications survived many dramatic upheavals including the restoration and re-abolition of the royal rule, the Republic and the Empire, as well as both World Wars. A new Penal Code (*Nouveau code pénal*, N.C.P.) replaced the Napoleonic Penal Code in 1994 and the two procedural codes have been replaced by the *Code de procédure pénale* (C.P.P.) of 1958 and the *Nouveau code de procédure civile* (N.C.P.C.) of 1976. On the other hand, public law, apart from the Constitution, has so far not been subjected to a codification in the form of a comprehensive code. The present Constitution is from 1958.

The Napoleonic Civil Code and Commercial Code are thus still in force, even though with numerous amendments. The relationship between the Civil Code and the Commercial Code is often misunderstood by foreign jurists. The Commercial Code does not contain an exhaustive regulation of commercial transactions, which remain in principle governed by the relevant rules in the Civil Code, such as the rules concerning contracts. The Commercial Code deals rather only with issues that are specific to commercial matters, such as accounting, partnerships, corporations, and maritime transportation of goods. Many rules relevant to commercial transactions are however found today in special statutes, for instance rules regarding bankruptcy.

In addition to the above-mentioned traditional codes, France has today several other large legislative texts in various areas, and they are also called "codes", such as the *Code du travail* covering labour law and *Code de la consommation* dealing with consumer law.

11.2 The Napoleon Code

The Napoleonic Civil Code of 1804 has a very unique and central role in the French legal system, and even in French culture as a whole. The latter is due not the least to the elegant language of the Code; the French author Stendhal is said to have practiced his linguistic skills by regularly reading the

Napoleon Code. The Code is regarded, and not only by the French themselves, as one of France's most important contributions to human civilization. Without changing its basic character, the Code has survived ten French Constitutions and in spite of its age shows an amazing ability to adapt itself to changes and developments in the society. As early as in 1904, in connection with the Code's hundred-year anniversary, a special commission was established with the task of revising the entire Code, but the work of the commission has not resulted in any significant changes.

As mentioned above, certain important parts of private law, for instance labour and consumer law, are now regulated in separate legislation outside of the Napoleon Code, which is complemented by many supplementary statutes also in other respects. The Code, however, contains even today not only the core of French private law but also most of its detailed rules.

Aside from a few introductory provisions in the *Titre préliminaire*, the more than 2,500 articles of the Civil Code are today divided into five main sections, designated "books" (*livres*). The first deals with persons (*Des personnes*) and is concerned first and foremost with personal status and family matters. The second primarily deals with issues concerning property and property rights *in rem* (*Des biens, et des différentes modifications de la propriété*). The third and largest book deals with different manners of acquiring property rights (*Des différentes manières dont on acquiert la propriété*) and contains rules not only on different kinds of contracts but also on i.a. torts, inheritance, wills and marital property regime. The fourth and the fifth books were added as late as in 2008 and deal with security interests (such as suretyships, pledges and mortgages) and some special features of the Code's application in Mayotte (a small French possession in the Indian Ocean). Even apart from the last-mentioned book, this structure looks today quite peculiar in certain respects, for instance the division of family law between the first and third book is less than appropriate from a purely pedagogical point of view.

The Napoleon Code is naturally a child of its time. It does not have the logical perfection of the German Civil Code written almost a hundred years later. The latter, on the other hand, cannot be compared to the Napoloeon Code when it comes to linguistic elegance. Concerning the substantive content, the Napoleon Code is said to have been influenced on certain points by such incidental factors as Napoleon's personal preferences, related to his own family situation, regarding matters such as the simplification of divorce and adoption (he was at the time still married to Joséphine, who was unable to provide him with an heir to the throne). It is also said that the rather "sexist" rules originally found in the Code concerning, for example, the wife's subordinate position, were due to Napoleon's own bad experiences with Joséphine's extravagance and wastefulness while he was constantly away at war. As a whole, the entire Code expressed rather well the new bourgeois society's liberal and individualistic values prevailing at the time. The fundamental ideology behind the Code's rules was based upon the belief in natural law and the common sense of human beings. Among the more concrete underlying values, the following can be mentioned: the formal equality of every person in the eyes of the law, an extensive protection for private property (e.g. Article 544[2]), an almost unconditional respect for contractual obligations (e.g. Article 1134[3]) and a somewhat sanctimonious veneration for the traditional, patriarchal family structure (this last leading to a prohibition in former Article 340, subsequently abolished, of paternity actions by childred born outside of marriage[4]). The authors of the Code were most probably more concerned with a well-to-do, responsible, and enterprising patriarchal family father, than with a poor unmarried pregnant cleaning woman. Many of the Code's original values have later on gradually been abandoned, this not only within family law but also within e.g. the law of contracts, for instance through the enactment, outside of the Civil Code, of mandatory rules for the protection of consumers, employees, tenants and other weaker parties.

The ambition of the authors of the Civil Code was to achieve a comprehensive rational regulation of legal relationships in the field of private law. The fiction was created that the Code had no gaps: it was considered that one could find the answer to all questions within the Code, provided that one looked carefully enough. Article 4 of the Code therefore provides that a judge, who refuses to render a decision pretending that there are no applicable legal rules (*sous prétexte du silence, de l'obscurité ou de l'insuffisance de la loi*), shall be punished for denial of justice (*déni de justice*). The same idea about the Code's comprehensiveness also lies behind its Article 5, which forbids judges to create new general rules by means of precedents.[5] The Code was originally regarded to be complete and clear to such a degree that any legal scholarly interpretation and workmanship was regarded not only as unnecessary but even as being harmful. It is said that Napoleon himself, when he heard that a commentary to the Civil Code had been published, exclaimed "My Code is lost!"; there is also the story about a nineteenth-century French law professor who emphatically defended himself against assertions that he taught civil law, and with pride maintained that he taught the Napoleon Code. This attitude, according to which the Code was entirely comprehensive and contained the answer to all conceivable questions, prevailed in France practically throughout the entire nineteenth century.

It was of course known to most French jurists that the Code's comprehensiveness was only a fiction, but the filling in of any possible lacunae, whose existence one was not prepared to openly acknowledge, has in this manner simply been entrusted to the courts. The judgments of the Court of Cassation, and to a certain extent also of the appellate courts, are published, studied, and ordinarily followed in judicial practice, even though they are not formally

---

[2]   "*La propriété est le droit de jouir et disposer des choses de la manière la plus absolue, pourvu qu'on n'en fasse pas un usage prohibé par les lois ou par les règlements.*"

[3]   "*Les conventions légalement formées tiennent lieu de loi à ceux qui les ont faites.*"

[4]   "*La recherche de la paternité est interdite.*"

[5]   "*Il est défendu aux juges de prononcer par voie de disposition générale et réglementaire sur les causes qui leur sont soumises.*"

binding. French judges are not mechanical appliers of the text of the Code, but rather have shown themselves to be creative, and good at filling in the gaps and adapting the interpretation of the text to new situations in the society, however without openly acknowledging it. One of the best examples of this is the entire French law of torts, which over the years has been created by the courts, only formally on the basis of five short articles in the Napoleon Code. The courts have also developed some corrective instruments that can be used when the legislated provisions lead to undesirable results; an example of this is the concept of misuse of rights (*abus de droit*), whereby one for instance can to a certain extent restrict property owners from exercising their rights in an improper manner.

The fact that the Napoleon Code was a product of the new, post-revolutionary society and its values, did not mean that it lacked roots in pre-revolutionary legal traditions. The drafters of the Code were jurists educated in and with extensive experience of *ancien droit*, which left important traces in the new codification. With some simplification, it may be asserted that certain parts of the Code, for instance the law of contracts, were built to a great extent upon the Roman-inspired *droit écrit*, while other parts, such as family and inheritance law, had more in common with the North French customary law of Germanic origins. In that manner the Code, on certain points, has become more "Germanic" than the later German Civil Code of 1896, which to a greater degree was built upon the reception of Roman law.

Judicial System in France (Simplified Diagram)

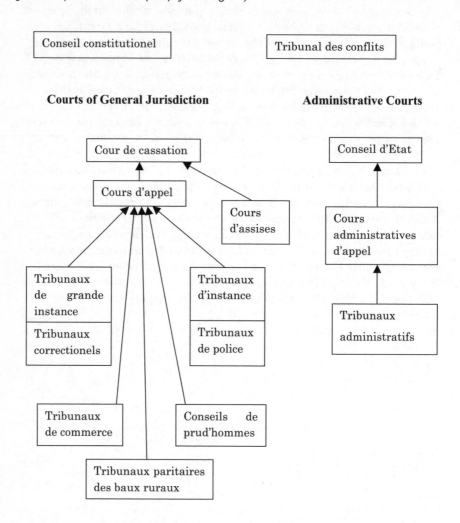

11.3 The Judiciary

At the top of the French judicial system, for other than administrative law cases, is the Court of Cassation (*Cour de cassation*). As the name implies, this court functions according to the cassation principle, i.e. it can annul the decision of a lower court, but normally does not replace it with its own final decision in the case. An appeal to the Court of Cassation is therefore regarded as an extraordinary legal measure and is not called an *appel* but instead a *pourvoi en cassation*. If the lower court's judgment is annulled, the case normally returns to a lower court for a new decision. In France the remanding of the case occurs, however, not to the same court whose judgment has been annulled (normally one of the appellate courts), but rather to a different court at the same level. This court is not formally bound to follow the Court of Cassation's position on the point of law in question. However, if this second judgment is appealed to and annulled by the Court of Cassation (which in this case would occur by means of a decision of the Cassation Court in plenum), then the third Court of Appeal to which the case is referred will be bound by the Cassation Court's view on the legal issue. The Cassation Court is concerned exclusively with questions of law and is regarded to be bound by the findings of fact upon which the appealed judgment is based (one speaks about *"appréciation souveraine des juges du fait"*), which means, among other things, that the interpretation of contracts can be reheard only in certain special cases. In contrast to the highest courts in many countries, the Court of Cassation cannot, since 1958, regulate its own workload by means of granting or denying leave to appeal. This creates long delays as the court is forced to decide thousands of cases annually, including many cases of no great importance. The Court of Cassation is divided into six divisions (*chambres*), five of which deal with civil and one with criminal cases. A French institution that has been transplanted to the Court of Justice of the EU is the Advocate General (*Avocat général*) at the Court of Cassation, whose function in individual cases is to submit to the Court an independent opinion representing the public interest in the correct application of the law.

Under the Court of Cassation there are some 35 Courts of Appeal. These are found in the larger cities and decide appeals of decisions rendered by the various types of first instance courts. The Courts of Appeal are denoted by the name of the city, for example *Cour d'appel de Bordeaux*. Each case before a Court of Appeal is heard by three professional judges.

The trial courts for the more important civil cases are the approximately 165 *tribunaux de grande instance* (*tribunaux* is the plural form of *tribunal*), which, like the Courts of Appeal, are composed of three professional judges. In criminal cases, the corresponding courts are the *tribunaux correctionnels*. Small claims cases are heard by one of the approximately 300 *tribunaux d'instance* and minor criminal cases by the *tribunaux de police*. In these courts the case is decided by a single professional judge. There are a number of special courts, including the approximately 140 commercial courts (*tribunaux de commerce*), staffed by lay judges who are elected from among businessmen themselves, and the *conseils de prud'hommes*, which deal with cases relating to labour law and include representatives for the employees as well as the employers. Cases concerning lease of agricultural land are heard by one of the *tribunaux paritaires des baux ruraux*, which are also composed of members representing the particular interests. The decisions of all of these courts can, with the exception of some small claims, normally be appealed to a Court of Appeal and further to the Court of Cassation. It should be noted that appeals directly to the Court of Cassation are possible even in those minor cases decided in a first instance court that cannot be appealed to a Court of Appeal. Very serious criminal matters are heard, however, in first instance before a jury in one of the non-permanent *cours d'assises*, whose decision can be appealed to another *cour d'assises* and from there to the Court of Cassation.

The division of competence between the courts of general jurisdiction and the commercial courts is of great importance. When only the defendant is a business enterprise (*commerçant*), the plaintiff can most often choose between the two types of courts, while a *commerçant* may only sue a private person in a court of general jurisdiction. If both parties are *commerçants*, the commercial courts have as a rule exclusive jurisdiction.

France also has a number of administrative courts. A decision rendered by any of the 42 *tribunaux administratifs* can be appealed to one of the 8 *cours administratives d'appel*. At the top of the administrative courts there is a cassation instance, the *Conseil d'Etat*. The *Conseil d'Etat* functions at the same time as a consultation organ, providing expert opinion on proposed legislation. In such rare cases where a jurisdictional conflict arises between the courts of general jurisdiction and the administrative courts, the *Tribunal des conflits*, composed of judges from both the *Conseil d'Etat* and the Court of Cassation, will decide the appropriate manner of proceeding.

A quasi-judicial body of special character is the Constitutional Council (*Conseil constitutionnel*), consisting of all former French presidents and nine additional members. The Constitutional Council cannot declare an enacted law to be unconstitutional, but it can stop a proposed statute if it finds it to be in conflict with the Constitution. It will only consider the matter on the application of the President of the Republic, the Prime Minister, the chairman of either of the French parliament's two chambers (the Senate and the National Assembly), or a group of at least 60 members of either chamber.

A typical French trial in a civil case begins with the issuance and serving of a summons called *assignation* on the defendant (*le défendeur*), whereafter comes the filing of a number of documents on which the plaintiff (*le demandeur*) bases his case (*communication des pièces*). The defendant answers the summons and files his documents by means of *conclusions*. At the trial itself, the attorney's oral presentation and arguments (*plaidoiries*) play a central role; they are regarded as constituting the very essence of the attorney's profession. Witnesses are rare in civil cases and their questioning is conducted by the court, not by the parties or their advocates, who may, however, ask the court to put a certain question to the witness. In situations where the facts are very unclear, French courts can make use of the services of an *"expert"*, who is expected to investigate and present the facts of the case in an impartial manner. He does not necessarily have to be an expert in the ordinary sense of the word, i.a. a person with special knowledge or qualifications in a particular field. French court judgments are usually very short and often consist of one single long sentence with numerous subordinate clauses starting with *"Attendu que..."* or *"Considérant que..."*, meaning roughly "With regard to that...". They pretend that it is the "naked" text of the statute speaking: earlier decisions and legal authors are ordinarily not cited, despite the fact that the grounds of a decision frequently contain formulations that have obviously been taken over directly from them. Nor do the French courts ordinarily take openly into consideration the needs of society and demands of justice, but it is clear that such considerations influence the courts in reality. Dissenting opinions are kept in the files but they are not published; in fact, even their existence is kept secret from the parties. The published judicial reasoning of a French judgment consequently does not reveal the entire truth behind the court's decision. A special feature of French legal writing is therefore the role of the notes in the legal periodicals that usually accompany reports of judicial decisions. Such *note d'arrêt*, normally written by a legal scholar or an experienced judge or legal practitioner, is frequently much more extensive that the judgment itself and has the purpose of explaining the meaning of the new judgment and to place it into context.

11.4   Legal Education and the Legal Profession

A university law degree (*maîtrise en droit*) is a necessary precondition for any legal career in France. A person who wishes to pursue a judicial career may, after his or her university studies at a law faculty (which normally take four years to complete), apply to be accepted into a judicial education programme, which is concentrated to one particular school, *Ecole nationale de la magistrature* (ENM, formerly called *Centre national d'études judiciaires*) in Bordeaux. The entrance examination is regarded as being very demanding and the competition for places is severe. The judicial education program, which is the same for future judges (*magistrats de siège*) and future prosecutors (*magistrats du parquet*), lasts for 31 months and the participants (called *auditeurs de justice*) receive a salary. After successfully completing the programme, which also contains important practical work (*stage*), the graduates are usually appointed to various judicial or prosecutorial positions. The appointment of judges is made through a decree of the President of the Republic upon the recommendation of a special organ, *Conseil supérieur de la magistrature*, which is also in charge of disciplinary proceedings concerning judges. A similar institution exists also for the administrative courts; however administrative judges receive their judicial training not from the above-mentioned school in Bordeaux, but together with other high civil servants at the prestigious *Ecole nationale d'administration* (ENA) in Paris.

Practicing lawyers used to be divided into many different categories (such as *avocats, conseils juridiques, avoués* and *agréés*), which after several reforms have been amalgamated, with some minor exceptions, into one legal profession (*profession d'avocat*). Membership in a local bar association (*barreau*) is a mandatory condition for the practice of the legal profession, which in some respects is restricted geographically. The local *barreaux* are joined into the *Conseil national des barreaux*. Admittance to a *barreau* requires a university law degree, the completion of a one-year special course at a regional *Centre de formation profes-sionelle des avocats* and two years of practical experience under the guidance and supervision of a practicing lawyer. Except in small claims courts, a party before a court must in principle always be represented by an advocate.

Another category of lawyers is the *notaires*, who among other matters deal with the drafting of wills, marital property agreements, and transfers of real property. Judgments are enforced by semi-private *huissiers de justice*. The number of *notaires* and *huissiers* is limited by statute, which means that for a lawyer who desires to enter either of these careers it is not sufficient to fulfil the stipulated requirements concerning education and practical experience; he must also wait until a vacancy arises, which as a rule means that he has to purchase an existing practice from someone who is retiring (or from his estate).

11.5 Geographic Spread of French Law

French law began to spread outside of the borders of France in connection with the French colonial expansion even prior to the revolution of 1789, for instance to Québec (now a province of Canada). Considerably more extensive and important however was French colonialism at the end of the nine-teenth and the beginning of the twentieth century, when great parts of North Africa, West Africa, Central Africa and Indo-China were governed from Paris, in addition to the colourful group of further territories ranging from French Guyana in South America and Madagascar in the Indian Ocean to Tahiti in the South Pacific. Minor remnants of this great empire still exist today, but most of the territories became independent states many years ago. They have, never-theless, retained more often than not the French-inspired legal system, even if frequently in combination with local rules such as those pertaining to land and family law. Certain of these countries have for a period of time adopted some form of socialist model, with the resulting changes in the legal system, but they seem to return under French legal influence when reverting to a market econ-omy. The influence of French law is furthermore strengthened by the fact that many former French colonies continue to educate a significant part of their elite, including their jurists, in France or in local law schools supported by France and staffed with French professors teaching French law.

Perhaps of even greater importance for the spread of French law has been its influence in the other countries in Europe. In connection with the Napo-leonic wars or later, French law gained a foothold or was copied in Belgium, Luxemburg, the Netherlands, Italy, Spain and Portugal, whereby it indirectly also influenced the law in these countries' colonies, such as Angola, Congo and Indonesia. These territories are now independent states, but they have retained most often the former colonial power's legal traditions, combined in certain fields (most often family law) with local customary law or legislation.

Practically all of the Latin American countries adopted great codes based on the French model relatively quickly after having attained their independence, much of the substantive contents of these codes also having been imported from France (the civil code of Brazil is, however, influenced by German law as well). In South America, at least in the old days, it occurred that French legal experts were commissioned to write expert opinions concerning the interpretation of the local civil code. Within public law, especially constitutional and penal law, the Latin American countries seem however to have subsequently been more influenced by American law.

Except for the fields of family and inheritance law, French law has played a significant role in the design of the private law in many countries in the Middle East, first and foremost Egypt and Lebanon. Via Egypt, French law came to influence the law in other Arab countries in the region, such as Libya and Iraq.

Considerably more recent is the significant influence of French law within the European Union. One should keep in mind that France was the politically dominant power among the six original Member States of the European Economic Community, and that the law in four of the other five (in other words, all the other original Member States except West Germany) was by tradition very close to French law. The basic foundations of EU law, laid during the first two decades of the European integration process, often carry distinct traces of French legal influence; the institution of Advocates General of the Court of Justice of the EU can be mentioned as an example. French was, and continues to a great extent to be, the most important working legal language of the EU, especially in the Court of Justice.

A number of territories first colonized by France were later taken over by Great Britain or another country with a common-law legal system. Due to the historical developments of the balance of power between the two most important colonial empires, there are no examples of a transfer of territory in the opposite direction. In connection with the transfer of power, the local population was often promised that they could retain their French-inspired law, but English law successively gained greater and greater importance, for instance due to the numerous English-inspired amendments, the isolation from the legal developments in France, the English education of the judges and other jurists, and the transition to English as the language of the courts. In this manner, a number of "mixed legal systems" came into being, and these can be very interesting for comparative law purposes (see Chapter 7 above). Some of the mixed legal systems, such as the one existing in the Canadian province of Québec, have abundant legal resources of their own, which have made them resistant to common-law influences. The continued use of the French language by the overwhelming majority of the population of Québec has also played an important role. Québec has succeeded, to a high degree, to retain its special legal characteristics. Instead of going over to common law, Québec for many years continued to apply *Coutume de Paris*, i.e. the pre-revolutionary Parisian customary law (Québec was taken over by the British before the Napoleonic codification took place in France). When Québec finally adopted its own Civil Code, which entered in force in 1866, its rules were to a predominant extent based neither on common law nor on the Napoleon Code but rather constituted a codification of the *Coutume de Paris* (today Québec has a civil code of 1994). On the other hand, the small mixed legal systems, often on little islands dependent for their legal development on outside influences, have moved closer to the common-law family. The two island countries Mauritius and the Seychelles in the Indian Ocean can be mentioned as examples; they became British possessions in 1814, after having for many years been part of the French colonial empire and endowed with the Napoleonic Civil Code. This Code is still applicable in Mauritius, while the Seychelles adopted in 1975 its own Civil Code in the English language, which however is inspired to a great extent by the Napoleon Code. The penal and procedural law of both countries is on the other hand predominantly of British origin. At the same time as France lost Mauritius and the Seychelles, it also lost the Caribbean island of Saint Lucia, where however the Napoleon Code had not been introduced. Saint Lucia continued therefore to apply the pre-revolutionary customary law of Paris, which in 1879 was replaced by its own Civil Code based upon the Civil Code in Québec. In reality today, the legal life on the island is predominantly based on English legal thinking, since large parts of the Civil Code were subsequently adapted to English law and all of the lawyers now have a common-law legal education. Another unique mixture of French and English law can be found also in Vanuatu in the South Pacific, as this territory before its independence in 1980 constituted a British-French condominium named New Hebrides, but even there the importance of common law has been growing at the expense of French law.

CHAPTER 12

German Law

12.1 Historical Background

In contrast to pre-revolutionary France, which despite the lack of a uniform legal system was one centrally-governed state, Germany as a state did not really exist until the nineteenth century. Although it formally had an Emperor, Germany lacked most of the important attributes of a sovereign state; it was composed of a large number of different kingdoms and principalities, some of which were even occasionally at war with each other. In 1806 this weak Empire was formally dissolved, and Germany was not reestablished until 1871.

Taking this into account, it is not surprising that Germany as such did not have its own legal system until the end of the nineteenth century. Some codifications intended for all of Germany came into existence even prior to the reestablishment of German statehood, such as a uniform Act on Bills of Exchange of 1848 and a uniform Commercial Code of 1861. In the field of procedural law, the reestablished Germany introduced, i.a., a Civil Procedure Code and a Bankruptcy Act of 1877, but the private law for instance remained fragmented, consisting of many local rules. In certain parts of Germany, the Rheinland for instance, the French Civil Code was applicable, since it had been introduced there during the time of Napoleon. In Prussia, private and penal law as well as procedural law was condified as early as in 1794 with the *Allgemeines Landrecht für die Königlich-Preussischen Staaten*. In most of the German mini-states, a local customary law was applied since the Middle Ages. This local law, which was occasionally written down in ancient works such as the *Sachsenspiegel* from the thirteenth century, was complemented, remarkably, with Roman law.

The extensive reception of *Corpus juris civilis* had several explanations, some of which were ideological and psychological: the German Empire that formally existed between 962 and 1806 (*Das heilige römische Reich deutscher Nation*) represented itself as the successor to the Roman Empire. Roman law was studied at the German universities and served as a kind of subsidiary source of law, i.e. it was applied when local statutes or customary law did not provide a solution. When one spoke about the law applicable for the entire Empire (*gemeines Recht*), one was thus speaking about Roman law. This influence of Roman law was however not equally strong in all of Germany, due to the fact that certain parts of the territory had many local rules of their own, which reduced the need of the subsidiary application of Roman law. The Roman law used in Germany (*usus modernus pandectarum*) contained additionally Germanic elements and was somewhat different from the classic original.

The German civil law was not unified until the 1st of January 1900, when the 1896 German Civil Code (*Bürgerliches Gesetzbuch*, BGB) entered into force. With a number of amendments, it remains in force until today and there are no plans to replace it. Certain minor differences between the law common for the entire country (*Bundesrecht*) and the law of each *Land* (*Landesrecht*), as well as differences between the laws of the different *Länder* (plural of *Land*), remain though, albeit more within public than within private law. Due to Germany's federal structure (the country consists after the reunification in 1990 of 16 *Länder*), each *Land* has its own parliament with certain limited authority to legislate, but almost all important legislation is either applicable for the entire country or is worded in a uniform manner. German federalism is thus somewhat different on this point from the situation in for instance the USA.

In addition to the BGB, Germany has a number of other important codes, such as a Commercial Code (*Handelsgesetzbuch*, HGB), a Code of Civil Procedure (*Zivilprozessordnung*, ZPO), a Penal Code (*Strafgesetzbuch*, StGB), and a Code of Criminal Procedure (*Strafprozessordnung*, StPO). Also of significant importance are the two administrative codifications, the Administrative Code (*Verwaltungsverfahrensgesetz*, VwVfG) and the Administrative Judicial Procedures Code (*Verwaltungsgerichtsordnung*, VwGO). In the same manner as in France, the Commercial Code constitutes, with its rules on i.a. accounting, commercial registers, partnerships, commercial agents and carriage by sea, only a complement to the BGB, whose rules, in principle, are also applied to transactions between businessmen. Important parts of the private and commercial law are regulated in separate statutes, such as those concerning intellectual property and corporations. For example, there are two separate statutes dealing with two different types of corporations, namely *Aktiengesellschaft* (AG) and *Gesellschaft mit beschränkter Haftung* (GmbH), the latter form being especially adapted for and used by smaller enterprises.

In the same manner as French law, the German legal system is based primarily on written statutory legal rules, established by legislation. Precedents are not binding on future cases, but are published and normally followed in practice and therefore play an important role, especially for the uniform interpretation of written legal rules. As in France, the impact of EU (previously EC) law in Germany has not given rise to significant difficulties relating to the legal techniques, due to the Continental European nature of both German and European law. A salient feature of German law is the influential role played by academic legal authors, whose works are cited and taken into account by the courts. Among German legal writings, a prominent place is taken by refined commentaries on the various codes and other more important statutes. The BGB has most commentaries, among which some are very detailed and voluminous but with longer time intervals between editions, while there are also concise commentaries in a single volume published annually.

12.2 The German Civil Code (BGB)

Despite the absence until 1900 of a common uniform codification of private law, the private law in the different parts of Germany was to a great extent similar, first and foremost due to the reception during the latter part of the Middle Ages of Roman law, which, as mentioned above, constituted a subsidiary source of law. It therefore became natural to use Roman law as a basis also for the new Civil Code. As contrasted with the Napoleon Code, which was the work of experienced practitioners, the BGB is regarded as the product of scholarly minds (it has also obtained the nickname *Professorenrecht* or "professorial law"). This should not be seen, however, as the result of the dominating influence of legal theoreticians on the design of the Code, but can be explained to a large extent with the political need to create a new German legal terminology and new legal concepts for the purpose of avoiding accusations of giving some of the local legal systems preference over others.

It is true that the BGB appears, in certain respects, to be more modern than the Napoleon Code, but this is due less to the predisposition of the authors than to the simple fact that the BGB is almost a century younger. In similarity with the Napoleon Code, the BGB is also based upon individualistic liberalism, protection of private ownership and freedom of contract, but in a somewhat weakened form due to a number of general clauses. Some of the BGB's general clauses have played a very prominent role in that regard, probably more than what was originally intended. For instance § 242, according to which the debtor is obligated to fulfil his obligations in accordance with good faith (*Treu und Glauben*), has been used as the basis for many different social and ethical considerations, such as to avoid the unreasonable consequences of hyperinflation upon contracts or to protect the weaker parties against unfair contractual provisions. At the time of its entry into force, the BGB shared several of the Napoleon Code's original values in the field of family law, such as a prejudice against children born out of wedlock, who in a legal context were regarded as being unrelated to the father and were merely entitled to a limited financial support that ceased when the child became 16 years old (*Zahlvaterschaft*). This rule and some other out-of-date rules have, however, over the years been removed from the Code.

The BGB is accompanied by a special Promulgation (Introductory) Act (*Einführungsgesetz*), containing i.a. private international law rules and rules on the relationship between the BGB and other German statutes. The BGB itself consists of almost 2,400 sections, grouped into five parts called "books" (*Bücher*). The first book is a novelty in comparison with the Napoleon Code and contains the Civil Code's general part (*Allgemeiner Teil*), with rules on matters common for the remainng parts, such as legal capacity, legal acts, calculation of time, and statute of limitations. The second book covers the law of obligations (*Recht der Schuldverhältnisse*) including both contracts and non-contractual obligations such as torts; this book has undergone a substantial reform in 2002. The third book concerns rights *in rem* (*Sachenrecht*), the fourth family law (*Familienrecht*), and the fifth the law of succession (*Erbrecht*). In contrast to the Napoleon Code, the BGB did not have the unrealistic ambition to be entirely comprehensive. More controversial questions were assigned to special statutes. There are, however, also private law questions that remain unanswered, be it in the BGB or in special private law legislation. In these cases, the German judge is expected to place himself in the position of the law-maker and create an appropriate rule, which however, in accordance with the German system of sources of law, never binds judges in future cases.

The BGB cannot be accused of being hastily put together; it constitutes the result of approximately a quarter-century of preparatory work. Characteristic for the BGB is its logical structural design and clarity, which was however obtained at the expense of the textual elegance and comprehensibility for non-jurists. For example, the frequent cross-references between sections contribute to clarity, but they hardly make the reading enjoyable. Behind the structure of the Code is the idea that the rules should be arranged from the general to the specific, as is evidenced by i.a. the previously-mentioned general part in the beginning of the Code. This intention is however accomplished with such a consistency that, for instance, a rule one may be looking for regarding a dispute between a buyer and a seller can be found among the general provisions, the provisions on obligations in general, the provisions on contracts in general, the provisions on reciprocal contracts in general, or the provisions on contracts of sale, all depending upon if the rule is specific for just sale or is also applicable to other reciprocal contracts, all contracts, all obligations, etc. This does not contribute to making the law accessible to those who have not become familiar with the entire Code, i.e. for those who are not professionally trained jurists.

The authors of the BGB expended great efforts to provide definitions of the various terms and concepts so that they would have the same meaning in the entire field of private law. This well thought-out and well-defined terminology is undoubtedly of very great value but the perhaps somewhat exaggerated attention it received has created a certain propensity among German jurists to reduce real economic, political and ethical conflicts to terminological quarrels and juggling with concepts. A certain amount of such conceptualism (*Begriffsjurisprudenz*) is perhaps unavoidable in connection with the application of a logically constructed Civil Code, where what decides the case is often whether the actual situation fits within one or another of the Code's definitions and terms. From a foreign jurist's point of view, it may however appear as less acceptable to seek a solution primarily in an abstract interpretation of concepts, which are detached from reality and live a life of their own, in a kind of "concepts heaven" (*Begriffshimmel*). The legal terms and concepts, which can be of great service for the legal system, should not be allowed to become its masters. After a few decades, even German jurists started to disassociate themselves, consciously or instinctively, from this excessive conceptualism. This is connected with the aging of the Code and the increasing need of a freer interpretation, which to a greater degree must take into consideration the actual interests of the society and the parties (*Interessenjurisprudenz* in place of *Begriffsjurisprudenz*).

12.3 The Judiciary

As has been mentioned above, Germany is a federal republic (*Bundesrepublik*), consisting of 16 *Länder*. Germany lacks however parallel federal and *Land* judiciary structures similar to those existing in the USA. The court system is characterized by the fact that the highest instances of the judiciary are federal organs, while the administrative and financial responsibility for the rest of the court system, including the appointment of judges, is under the control of the individual *Land* where the court is located.

At the top of the courts of general jurisdiction (*ordentliche Gerichte*) is the Federal Court of Justice (*Bundesgerichtshof*, BGH) in Karlsruhe (in criminal matters partly in Leipzig), which only considers legal questions and does not concern itself with purely factual or evidentiary issues. The BGH was established in 1950 as a successor to the *Reichsgericht* (RG), whose decisions continue to enjoy a high respect despite the lapse of time, at least within private law. The BGH consists of 15 private-law chambers, 5 penal-law chambers and 8 special chambers (of which one hears competition law cases). Cases are decided normally by a *Senat* consisting of five judges. Under the BGH are 24 courts of appeal called *Oberlandesgericht* (OLG). In Berlin, by tradition the counterpart of the OLG is called *Kammergericht* (KG). In the first instance, cases are adjudicated by one of the 116 regional courts (*Landgericht*, LG) or, if they involve small claims, the least serious criminal matters, landlord-tenant disputes, or family or non-adjudicatory matters, by one of the roughly 700 local courts (*Amtsgericht*, AG). The judgment of an AG is normally appealable to a LG. The Judiciary is complicated in that the same court can sit in a number of different compositions, depending upon the nature of the case.

Judicial System in Germany (Simplified Diagram)

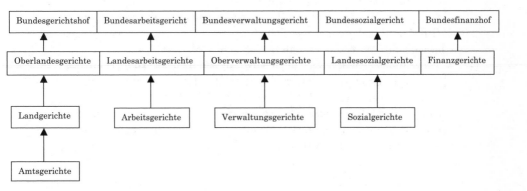

There are a number of administrative courts (*Verwaltungsgerichte*), social insurance courts (*Sozialgerichte*), labour courts (*Arbeitsgerichte*) and tax courts (*Finanzgerichte*). Of particular importance is the Federal Constitutional Court (*Bundesverfassungsgericht*, BVerfG), which is the first and final instance to deal with constitutional complaints from individuals (the clearly largest group of cases), the constitutionality of laws, and competence conflicts between the *Länder* and the Federal Republic. The examination of the constitutionality of a law (*Normenkontrolle*) can result in that the Federal Constitutional Court annuls the statute in question. The other German courts do not have the authority to render decisions on the constitutionality of statutes, but must turn to the Federal Constitutional Court if they consider that there is a conflict with the Constitution. The Federal Constitutional Court can practice *Normenkontrolle* even when the issue of the constitutionality of a statute has not arisen within the context of an actual case, but such "abstract" examination must be raised by the Federal Government, the government of a *Land*, or one-third of the members of the Federal Parliament (*Bundestag*). The Federal Constitutional Court is the only German court where dissenting opinions are made known and published.

12.4   Legal Education and the Legal Profession

The academic legal education, which takes at least four years to complete, is provided by the faculties of law at the German universities. The theoretical studies are completed with the "first state examination" (*Referendarexamen*), but relatively many – perhaps one tenth – of all German jurists also write a doctoral thesis (*Dissertation*) and receive a "dr.jur." degree. This doctoral degree ordinarily requires between one and two years of full-time work to complete. It is not formally a necessary precondition for any legal career, but has social status attached to it and is helpful in "opening doors", as it is also commonly used in everyday social contacts. In private business, a jurist without a doctor's title is regarded as having less chance of obtaining a top position. A positive consequence of this title-chase is that there are few legal problems that have not had at least one dissertation written about them. These works can be of great value also to foreign jurists studying German law. The dissertations are all published, although not necessarily in ordinary book form, and they can usually be located and obtained in or with the assistance of a law library.

The young German law graduate wishing to pursue a legal career applies to be admitted as a trainee (*Referendar*) in the Judiciary. This traineeship is completed in approximately two years with a "second state examination" (*Assessorprüfung*). It is not until the completion of this examination that one is regarded as a fully educated jurist (*Volljurist*). The choice between the various legal careers (judicial, practicing lawyer, etc.) therefore as as rule occurs only after passing this second examination.

Apart from some minor exceptions, a German attorney (*Rechtsanwalt*) has a protected position, since only attorneys, i.e. members of a bar association, are allowed professionally to represent others before a court of law. There is a bar association (*Rechtsanwaltskammer*) for the territorial area of each OLG, and they collectively constitute the *Bundesrechtsanwaltskammer* for the entire country. With the exception of trials before an AG, it is required in principle that each party be represented by an attorney. There are special requirements concerning minimum age and experience for an attorney to represent his client in an OLG or the BGH.

The enforcement of judgments is the task of officials called *Gerichtsvollzieher*. A kind of lesser practicing lawyer is a *Rechtsbeistand*, who is not fully qualified to be an attorney but is licensed to offer certain limited legal services to the general public, normally in specified fields of law only.

An important role in the legal community is played by the *Notar*, who concentrates primarily on the drafting and certification of written legal documents, such as wills and transactions concerning real property. His functions and his qualifications go far beyond the Notary Public in common-law countries, who merely certify the authenticity of documents. The number of *Notar* positions is limited by law. A *Notar* is regarded to be a public official and, in contrast to an attorney representing the interests of one of the parties, is expected to conduct himself in an impartial manner. To become a *Notar* one must, in addition to passing the first and the second state examination, have several years of practical experience. In most, but not all, *Länder* a lawyer can combine both functions and be both a *Notar* and a *Rechtsanwalt*.

12.5   Geographic Spread of German Law

The colonies of Imperial Germany (e.g. present-day Namibia, Burundi and parts of Cameroon and Tanzania in Africa, and Western Samoa in the South Pacific) were lost after Germany's defeat in World War I. Today there are practically no traces of German law in these countries.

That naturally does not mean that German law has not been exported by other means than via colonial expansion. The logic and stringency of the German Civil Code have given rise to admiration in many parts of the world. The BGB has been followed in for instance Japan, whose Civil Code (except for family and succession law) is predominantly built upon the German model. Remarkably enough, the copying was so quick and so efficient that the Japanese translation of the Code entered into force even before 1900, when the BGB entered into force in Germany iself! Even today Japanese scholars in the field of private law often do their postgraduate studies in Germany and German legal writing and judicial decisions continue to enjoy a significant authority in Japan. Japanese public law has, on the other hand, after World War II found inspiration first and foremost from the USA. Either via Japan or directly, the BGB has influenced Korea, Thailand and partly also China. Additionally, Greece has shaped its Civil Code substantially according to the German model (the Greek Commercial Code of 1835 is however a close copy of the French *Code de commerce*). Also the private law codifications of Brazil and Portugal have been heavily influenced by the BGB.

Even the first codifications of Soviet civil law in the 1920s show similarities to the BGB, which at the time was possibly regarded as the most progressive, modern and comprehensive set of legal rules in most fields of private law. Both via the Soviet Union and directly, the BGB influenced most of the legal systems in the formerly socialist countries in Central and Eastern Europe. The present-day economic strength and political weight of Germany, together with long-time linguistic and historic ties, are reasons behind the significant influence enjoyed by German law in connection with the restoration of market-oriented legal system in these countries.

A country which deserves special mention is Austria, whose Civil Code (*Allgemeines Bürgerliches Gesetzbuch*, ABGB) från 1811 is considerably older than the BGB. Even the ABGB is to a significant degree influenced by Roman law. The German law's influence in Austria has been apparent in connection with different legal reforms during the twentieth century. During the Nazi occupation, which for a time incorporated Austria into the German Third Reich, the geographic field of applicability of the German Commercial Code (but not of the BGB) was extended to even include Austria where, in spite of the outcome of the war, this Code continues to be applicable even today.

CHAPTER 13

Chinese Law

13.1 Confucianism

To understand the Chinese attitude towards law and the legal developments in China, it is necessary to go more than two thousand years back in time to the great thinker Confucius (551–479 B.C.), whose influence on the everyday Chinese way of life up to today lacks a parallel in any other part of the world. Even though Confucius never made any claim of divinity, the ethics and moral beliefs of Confucianism were elevated almost to a form of state religion in imperial China and gained very strong influence upon the population in general. Only to a minor degree has traditional Chinese society been influenced by other ways of thinking, with perhaps the exeption of Buddism.

One of the cornerstones of the Confucian view of the world is represented by the concept of "cosmic harmony", in other words a harmoniously ordered, peaceful, and well-balanced universe. Individuals, presumed to be fundamentally good, should not disturb this harmony by mutual conflicts, but should rather humbly keep in their place and conscientiously follow the ethical rules of conduct applying to them. These rules, based upon established custom, were very complicated, carefully balanced, and adapted to different relationships and situations between individuals. Particular ethical rules existed, for instance, on how an older brother should treat a younger brother, how a younger brother should treat an older brother, how a businessman should behave towards a customer, an employer towards an employee, a nobleman toward a commoner, etc. The idea was, consequently, that individuals should be governed by means of moral rules *(li)* instead of by legal rules enforced by the authority of the state *(fa)*. According to Confucius, judges and laws were a necessary evil to punish criminals, but they were not needed to regulate the affairs between honest people. In other words, criminal law was necessary but private law was not. If all people conducted themselves in accordance with the moral rules, then no conflicts would arise. A legal rule, formulated in advance by outsiders and applied mechanically, and which made it impossible to take into consideration factors relevant to the situation from an ethical point of view, was regarded as causing more harm than good. The role of law as an instrument of social control was thus weaker than in the West and was to a significant extent replaced by concepts of honour, shame and "loss of face".

Disputes between individuals should be resolved – or more accurately said dissolved – by means of conciliation and compromise in accordance with ethical principles, where the parties involved could engage prominent members of their respective families as conciliators. More important than the victory of the deserving party was that harmony should be restored so that no one would experience being the loser. This depended upon the resolution of the conflict being voluntarily accepted by both parties and not being forced upon them from outside. An individual who refused to go along with a friendly settlement was regarded as not being a good person. This applied especially to the party who instead aggravated the conflict by going to a court; he stood out as someone who was disturbing the harmony in society and became as such exposed to social criticism by those around him and harsh treatment by the judge. The social pressure to resolve the matter was so strong that, for instance, sympathy for a victim of an accident would disappear if he filed a lawsuit in a court claiming compensation that he was legally entitled to – in the same manner as the person who caused the injury lost face if he refused to pay reasonable compensation relying upon some legal technicality which did not fit in with the ethics of Confucianism. An important role in this social pressure was played by the traditional concept of the extended family, as the entire family was seen as carrying the moral responsibility for the acts and behaviour of each family member. To save face for both of the families involved, the most respected members of the families sought to find a settlement and the parties were exposed to extraordinarily strong social pressure from their relatives. Arbitration was regarded, from that point of view, as being not much better than a court proceeding, as in both cases a resolution was forced upon the parties from outside, which by definition meant that they lost face.

It has been said that the Chinese people associate law and judicial proceedings with disgraceful events such as prosecution for crimes and imprisonment; they have difficulty in understanding that in the West *Justitia* is glorified as being a goddess (even though a goddess with blindfolded eyes).

It is important to point out that the continued survival of this traditional attitude to law cannot be explained simply by saying that the Chinese have not been exposed to any other system. Approximately 250 years after Confucius, China was in fact dominated by the so-called legalistic school, with its preference for comprehensive regulation by laws and a detailed state control over their implementation. However, these ideas had official support for only a very short period of time and disappeared with the change of dynasty in 202 B.C.

13.2 Main Features of Legal Development

The Confucian order of society, based on social pressure, functioned quite well in feudal China for many centuries; consequently, no private law in the Western sense was developed. The system became, however, hopelessly insufficient when China commenced its modernization after the fall of the last Emperor in 1911. The Kuomintang government introduced a number of major codifications based on the Continental European model, including a civil code. These codifications are to a large extent still applicable in Taiwan, which regards itself as a state identical to the Republic of China that existed between the two world wars. In the years between the two wars, many Chinese jurists studied in Germany and France. These modernizations of the law played no doubt an important role for commerce in the coastal cities, but they have never reached the people as a whole, especially not in the countryside.

In connection with the establishment of the People's Republic of China
(P.R.C.) in 1949, the Kuomingtang codes were abolished with the stroke of a
pen. The legal vacuum that arose was not considered to be a significant problem,
which probably was a realistic judgment. Private enterprises, which need clear
legal rules of conduct, were transferred for the most part into the hands of the
state and in any case the codified laws had never played much of a role in the
everyday life of the people. While awaiting the planned new legislation, based
upon the Soviet model, the judicial "cadres" were guided by various political
directives. Gradually some few statutes were enacted, for instance in family
law, but the main fields of law remained unregulated at the time an intensive
campaign against the so-called right-wing reactionaries was launched in 1957.
This campaign was a reaction against the comparatively liberal political climate
prevailing some months earlier under the slogan "let a hundred flowers blos-
som". Among those accused of being right-wing reactionaries were many jurists,
mostly educated before the Communists took power, who had criticized the
lack of rule of law that was a consequence of the lack of legal rules and of the
deficiencies in the implementation of those in existence. The reaction from the
left was very severe. The Ministry of Justice was abolished in 1959, many law
students were sent together with their teachers to the countryside to work on
collective farms, and all legal research and work to create new legislation ceased.
In China the development of the law was thus significantly different from the
development in the Soviet Union and the Eastern European socialist states,
where the pace of new legislation was substantial and the society, at least on
paper, was regulated by means of law.

A drastic further deterioration came in connection with the Cultural Revolution (1966–1976), when legal nihilism and lawlessness with accompanying
chaos prevailed in the entire country. Legal rules were replaced by the political
mood of the day, which depended upon the latest interpretations of the sayings
of the cult figure Mao Zedong. Excesses, including summary executions of
supposed political opponents, were commonplace. The few jurists that China
had at that time were regarded with suspicion and almost all of them were
persecuted in one way or another.

Even though the Maoist form of Marxism can in many respects be regarded
as the very opposite of conservative Confucianism, one may find certain
interesting similarities between the two, even in the legal area. The catastrophe
for China's legal life, which culminated with the Cultural Revolution, possibly
could not have occurred without the old Confucian way of thinking. Legal rules
and courts were something strange for the masses. The situation where laws
were replaced with political slogans was perhaps seen as being quite natural by
a people who were accustomed to be governed by non-legal principles and for
whom the political ideals of Maoism were perhaps an adequate substitute for
Confucian ethics (which however also survived, especially within family relationships). Certain similarities between Mao and Confucius are almost striking,
such as when Mao in a speech he gave in 1957 made a distinction between on

the one hand "conflicts between the class enemy and us", for which he recommended strong repressive state measures, and on the other hand "conflicts among the people", which according to his opinion ought to be resolved with help of proper education. Private law disputes should, according to this classification, belong to the category "conflicts among the people" and as such consequently required no legal regulation. Old Confucius would have most probably rejected Mao's values, but he would not have had a difficult time recognizing the methods as his own.

The new Chinese leadership that came to power after the Cultural Revolution decided to transform China into a modern industrial nation. This should be achieved with the help of such proven methods as a functioning market economy based upon competition between enterprises, private ownership of businesses, and foreign investments. The new leadership soon realized that a reform of the economic life in that direction was not possible without a functioning legal system. To establish such a system was, however, a very difficult task.

The legislative process after the Cultural Revolution had to start over again practically from nothing. One of the greatest problems of the newly opened law faculties at the end of the 1970s was the lack of laws to teach on. One cannot help, however, but be impressed by the quick adoption of legislation, especially in the course of the 1980s (the Ministry of Justice was reestablished in 1979). Today China has a legal system that is substantially comprehensive. The present Constitution, dating from 1982, promises, in Article 5, allegiance to the principle of rule of law. The most important enactments have the form of laws passed by the National People's Congress or its Standing Committee, but there are also many administrative rules adopted by the State Council (i.e. the Government). Judicial precedents are not a source of binding legal rules, but the normative statements made by the Supreme People's Court are generally followed by the lower courts (the "Basic" or "Grassroots" People's Courts, the Intermediate People's Courts, and the Higher People's Courts plus a number of courts of special jurisdiction such as military courts and maritime courts).

The most important codification, without doubt, was the Civil Law of 1986, whose official heading in the English-language translation reads "General Principles of Civil Law of the People's Republic of China".[1] It is sometimes referred to as China's "Civil Code", despite the fact that its arrangement and ambitions are significantly different from the Civil Codes of, for example, France and Germany. The most conspicuous difference concerns the size, the Chinese Civil Law having only 156 articles. In addition, the Chinese Civil Law consists of very general legal rules and seems to presuppose a more detailed set of rules to be found elsewhere. Such supplementary rules do exist for instance on questions concerning property (2007), anti-trust (2007) and contracts (1999). Article 151 of the Civil Law gives each of China's autonomous regions certain rights to adopt "modified or supplementary statutes or regulations in light of its special national characteristics". Other important pieces of legislation are the Penal Law, the Law on Civil Procedure and the Law on Penal Procedure.

---

[1] An English-language translation of the text of the law can be found in e.g. 34 *A.J.C.L.* 715-743 (1986).

The reestablishment of legal rules should not be interpreted as a clear departure from the traditional negative view of legal solutions. It has clearly been recognized that modern business activity cannot function without regulation by law, but at the same time conciliation and compromises are still encouraged as alternatives to court trials. Thus, pursuant to Article 111 of the Constitution, People's Mediation Committees are set up on the local level to mediate civil disputes. Mediation and conciliations play more significant role also in the practice of the Chinese arbitration institutions, active within international trade, than in similar arbitration institutions in other countries.

The state and Communist Party leadership of China appears not to have become quite accustomed to using legal instruments as the main means of control over society. It is still common that political directives ("party policy") are preferred in sensitive areas, for example regarding forced family planning. Within commercial law the existing legal regulation is, however, respected to a relatively high degree. In view of the power monopoly of the Communist Party, which is explicitly stipulated in the Chinese Constitution, it is clear that the role and rule of law in the Chinese society depends on the extent to which the Party finds it compatible with its interests and policies.

13.3   Legal Education and the Legal Profession

Concerning the legal profession, one should keep in mind that in China for over two decades subsequent to 1957 there was in fact no higher legal education, at least not to any mentionable extent. New law faculties were opened at the end of the 1970s, with the first law degrees being granted around 1983; this meant that during a full quarter-century there were no new jurists. The older generation, who even prior to the purges had in any case been few in number, was decimated, demoralized, and after two decades of forced inactivity could hardly be regarded as highly qualified.

The undergraduate study of law program at a Chinese university takes normally three years to complete. There is even today a shortage of university-educated jurists. Many older judges and prosecutors have no law degree and their social status is not very high, partly due to wide-spread corruption.

In 1980 the first regulations on the practice of law were issued, however it was not until 1986 that an association of lawyers covering the entire country, the All-China Lawyers' Association, was established, and a uniform qualifying examination was introduced. The present Lawyers' Act was promulgated in 1996. At the beginning Chinese lawyers were not allowed to establish themselves as private practitioners, but had rather to work within a state-owned law office or a cooperative. Today, however, the formation of private law firms is encouraged. Membership in the Bar Association is compulsory. At the turn of the Millennium there were about 100,000 practicing lawyers, but this is a very low figure in view of the size of the country and its population. In the countryside there are still many "barefoot lawyers", with a minimal formal legal educa-tion, who assist the public with simple legal matters.

13.4 Geographic Spread of Chinese Law

China has traditionally been playing the same role for the Fast East as the Roman Empire played for Europe, i.e. the role of the permanent source of inspiration in matters of culture, religion, philosophy and science. Even though this influence has been substantial, Chinese law as such has not been exported to a large extent, probably due to its low position held in China itself. On the other hand, the negative attitude in China toward judicial resolu-tion of disputes has gained a foothold in a number of Asian countries, and one can therefore speak about a significant geographic spread of this traditional Con-fucian approach, which even today continues to play an important role in the legal life of these countries.

When discussing the influence abroad of the Chinese approach to law, one must first consider those countries other than the People's Republic of China which in a wider sense nevertheless may be considered to be "Chinese". This refers to countries where the majority of the population is predominantly ethnic Chinese with deep roots in the Chinese culture. Included here are Taiwan and Singapore, but also the territories of Hong Kong and Macao (today formally parts of the P.R.C. but with Western-inspired legal systems of their own). Confucianism plays a significant role even in countries such as Japan and South Korea (and in disguise also in North Korea). From the point of view of compara-tive law, an interesting aspect to study is the extent to which the legal systems of these countries, whose external forms were taken over from various European legal systems (e.g. English law in Singapore, Continental European law in Japan, Soviet law in North Korea, etc.), show similarities in the everyday legal life. The formally applicable legal rules have not quite penetrated the shield of Confucian-ism. They play a subordinate role in the life of the people, as most disputes are resolved primarily by means of various kinds of compromises and settlements. It is therefore not surprising that the number of licensed attorneys (*bengoshi*) in all of Japan is said to be less than the number of lawyers in New York City.

Aside from North Korea, the above-mentioned countries of the Far East have become or are becoming industrialized free-market societies, and have addi-tionally been subjected to strong ideological and cultural influences from the West. This has to an important degree weakened the influence of Confucian-ism. Confucianism functioned quite well as long as the contacts and conflicts between people were limited to those who lived in the same village or who had otherwise known each other and each other's families, but the moral and social pressure, which lies behind the strong inclination to compromise and save face, does not function with equal effectiveness in relations that develop in large anonymous cities, especially since the traditional family concept is also being weakened. One can therefore observe a development, also in China itself, toward a greater use of judicial resolutions of conflicts.

Within the increasing foreign trade, business has since long ago relied upon law, in any case when entering into commercial relationships with Westerners who have not been exposed to the teachings of Confucius. The influence of Confucianism on commercial transactions in foreign trade cannot, however, be entirely disregarded. Among businessmen from Western countries it is, for instance, generally known that even a relatively simple new business relationship, which in the West would result in a contract after a brief negotiation, must often begin, in Japan and South Korea, with creating a personal relationship through, for example, sharing numerous meals. The reason for this is not that the Japanese and South Korean businessmen have a lot of time to spare, or that they are looking for every opportunity to have a good meal, but rather that in business dealing they rely more upon personal relationships than on formal legal means. It is unusual, in contrast to the situation in Western countries, especially in the USA, that a party in violation of a contract will find itself immediately threatened with a lawsuit. This affects to some extent also the Confucian attitudes to contracts as such. It is often assumed that the terms of the contract can be renegotiated if circumstances change; the contract is seen as the beginning of a flexible business relationship rather than a final agreement stipulating the detailed rights and obligations of the parties in a legal meaning. It is also common that a contract contains clauses stating that any disputes that may arise shall be resolved "by mutual agreement", by means of "friendly renegotiations" or similar expressions.

As a curiosity it can be mentioned that the Confucian attitude toward law has in certain respects survived among Chinese immigrants and their descendants in the West, including in litigious societies such as the USA. The place to which Chinese businessmen in the USA turn to resolve mutual disputes is almost never the courts. Conflicts that arise between them are normally resolved by means of private mediation and a compromise. Group pressure and the threat of social isolation continue to play an important role in that connection.

CHAPTER 14

Moslem Law

14.1 Sources of Law

Moslem law, or Islamic law, in Arabic called *sharia* (the right way), is a religious system of rules, comparable for example to the canon law of the Catholic Church or the Old Testament of Judaism. To the extent the Moslem rules are discussed as a religious phenomenon, their existence is naturally independent of any government support, and they in fact do not constitute legal rules in the meaning of the term as it is used in the other chapters of this book. The "pure" Moslem law, undefiled by state interference and independent of any state backing, is studied by scholars in a similar way as Roman law was studied at the universities during the Middle Ages in Europe, i.e. as an "ideal law". In their practical legal activities, the same scholars are forced to learn and apply the individual state's own positive law. A large number of states have, however, formulated their legal systems under the strong influence of and/or with direct reference to Moslem law. The legal systems of these states can, for pedagogical purposes, be considered to collectively form a special family of their own, the understanding of which requires a certain basic knowledge of Moslem legal thinking and of the sources of Moslem religious law.

The *sharia* plays naturally an important role first and foremost within those legal areas that in some detail are regulated in the Islamic legal sources, primarily within family law and succession law, and to a certain degree within criminal law, while the influence of Moslem law on, for example, the law of property or contracts is much weaker (however not without some importance, as indicated by the prohibition on interest and the sensitive relationship between the modern insurance industry and the Islamic prohibition against gambling). Moslem law interferes even in some areas, which in the West are considered as being quite outside the domain of law, ranging from the appropriate times for prayer to the proper manner of brushing one's teeth. To differentiate between the religious and the legal rules is not always easy for many Moslems, as they consider religion and law to be one and the same. In the same manner, they sometimes find it difficult to distinguish legal science from theology, and a priest from a jurist. In reality Moslem law contains, however, a number of commandments and prohibitions that are not associated with any actual legal sanctions and therefore, in the Western view, more closely belong to the religious or moral sphere. While Western law can be said to divide human conduct into three categories (prohibited, mandatory, and legally indifferent), Moslem legal scholars add two additional categories, namely recommended and reprehensible. The Koran criticizes, for example, those who enter into commercial agreement on a Friday before the Friday noon prayer, but despite this a contract entered into on a Friday morning is not void, nor are the parties who act against this admonition threatened with punishment.

The most central and highest source of Moslem law is the Koran (*Qur'an*), the holy book of Islam, which is regarded as being of divine origin and as containing God's (Allah's) revelations before Prophet Muhammed, who lived

IVERPOOL JOHN MOORES UNIVERS···
LEARNING SERVICES

during the years 570–632 A.D. The revelations are said to have occurred gradually over a period of about 23 years. The Koran is divided into 30 main parts,
which together contain 114 chapters, which in turn are divided into more than
6,200 verses of a few lines each. Only a small part, about 3 percent, of these are
concerned with matters that in the West are regarded as relating to law. Family
law relationships are regulated in about 70 verses. Other private law matters
are covered also in about 70 verses, and some 30 verses can be characterized as
concerning penal matters. Constitutional and fiscal issues are touched upon in
about 20 verses, and approximately the same number can be regarded to be of
relevance for international law.

Next in the hierarchy of the sources of law is the *Sunna*, which is a collection
of a large number of stories (*hadíth*) about the Prophet Muhammed's pronounce-
ments, deeds, and other behaviour. The Sunna is meant to serve as a model for
the faithful believers. It is said to originate from eyewitnesses in the vicinity
of Muhammed, and has been written down on the basis of oral accounts and
traditions by several Moslem authors who lived during the ninth century. As
Muhammed was a child of his time, and normally conducted himself in accordance with the then prevailing customs and practices, many ancient traditions
from the pre-Islamic times have become part of the Islamic law via *Sunna*.
Sunna often serves as a set of rules for matters on which the Koran is silent. The
Koran forbids, for example, the consumption of wine, but says nothing about the
applicable sanctions; these can be found in the *Sunna*, which describes how the
Prophet in such cases ordered – and even himself administered – flogging.

A further source of law is the *idjmá*, i.e. the generally accepted view among
the faithful, primarily the legal scholars, on the interpretation of the first two
main (primary) sources. There are divided opinions on whether it is a condition that a particular view is accepted by all true believers, all legal scholars, all
legal scholars belonging to a particular school, etc. As an example of an *idjmá*
rule, the principle in some Islamic countries that a woman cannot be a judge
can be mentioned. Such a rule is not found in the Koran, nor in *Sunna*, but its
adherents derive it from the view of a part of Moslem legal scholarship. The
Islamic legal science (*fiqh*) enjoys considerable authority, but certain authors
are accorded greater respect than others depending on the opinion of the reader
and the school of Islam he happens to belong to. Respected legal scholars are
frequently commissioned to write a legal opinion (*fatwa*) on a difficult question
of law. Nowadays many scholars can be contacted and even paid for their work
through the Internet.

The great body of available legal literature means that a Moslem judge
today seldom feels the need to turn to primary sources of law (the Koran or the
Sunna), as these have been authoritatively commented on since more than a
thousand years ago by renowned legal scholars. Even the modern scholars are
considered to be bound by *taqlíd*, i.e. the obligation to recognize and respect the
authority of certain old "classics", which thereby have become an almost independent source of law. *Taqlíd* means that modern authors may not add anything

new to the classical conclusions and modern Islamic legal scholars limit themselves formally to commenting on and analyzing these classical texts. The door
to independent creative thinking (*idjtijád*) is regarded to be closed. The Shi'ite
Moslems (see below) and the modern Islamic reform movements are however,
on this point, more liberal than the more orthodox Sunni schools.

Among the legal methods used, reasoning by analogy (*qiyás*) plays a prominent role (see section 14.2 below), primarily when searching for the regulation
of situations not directly covered by the basic sources. The general prohibition on the consumption of alcohol is, for example, built on the analogy from
the Koran's prohibition of drinking wine; the prohibition on alcohol has been
extended further by analogy to encompass even hard narcotics. Analogy can,
however, also be used to establish rules for situations that were unknown or
even nonexistent during the time of the Prophet. The great significance of analogy has resulted in that Sunni Moslems sometimes regard it as an independent,
fourth source of law after the Koran, *sunna* and *idjmá*. Additionally, there are
also certain subsidiary sources, such as judicial precedents, customs, and the
"common good".

The Moslem faith is divided into many different religious schools (called
rites, *madhhab*), which however are more closely related to each other than
the various Christian religions are. The differences concern only details and
the various schools recognize each other's practices as being legitimate and in
accordance with the true faith. The great mutual tolerance between the different
rites is evidenced by i.a. the fact that it is in principle acceptable that a Moslem,
who normally follows one rite, chooses to perform a particular individual act
in accordance with another rite, which in the particular case is more advantageous for him. The most important and most known division is between the
Shi'ite and the Sunni Moslems. Shi'ites, who make up only about 15 percent
of all Moslems, are in the majority in Iran, Bahrain and Iraq, and constitute a
significant part of the Moslem population in i.a. Lebanon, Indonesia, India and
Pakistan. Both the Sunni and the Shi'ite Moslems can be divided into several
"sub-schools", each of which bears the name of its founder and spiritual father.
The four most important Sunni schools are Shafi'i, Maliki, Hanafi and Hanbali,
while the dominant Shi'ite school is the Djafari.

14.2   Legal Method

Due to the fact that the two fundamental and primary sources
of Islamic law are considered to originate either directly from God (the Koran)
or from his Prophet Muhammed (*Sunna*), they are regarded by faithful Moslems
to be eternally valid and immutable, i.e. the ultimate and perfect law, which at
some time in the future will be recognized and followed by all humankind. The
national legislatures of various countries, according to that view, cannot change
the law, but can only regulate such details and modalities that have been left
unregulated by the *sharia*.

This might lead one to believe that the unchangeable and set-in-stone Moslem law, which is built on sources which are well over a thousand years old, cannot be adapted to and made compatible with a modern society and modern values. The truth is, however, that Moslem law can be an exceptionally flexible system of rules, in any case if the court or authority interpreting and applying it strives to achieve such flexibility.

To begin with, it must be pointed out that many of the Moslem rules are so broadly formulated that they can be relied upon for support for feudal as well as modern ideas. The stipulated obligation to practice charity can, for example, be complied with by means of giving alms to poor beggars in the street, but can also be relied upon for support by politicians or legislators who desire to introduce a social insurance system of the Western welfare-state type.

A part of the more outdated rules can be "disarmed", without being formally overruled, by means of interpretation or the use of contracts. A well-known rule of Moslem family law provides, for example, that a marriage can be unilaterally dissolved by the husband, which occurs by his saying to his wife three times "I divorce you" (*talaq*). In some Moslem countries, such *talaq* divorce is only recognized, however, under the precondition that a court or some other state or religious authority has affirmed it after having investigated the circumstances, to a large extent in the same manner as in the legal systems of many Western countries, although formally the investigation is merely for the purpose of making sure that the divorce has voluntarily and seriously been carried out by the husband.

Several Western countries have today liberal divorce laws giving each spouse an unconditional right to divorce, without there being any need to investigate the grounds. The Moslem law gives such a right to the husband only. This gender discrimination can, however, be corrected without violating any mandatory Islamic legal rule, for instance in the manner that the husband in connection with the entry into marriage gives to his (future) wife an irretrievable power of attorney authorizing her, if she wishes, to divorce herself on his behalf! On the other hand, the husband can, when entering into a marriage, renounce in a binding manner his right to divorce; paradoxically enough this effect can among the Shi'ite Moslems be achieved by entering into a temporary marriage, for instance for 100 years.

Another example is polygamy, i.e. the right of the husband to be married to up to four wives at the same time, which is one of the most well-known characteristics of Moslem family law. Polygamy is nowadays forbidden in some Moslem countries, which has been accomplished without violating the *sharia*: Islamic law does not make polygamy obligatory, but only makes it permissible under the precondition that the husband treats all of his wives fairly and in the same manner, something which no man, according to certain statements in the Moslem sources, can possibly achieve. Moslem law additionally accepts that the husband, in a marriage contract concluded at the time of the first marriage, renounces his right to enter into further marriages.

Some of the Moslem family law traditions show themselves at a closer look to play another role, and function in another manner, than how jurists in Western countries ordinarily see them. As an example the tradition of "purchasing" the bride can be mentioned. According to Moslem law, marriage is regarded as being based on contract. The marriage contract stipulates, among other things, the *"mahr"*, which the bridegroom pays or promises to pay to his bride. This price, which can be set in money or in another manner, can be purely symbolic (e.g., it can consist of "a copy of the Holy Koran and twenty roses"), but can also be very high and exceed the bridegroom's ability to pay. In reality, often no price is actually paid out at all, as the amount at the same time serves as the bride's dowry. Considering that Moslem law does not recognize any form of matrimonial community property, the wife is entitled in the case of a divorce to take the dowry with her, i.e. the husband is now forced to pay out the price. The system in fact is an economic guarantee that the bridegroom ensures his future wife. A tradition that at a superficial glance may seem to treat the woman as a commodity for sale, can in reality have an entirely different purpose and actually be to her advantage.

Similar misunderstandings can arise in the field of penal law. Some very drastic punishments in Moslem law, such as the stoning to death of adulterous wives, play normally more the role of a moralistic admonishment than actually being used in practice. This is evidenced by the fact that the burden of proof has deliberately been placed so high that it is normally impossible to meet (for instance the requirement of four male eyewitnesses to the above-mentioned crime, with the addition that anyone who without such full proof accuses another of committing adultery shall be punished with flogging).

Paradoxically, the Moslem law's divine status and unchangeability can sometimes be utilized for circumventing its commandments and prohibitions. The *raison d'être* of an Islamic rule is in principle not connected to any rational purpose that it may serve and in relationship to which it should be interpreted, but instead depends on the rule's divine origin. It is possible therefore, if one wishes, to interpret the rule strictly to the letter, without taking into account that one thereby makes it possible to evade or circumvent its (presumed) purpose. This can be illustrated by the Moslem law's prohibition against the taking of interest (*riba*), which is equated to usury. A manner that is often used to circumvent this prohibition is to engage in a fictitious sale-and-buy-back transaction. This is effected by the borrower first buying some object from the lender, which he pays for with a promissory note (of course without any promise to pay interest), and immediately thereafter selling the same object back to the lender for a lower cash payment. The economic result of such a transaction becomes the same as an interest-bearing loan, since the borrower has received the money and the lender has obtained a promissory note that does not become due until at a set time in the future but in return promises a higher amount. Formally, however, interest has neither been charged nor received. The remarkable thing about this type of transactions and other similar legal "fictions" (*hiyal*), obviously involving acts made *in fraudem legis*, is that they are accepted by numerous Moslem jurists and law-makers, in particular those who desire to respect the rules of *sharia* but at the same time wish to encourage economic development (the prohibition of interest would of course otherwise be a serious obstacle for credit and investments). What is tolerated and what is not tolerated by the state varies however from one Moslem country to another, so that something accepted in, for instance, Morocco can result in a heavy punishment in, for instance, Iran.

It should also be mentioned that Islamic law also contains general rules on necessity and emergency. A Moslem dying of thirst may in fact drink wine when there are no non-alcoholic alternatives available and a Moslem living far north of the Polar circle does not have to starve to death during the month of Ramadan (the month when one must not eat nor drink until the sun goes down), not even if it coincides with the time of the year when it is light throughout the twenty-four hours of the day.

14.3 Geographic Spread of Moslem Law

Islamic law constitutes an important source for the legal systems of a considerable number of countries. This primarily concerns of course countries with a predominantly Moslem population but sometimes also countries where Moslems constitute a minority (Israel and India are examples of countries where Moslem law is applied on certain matters concerning family relations regarding Moslems). According to a rough estimation, approximately one-sixth of humankind live in those more than fifty countries whose law to a significant degree is influenced by *sharia*. Included here is not only practically the entire Arab world, but even many other countries, geographically spread from West Africa (e.g. Guinea and Senegal) to the Far East (e.g. Malaysia and Brunei). It cannot be excluded either that *sharia* will acquire an increasing influence in the legal systems of some of the independent states in Central Asia that have arisen after the demise of the Soviet Union, as several of these countries have an overwhelmingly Moslem population. Almost all Islamic countries have legal systems that are mixed (see Chapter 7 above), with i.a. commercial law based on the law of the former colonial power (e.g. English law in Malaysia and French law in Morocco).

The relationship between the state and *sharia*, on the other hand, varies greatly even between countries traditionally considered to be Moslem. Some of these countries are practically entirely secularized and the state treats Islam merely as one religion among many, such as in Turkey. The opposite extreme cases are today Saudi Arabia and Iran, where the state is understood as being entirely subordinate to the religion and as being a mere tool for its implementation; it follows from this that *sharia* rules are automatically enforced by the state. In between these two extremes one can find countries with varying degrees of ties between the state and Islam, and varying degrees concerning the position of

Islamic rules as the state's valid law. In the majority of Moslem countries, Islam is the state religion, but that is frequently understood to mean that it is the state that decides if, when and how *sharia* shall or may be applied.

Bibliography

Agge, "Några ord om den allmänna rättsläran och dess ämnesområde", *SvJT* 1969, pp. 156-167.

Ajani, "La circulation de modèles juridiques dans le droit post-socialiste", *Rev.int.dr.comp.* 1994, pp. 1087-1105.

Ajani, "By Chance and Prestige: Legal Transplants in Russia and Eastern Europe", 43 *A.J.C.L.* 93-117 (1995).

Ancel, *Utilité et méthodes du droit comparé*, Neuchâtel 1971.

Ancel, "Valeur actuelle des études de droit comparé", *20th Century Comparative and Conflicts Law. Legal Essays in Honor of Hessel E. Yntema*, Leyden 1961, pp. 15-28.

Ancel, "Réflexions sur la recherche et sur la méthode comparatives", *Ius privatum gentium. Festschrift für Max Rheinstein*, vol.1, Tübingen 1969, pp. 211-219.

Ancel, "La fonction du droit comparé dans la société contemporaine", *Act.Jur.Hung.* 1971, pp. 187-199.

Ancel, "Les buts actuels de la recherche comparative", *Mélanges de droit comparé en l'honneur du doyen Åke Malmström*, Stockholm 1972, pp. 1-12.

Ancel, "Quelques réflexions sur l'évolution et la situation présente des études comparatives", *Multitudo legum – ius unum. Festschrift für Wengler*, vol. 2, Berlin 1973, pp. 43-52.

Arminjon, Nolde & Wolff, *Traité de droit comparé*, vol. 1-3, Paris 1950-1952.

Arvind, "The 'Transplant Effect' in Harmonization", 59 *I.C.L.Q.* 65-88 (2010).

Aubin, "Die rechtsvergleichende Interpretation autonominternen Rechts in der deutschen Rechtsprechung", *RabelsZ* 1970, pp. 458-480.

Baade, "Comparative Law and the Practitioner", 31 *AJ.C.L.* 499-510 (1983).

Backe, "Brottsbalkens terminologi på främmande språk", *TSA* 1968, pp. 386-390.

Backe, "Juridik och språkkunskap", *TSA* 1971, pp. 501-503.

Backe, "Om ordböcker med juridisk terminologi", *TSA* 1976, pp. 189-191.

Backe, "Mera om ordböcker och rättstermer", *TSA* 1977, pp. 311-312.

Banakas, "Some Thoughts on the Method of Comparative Law: the Concept of Law Revisited", *Revue hellénique de droit international* 1980, pp. 155-181.

Banakas, "The Use of Comparative Law in Public International Law: Problems of Method", *Revue hellénique de droit international* 1982-1983, pp. 121-129.

Banakas, "The Contribution of Comparative Law to the Harmonization of European Private Law", in Harding & Örücü, eds, *Comparative Law*, pp. 179-191.

Bartels, "Rechtsvereinheitlichung zwischen unterschiedlichen Gesellschaftsordnungen", *RabelsZ* 1981, pp. 106-123.

Batiffol, "Les apports du droit comparé au droit international privé", *Livre du Centenaire de la Société de législation comparée*, vol. 1, Paris 1969, pp. 131-142.

Batiffol, "Droit comparé, droit international privé et théorie générale du droit", *Rev.int.dr.comp.* 1970, pp. 661-674.

Baxi, "The Colonialist Heritage", in Legrand & Munday, eds, *Comparative Legal Studies*, pp. 46-75.

Beaulieu, "Québec et la formation d'un droit canadien", *Rev.int.dr.comp.* 1961, pp. 300-306.

Bell, "Comparing Public Law", in Harding & Örücü, eds, *Comparative Law*, pp. 235-247.

Bendermacher-Geroussis, "La méthode comparative et le droit international privé", *Revue hellénique de droit international* 1979, pp. 54-61.

Berger, "Auf dem Weg zu einem europäischen Gemeinrecht der Metode", *ZEuP* 2001, pp. 4-29.

Berman, "Comparative Law and Religion", in Reimann & Zimmermann, eds, *The Oxford Handbook*, pp. 739-751.

Bermann, "Le droit comparé et le droit international: alliés ou ennemis?", *Rev.int.dr.comp.* 2003, pp. 519-529.

Bernhardt, "Eigenheiten und Ziele der Rechtsvergleichung im öffentlichen Recht", *ZaöRV* 1964, pp. 431-452.

Birkmose, "A 'Race to the Bottom' in the EU?", *Maastricht Journal of European and Comparative Law* 2006, pp. 35-80.

Blagojević, "Le droit comparé – méthode ou science", *Rev.int.dr.comp.* 1953, pp. 649-657.

Blagojević, "Le caractère révolutionnaire du droit des états socialistes", *Rev. roumaine* 1968, pp. 19-35.

Blagojević, "La méthode comparative juridique", in Rotondi, ed., *Inchieste*, pp. 17-40.

Blanc-Jouvan, "Les différentes tendances et conceptions du droit comparé dans les pays romanistes", *Act.Jur.Hung.* 1971, pp. 143-158.

Blanc-Jouvan, "La formation au droit comparé. Le point de vue d'un universitaire", *Rev.int. dr.comp.* 1996, pp. 347-367.

Blomeyer, "Zur Frage der Abgrenzung von vergleichender Rechtswissenschaft und Rechtsphilosophie", *RabelsZ* 1934, pp. 1-16.

Bobek, "Socialistická srovnávací právní věda", in Bobek *et al.*, *Komunistické právo v Československu*, Brno 2009, pp. 401-424.

Bogdan, *Travel Agency in Comparative and Private International Law*, Lund 1976.

Bogdan, "General Principles of Law and the Problem of Lacunae in the Law of Nations", *NordTIR* 1977, pp. 37-53.

Bogdan, "Stöd för marknadsekonomiskt inriktad rättsutveckling i u-länderna", *SvJT* 1991, pp. 784-792.

Bogdan, "Some Reflections on Development Aid in the Field of Law", *Essays in Honour of Jan Štěpán*, Zürich 1994, pp. 7-15.

Bogdan, "Common Law versus Civil Law in International Development Aid", *Festskrift til Ole Lando*, Köpenhamn 1997, pp. 69-81.

Bogdan, "Den komparativa rättens betydelse för utbildningen i internationell rätt och EG-rätt", *Festskrift til Birger Stuevold Lassen*, Oslo 1997, pp. 203-208.

Bogdan, "On the Value and Method of Rule-Comparison in Comparative Law", *Festschrift für Erik Jayme*, vol. 2, München 2004, pp. 1233-1242.

Bogdan, "Is There a Curricular Core for the Transnational Lawyer?", 55 *Journal of Legal Education* 484-487 (2005).

Bonfils, "Die Funktion des Privaterbrechts in den sozialistischen Ländern", *Jahrbuch für Ostrecht* 1979, no. 1, pp. 85-105.

Borucka-Arctowa, "Methodological Problems of Comparative Research in Legal and Other Social Sciences", *Archivum Juridicum Cracoviense* 1973, pp. 13-29.

Bothe, "Die Bedeutung der Rechtsvergleichung in der Praxis internationaler Gerichte", *ZaöRV* 1976, pp. 280-299.

Bucher, "Komparatistik – Rechtsvergleichung und Geschichte", *RabelsZ* 2010, pp. 251-317.

Bullier, "Le droit comparé est-il un passe temps inutile?", *Rev.dr.int.dr.comp.* 2008, pp. 163-172.

Burg, "Law and Development: a Review of the Literature & Critique of Scholars in Self-Estrangement", 25 *A.J.C.L.* 492-530 (1977).

Bussani, "'Integrative' Comparative Law Enterprises and the Inner Stratification of Legal Systems", 8 *Eur.Rev.Priv.L.* 85-99 (2000).

Bussani & Mattei, "Le fonds commun du droit privé européen", *Rev.int.dr.comp.* 2000, pp. 29-48.

Cadere, "Quelques réflexions sur les études de science juridique comparative", *Rev.int.dr.comp.* 1971, pp. 849-855.

Castellucci, "How Mixed Must a Mixed System Be?", *E.J.C.L.*, vol. 12.1 (May 2008), www.ejcl. org.

Chanturia, "Recht und Transformation: Rechtliche Zusammenarbeit aus der Sicht eines rezipierenden Landes", *RabelsZ* 2008, pp. 114-135.

Chebanov, "Science du droit comparé en U.R.S.S.", *Rev.int.dr.comp.* 1975, pp. 121-129.

de Coninck, "The Functional Method of Comparative Law: *Quo Vadis?*", *RabelsZ* 2010, pp. 318-350.

Constantinesco, *Rechtsvergleichung*, vol. 1-2, Köln 1971-1972. Was also published in French: *Traité de droit comparé*, vol. 1-2, Paris 1972-1974.

Constantinesco, "La comparabilité des ordres juridiques ayant une idéologie et une structure politico-économique différente et la théorie des éléments determinants", *Rev.int.dr.comp.* 1973, pp. 5-16.

Constantinesco, "Les buts et les méthodes du droit comparé", *ZvglRW* 1975-1976, pp. 144-168.

Constantinesco, "Über den Stil der 'Stiltheorie' in der Rechtsvergleichung", *ZvglRW* 1979, pp. 154-172.

Constantinesco, "Die Kulturkreise als Grundlage der Rechtskreise", *ZfRV* 1981, pp. 161-178.

Constantinesco, "Der Rechtsbegriff in der Makro-Vergleichung", *ZvglRW* 1981, pp. 177-198.

Cotterrell, "Comparatists and Sociology", in Legrand & Munday, eds, *Comparative Legal Studies*, pp. 131-153.

Cotterrell, "Comparative Law and Legal Culture", in Reimann & Zimmermann, eds, *The Oxford Handbook*, pp. 709-737.

de Cruz, *Comparative Law in a Changing World*, ed. 3, London-New York 2008.

de Cruz, "Legal Transplants: Principles and Pragmatism in Comparative Family Law", in Harding & Örücü, eds, *Comparative Law*, pp. 101-119.

Dainow, "Le droit civil de la Louisiane", *Rev.int.dr.comp.* 1954, pp. 19-38.

Dainow, "Use of English Translation of Planiol by Louisiana Courts", 14 *A.J.C.L.* 68-97 (1965-1966).

Dannemann, "Comparative Law: Study of Similarities or Differences?", in Reimann & Zimmermann, eds, *The Oxford Handbook*, pp. 383-419.

David, *Traité élémentaire de droit civil comparé*, Paris 1950.

David, *Les avatars d'un comparatiste*, Paris 1982.

David, "Le droit comparé, enseignement de culture générale", *Rev.int.dr.comp.* 1950, pp. 682-685.

David, "Existe-t-il un droit occidental?", *20th Century Comparative and Conflicts Law. Legal Essays in Honor of Hessel E. Yntema*, Leyden 1961, pp. 56-64.

David, "La coopération internationale en matière de droit comparé", *Mélanges de droit comparé en l'honneur du doyen Åke Malmström*, Stockholm 1972, pp. 58-72.

David & Brierley, *Major Legal Systems in the World Today*, ed. 3, London 1985. This book is an English-language translation and revision of David, *Les grands systèmes de droit contemporains*, ed. 8, Paris 1982.

Dehousse, "Comparing National and EC Law: the Problem of the Level of Analysis", 42 *A.J.C.L.* 761-781 (1994).

Demleitner, "Challenge, Opportunity and Risk: An Era of Change in Comparative Law", 46 *A.J.C.L.* 647-655 (1998).

Derret, *An Introduction to Legal Systems*, London 1968.

Doucet & Vanderlinden, *La réception des systèmes juridiques: implantation et destin*, Bruxelles 1994.

Drobnig, "Rechtsvergleichung und Rechtssoziologie", *RabelsZ* 1953, pp. 295-309.

Drobnig, "Methodenfragen der Rechtsvergleichung im Lichte der International Encyclopedia of Comparative Law", *Ius privatum gentium. Festschrift für Max Rheinstein*, vol. l, Tübingen 1969, pp. 221-233.

Drobnig, "Methods of Sociological Research in Comparative Law", *RabelsZ* 1971, pp. 496-504.

Drobnig, "Rechtsvergleichung zwischen Rechtsordnungen verschiedener Wirtschaftssysteme. Zum Problem der intersystemaren Rechtsvergleichung", *RabelsZ* 1984, pp. 233-244.

Drobnig & Rehbinder, eds, *Rechtssoziologie und Rechtsvergleichung*, Berlin 1977.

Ehrenzweig, "Malmström's 'System of Legal Systems': an Unsystematic Comment", *Mélanges de droit comparé en l'honneur du doyen Åke Malmström*, Stockholm 1972, pp. 73-79.

Elias, "Common Law. Kodifizierungsprobleme und der Einfluss afrikanischen Gewohnheitsrechtes", *ZfRV* 1966, pp. 45-56.

Eminescu, "Sur le problème de la comparabilité des systèmes de droit différents", *Jahrbuch für Ostrecht* 1973, no. 2, pp. 75-96.

Engström & Wesslau, *Anteckningar rörande jämförande rättsforskning, approximering – harmonisering – unifiering, enhetlig tolkning av enhetlig rätt*, Karlshamn 1972.

Eörsi, *Comparative Civil (Private) Law – Law Types, Law Groups, the Roads of Legal Development*, Budapest 1979.

Eörsi, "Comparative Analysis of Socialist and Capitalist Law", *Co-existence* 1964, pp. 139-151.

Eörsi, "Réflexions sur la méthode de la comparaison des droits dans le domaine du droit civil", *Rev.int.dr.comp.* 1967, pp. 397-418.

Eörsi, "Some Aspects of Comparative Law", *Xenion. Festschrift für Pan.J.Zepos*, vol. 2, Athen-Freiburg-Köln 1973, pp. 87-97.

Eörsi, "On the Problem of the Division of Legal Systems", in Rotondi, ed., *Inchieste*, pp. 181-209.

Eörsi, "Unifying the Law: a Play in One Act with a Song", 25 *A.J.C.L.* 658-662 (1977).

Eörsi, "Convergence in Civil Law?", in Szabó & Péteri, eds, *A Socialist Approach*, pp. 45-94.

Erbe, "Der Gegenstand der Rechtsvergleichung", *RabelsZ* 1942, pp. 196-226.

Eustathiades, "Droit comparé et méthode comparative en droit international public", *Xenion. Festschrift für Pan.J.Zepos*, vol. 2, Athen-Freiburg-Köln 1973, pp. 117-157.

Faiziev, *Sovetskoe sravnitelnoe pravovedenie v usloviakh federacii*, Tashkent 1986.

Faust, "Comparative Law and Economic Analysis of Law", in Reimann & Zimmermann, eds, *The Oxford Handbook*, pp. 837-865.

Fauvarque-Cosson, "Droit comparé et droit international privé: la confrontation de deux logiques à travers l'exemple des droits fondamentaux", *Rev.int.dr.comp.* 2000, pp. 797-818.

Fauvarque-Cosson, "Comparative Law and Conflict of Laws: Allies or Enemies? Perspectives on an Old Couple", 49 *A.J.C.L.* 407-427 (2001).

Fauvarque-Cosson, "L'enseignement du droit comparé", *Rev.int.dr.comp.* 2002, pp. 293-309.

Fedtke, "Legal Transplants", in Smits, ed., *Elgar Encyclopedia*, pp. 434-437.

Feldbrugge, "Sociological Research Methods and Comparative Law", in Rotondi, ed., *Inchieste*, pp. 213-224.

Ferid, "Methoden, Möglichkeiten und Grenzen der Privatrechtsvereinheitlichung", *ZfRV* 1962, pp. 193-213.

Foster, "Transmigration and Transferability of Commercial Law in a Globalized World", in Harding & Örücü, eds, *Comparative Law*, pp. 55-73.

Frankenberg, "Critical Comparisons: Re-Thinking Comparative Law", 26 *Harvard International L.J.* 412-455 (1985).

Friedmann, *Law in a Changing Society*, ed. 2, 1972 (PenguinBooks).

Fuchs, "Recht und Entwicklungsländer", *ZvglRW* 1981, sid. 355-372.

Genzmer, "Über historische Rechtsvergleichung", in Rotondi, ed., *Inchieste*, pp. 235-254.

Gerber, "System Dynamics: toward a Language of Comparative Law?", 46 *A.J.C.L.* 719-737 (1998).

Germer, "De europæske fællesskabers erstatningspligt uden for kontraktsforhold: et praktisk anvendelseområde for den komparative retsforskning", *Juristen* 1967, pp. 449-463.

van Gerven, "A Common Law for Europe: the Future Meeting the Past?", 9 *Eur.Rev.Priv.L.* 485-503 (2001).

van Gerven, "Comparative Law in a Regionally Integrated Europe", in Harding & Örücü, eds, *Comparative Law*, pp. 155-178.

Gessner, "Soziologische Überlegungen zu einer Theorie der angewandten Rechtsvergleichung", *RabelsZ* 1972, pp. 229-260.

Gilissen, "Histoire comparée du droit. L'expérience de la Société Jean Bodin", in Rotondi, ed., *Inchieste*, pp. 257-297.

van Ginsbergen, "Qualifikationsproblem, Rechtsvergleichung und mehrsprachige Staatsverträge", *ZfRV* 1970, pp. 1-15.

Glendon, Gordon & Carozza, *Comparative Legal Traditions*, ed. 2, St.Paul 1999.

Glendon, Gordon & Picker, *Comparative Legal Traditions. Text, Materials and Cases on Western Law*, ed. 3, St.Paul 2007.

Glenn, *Legal Traditions of the World*, ed. 3, Oxford 2007.

Glenn, "Vers un droit comparé intégré?", *Rev.int.dr.comp.* 1999, pp. 841-852.

Glenn, "La tradition juridique nationale", *Rev.int.dr.comp.* 2003, pp. 263-278.

Glenn, "Aims of Comparative Law", in Smits, ed., *Elgar Encyclopedia*, pp. 57-65.

Glenn, "Comparative Legal Families and Comparative Legal Traditions", in Reimann & Zimmermann, eds, *The Oxford Handbook*, pp. 421-440.

Gomard, "Civil law, Common Law and Scandinavian Law", 5 *Sc.St.L.* 27-38 (1961).

Gordley, "Common Law und Civil Law: eine überholte Unterscheidung", *ZEuP* 1993, pp. 498-518.

Gordley, "Comparative Legal Research and its Function in the Development of Harmonized Law. An American Perspective", *De lege. Juridiska fakultetens i Uppsala årsbok* 1995, pp. 37-53.

Gordley, "Is Comparative Law a Distinct Discipline?", 46 *A.J.C.L.* 607-615 (1998).

Gordley, "Comparative Law and Legal History", in Reimann & Zimmermann, eds, *The Oxford Handbook*, pp. 753-773.

Grossfeld, *Kernfragen der Rechtsvergleichung*, Tübingen 1996.

Graveson, "L'influence du droit comparé sur le rapprochement des peuples", *Rev.int.dr.comp.* 1958, pp. 501-509.

Graveson, "Methods of Comparative Law in Common Law Systems", in Rotondi, ed., *Inchieste*, pp. 301-316.

Graziadei, "The Functionalist Heritage", in Legrand & Munday, eds, *Comparative Legal Studies*, pp. 100-127.

Graziadei, "Comparative Law as the Study of Transplants and Receptions", in Reimann & Zimmermann, eds, *The Oxford Handbook*, pp. 441-475.

de Groot, "Legal Translation", in Smits, ed., *Elgar Encyclopedia*, pp. 423-433.

Grossfeld, *The Strength and Weakness of Comparative Law*, Oxford 1990.

Grossfeld, *Kernfragen der Rechtsvergleichung*, Tübingen 1996.

Grossfeld, "Probleme der Rechtsvergleichung im Verhältnis Vereinigte Staaten von Amerika – Deutschland", *RabelsZ* 1975, pp. 5-28.

Grossfeld & Bilda, "Europäische Rechtsangleichung", *ZfRV* 1992, pp. 421-433.

Grosswald Curran, "Cultural Immersion, Difference and Categories in U.S. Comparative Law", 46 *A.J.C.L.* 43-92 (1998).

Grosswald Curran, "Comparative Law and the Legal Origins Thesis: [n]on scholae sed vitae discimus", 57 *A.J.C.L.* 863-876 (2009).

Grosswald Curran, "Dealing in Difference: Comparative Law's Potential for Broadening Legal Perspectives", 46 *A.J.C.L.* 657-668 (1998).

Grzybowski, "Continuity of Law in Eastern Europe", 6 *A.J.C.L.* 44-78 (1957).

Grzybowski, "Le but des recherches et les méthodes des travaux sur le droit comparé", in Rotondi, ed., *Inchieste*, pp. 319-335.

de Gusmao, "Droit comparé", *Etudes offertes à Jacques Lambert*, Paris 1975, pp. 489-494.

Gutteridge, *Comparative Law*, ed. 2, Cambridge 1949.

Gutteridge, "Comparative Law and the Law of Nations", 21 *B.Y.I.L.* 1-10 (1944).

Göranson, "Komparativa reflexioner. Några metodproblem vid rättsjämförande studier", *Festskrift till Anders Agell*, Uppsala 1994, pp. 193-207.

Hagelmayer, "Agreements by Collective Bargaining in the Socialist Countries", *Act.Jur.Hung.* 1973, pp. 399-416.

Hailbronner, "Ziele und Methoden völkerrechtlich relevanter Rechtsvergleichung", *ZaöRV* 1976, pp. 190-226.

Halász, "The comparative study of public administration", in Szabó & Péteri, eds, *A Socialist Approach*, pp. 163-182.

Hanisch, "Rechtsvergleichung – aber wie?", *Beihefte zur Zeitschrift für schweizerisches Recht*, no. 16, 1994, pp. 125-134.

Harding, "Comparative Law: Some Lesssons from South East Asia", in Harding & Örücü, eds, *Comparative Law*, pp. 249-266.

Harding & Örücü, eds, *Comparative Law in the 21st Century*, London-The Hague-New York 2002.

Harmathy, "Comparison in the Sphere of Economic Contracts", in Szabó & Péteri, eds, *A Socialist Approach*, pp. 183-212.

Hazard, *Communists and Their Law – a Search for the Common Core of the Legal Systems of the Marxian Socialist States*, Chicago-London 1969.

Hazard, "Socialist Law and the International Encyclopedia", 79 *Harvard L.R.* 278-302 (1965-1966).

Hazard, "Area Studies and Comparison of Law: the Experience with Eastern Europe", 19 *A.J.C.L.* 645-654 (1971).

Hazard, "Marxian Socialist Law as an Instrument of Comparison", *Problèmes de droit contemporain. Mélanges Louis Baudouin*, Montréal 1974, pp. 489-502.

Hazard, "Pourquoi le droit comparé? L'URSS et les Etats-Unis", *Rev.dr.int.dr.comp.* 1979, pp. 292-308.

Heiss, "Hierarchische Rechtskreiseinteilung. Von der Rechtskreislehre zur Typologie der Rechtskulturen?", *ZvglRW* 2001, pp. 396-424.

Heldrich, "Sozialwissenschaftliche Aspekte der Rechtsvergleichung", *RabelsZ* 1970, pp. 427-442.

Henrÿ, "Kulturfremdes Recht erkennen. Warum? Wie?", *ZfRV* 1997, pp. 45-55.

Herzog, "Les principes et les méthodes du droit pénal comparé", *Rev.int.dr.comp.* 1957, pp. 338-352.

Hirsch, "Vier Phasen im Ablauf eines zeitgenössischen Rezeptionsprozesses", *ZvglRW* 1968, pp. 182-223.

Van Hoecke, ed., *Epistemology and Methodology of Comparative Law*, Oxford-Portland 2004.

Van Hoecke, "Deep Level Comparative Law", in Van Hoecke, ed., *Epistemology*, pp. 165-195.

Van Hoecke & Warrington, "Legal Cultures, Legal Paradigms and Legal Doctrine: towards a New Model for Comparative Law", 47 *I.C.L.Q.* 495-536 (1998).

Hondius, "The Supremacy of Western Law", *Viva vox iuris romani. Essays in honour of Johannes E. Spruit*, Amsterdam 2002, pp. 337-342.

von Hülsen, "Sinn und Methode der Rechtsvergleichung, insbesondere bei der Ermittlung übernationalen Zivilrechts", *JZ* 1967, pp. 629-633.

Husa, "Law in Constitutional Comparative Law", *FJFT* 1997, pp. 407-423.

Husa, "Legal Families in Comparative Law – Are They of Any Real Use?", *Retfærd* 2001, no. 4, pp. 15-24.

Husa, "Farewell to Functionalism or Methodological Tolerance?", *RabelsZ* 2003, pp. 419-447.

Husa, "Classification of Legal Families Today: Is it Time for a Memorial Hymn?", *Rev.int. dr.comp.* 2004, pp. 11-38.

Husa, "Methodology of Comparative Law Today: From Paradoxes to Flexibility?", *Rev.int. dr.comp.* 2006, pp. 1095-1117.

Husa, "Legal Families", in Smits, ed., *Elgar Encyclopedia*, pp. 382-392.

Husa, "Familjer inom jämförande juridik – släktforskning, ätter och stamtavlor eller något annat?", *Juridiska fakultetens i Uppsala årsbok* 2011, *Vänbok till Rolf Nygren*, Uppsala 2011, pp. 29-41.

Husa, "Metamorphosis of Functionalism – or Back to Basics?", *Maastricht Journal of European and Comparative Law* 2011, pp. 548-553.

Ionasco, "Quelques considérations sur le droit comparé et les systèmes sociopolitiques", *Rev. roumaine* 1974, pp. 47-52. Also published in Rotondi, ed., *Inchieste*, pp. 445-451.

Jacobs, "Das Eigentum als Rechtsinstitut im deutschen und sowjetischen Recht", *RabelsZ* 1965, pp. 694-725.

Jaluzot, "Méthodologie du droit comparé. Bilan et prospective", *Rev.int.dr.comp.* 2005, pp. 29-48.

Jamieson, "Source and Target-Oriented Comparative Law", 44 *A.J.C.L.* 121-129 (1996).

Jayme, "Die kulturelle Dimension des Rechts – ihre Bedeutung für das Internationale Privatrecht und die Rechtsvergleichung", *RabelsZ* 2003, pp. 211-230.

Jenks, *The Common Law of Mankind*, London 1958.

Jeschek, *Entwicklung, Aufgaben und Methoden der Strafrechtsvergleichung*, Tübingen 1955.

Kahn-Freund, "Comparative Law as an Academic Subject", 82 *L.Q.R.* 40-61 (1966).

Kahn-Freund, "On Uses and Misuses of Comparative Law", 37 *M.L.R.* 1-27 (1974).

Kaiser, "Vergleichung im öffentlichen Recht", *ZaöRV* 1964, pp. 391-404.

Kakouris, "L'utilisation du droit comparé par les tribunaux nationaux et internationaux", *Revue hellénique de droit international* 1994, pp. 31-45.

Kamba, "Comparative Law: a Theoretical Framework", 23 *I.C.L.Q.* 485-519 (1974).

Kaufmann, "Le droit social comparé", *E.J.C.L.*, vol. 8.1 (March 2004), www.ejcl.org.

Kiralfy, "The Anglo-Saxon Conception of Comparative Law", *Act.Jur.Hung.* 1971, pp. 159-174.

Kisch, "Droit comparé et terminologie juridique", in Rotondi, ed., *Inchieste*, pp. 407-423.

Kiss, "Droit comparé et droit international public", *Rev.int.dr.comp.* 1972, pp. 5-12.

Kjær, "Ret og sprog i EU: mangfoldighed, sprogforbistring – og grænser for integration?", *Retfærd* 1998, no. 83, pp. 4-14.

Kjær, "Europas retskulturelle pluralisme: grænser for den EU-retlige integration?", *TfR* 2001, pp. 870-905.

Kjær, "A Common Legal Language in Europe?", in Van Hoecke, ed., *Epistemology*, pp. 377-398.

Knapp, *Základy srovnávací právní vědy*, Praha 1991.

Knapp, *Velké právní systémy. Úvod do srovnávací právní vědy*, Praha 1996.

Knapp, "Verträge im tschechoslowakischen Recht. Ein Beitrag zur Rechtsvergleichung zwischen Ländern mit verschiedener Gesellschaftsordnung", *RabelsZ* 1962-1963, pp. 495-518.

Knapp, "Quelques problèmes méthodologiques dans la science du droit comparé", *Rev. roumaine* 1968, pp. 75-85. Also published in Rotondi, ed., *Inchieste*, pp. 427-441.

Knapp, "Champ d'application du droit comparé: le droit comparé interne et le droit étranger", *Mélanges de droit comparé en l'honneur du doyen Åke Malmström*, Stockholm 1972, pp. 132-140.

Koch, "Prozessrechtsvergleichung: Grundlage europäischer Verfahrensrechtspolitik und Kennzeichnung von Rechtskreisen", *ZEuP* 2007, pp. 735-753.

Kokkini-Iatridou, ed., *Een inleiding tot het rechtsvergelijkende onderzoek*, Deventer 1988.

Kokkini-Iatridou, "Some Methodological Aspects of Comparative Law. The Third Part of a (Pre-)Paradigm", *NILR* 1986, pp. 143-194.

Koopmans, "Comparative Law and the Courts", 45 *I.C.L.Q.* 545-556 (1996).

Kötz, "Über den Stil höchstrichterlicher Entscheidungen", *RabelsZ* 1973, pp. 245-263.

Kötz, "Comparative Legal Research and its Function in the Development of Harmonized Law. The European Perspective", *De lege. Juridiska fakultetens i Uppsala årsbok* 1995, pp. 21-36.

Kötz, "Abschied von der Rechtskreislehre?", *ZEuP* 1998, pp. 493-505.

Kramer, "Topik und Rechtsvergleichung", *RabelsZ* 1969, pp. 1-16.

Kreuzer, "Entnationalisierung des Privatrechts durch globale Rechtsintegration?", *Raum und Recht. Festschrift 600 Jahre Würzburger Juristenfakultät*, Berlin 2002, pp. 247-295.

Kropholler, *Internationales Einheitsrecht*, Tübingen 1975.

Kropholler, "Die vergleichende Methode und das internationale Privatrecht", *ZvglRW* 1978, pp. 1-20.

Kuss, "Methodische Fragen der Ost-West-Rechtsvergleichung im Zeichen des Systemwechsels in Osteuropa", *ZvglRW* 1992, pp. 405-422.

Lando, *Kort indføring i komparativ ret*, ed. 3, København 2009.

Lando, "Konturerne af et juridisk Verdensatlas", *Erhvervsøkonomisk tidsskrift* 1963, pp. 153-163.

Lando, "Om de store europæiske retssystemer og om inddelingen af retssystemerne i familier", *Juristen* 1965, pp. 37-49.

Lando, "Komparativ ret som emne for forskning og undervisning", *FJFT* 1966, pp. 261-271. Also published in *Juristen* 1966, pp. 289-295.

Lando, "The Contribution of Comparative Law to Law Reform by International Organizations", 25 *A.J.C.L.* 641-657 (1977).

Lando, "Emner og metode for retssammenligning på privatrettens område", *TfR* 1998, pp. 389-403.

Lando, "The Worries of a Comparatist", *D'ici, d'ailleurs: harmonisation et dynamique du droit. Mélanges en l'honneur de Denis Tallon*, Paris 1999, pp. 139-148.

Langrod, "Quelques réflexions méthodologiques sur la comparaison en science juridique", *Rev. int.dr.comp.* 1957, pp. 353-369.

Lawson, "Comparative Judicial Style", 25 *A.J.C.L.* 364-371 (1977).

Legrand, "Une institution universelle: l'ombudsman", *Rev.int.dr.comp.* 1973, pp. 851-861.

Legrand, "The Impossibility of 'Legal Transplants'", *Maastricht Journal of European and Comparative Law* 1997, pp. 111-124.

Legrand, "Questions à Rodolfo Sacco", *Rev.int.dr.comp.* 1995, pp. 943-971.

Legrand, "Comparative Legal Studies and Commitment to Theory", 58 *M.L.R.* 262-273 (1995).

Legrand, "Comparer", *Rev.int.dr.comp.* 1996, pp. 279-318.

Legrand, "European Legal Systems Are Not Converging", 45 *I.C.L.Q.* 52-81 (1996).

Legrand, "Against a European Civil Code", 60 *M.L.R.* 44-63 (1997).

Legrand, "John Henry Merryman and Comparative Legal Studies: a Dialogue", 47 *A.J.C.L.* 3-66 (1999).

Legrand, "The Same and the Different", in Legrand & Munday, eds, *Comparative Legal Studies*, pp. 240-311.

Legrand & Munday, eds, *Comparative Legal Studies: Traditions and Transitions*, Cambridge 2003.

Lenaerts, "Interlocking Legal Orders in the European Union and Comparative Law", 52 *I.C.L.Q.* 873-906 (2003).

Loeber, "Rechtsvergleichung zwischen Ländern mit verschiedener Wirtschaftsordnung", *RabelsZ* 1961, pp. 201-229.

Lorenz, "Rechtsvergleichung als Methode zur Konkretisierung der allgemeinen Grundsätze des Rechts", *JZ* 1962, pp. 269-275.

Loussouarn, "Le rôle de la méthode comparative en droit international privé français", *Revue critique de droit international privé* 1979, pp. 307-339.

Lukic, "Notions de la propriété dans l'Europe socialiste et dans les états capitalistes", *RabelsZ* 1961, pp. 238-254.

Lukic, "Les méthodes sociologiques en droit comparé", in Rotondi, ed., *Inchieste*, pp. 455-463.

Lögdberg, "Some Aspects of Comparative Law, Particularly the Importance of Foreign Law in Shaping the Swedish Legal System", *Mélanges de droit comparé en l'honneur du doyen Åke Malmström*, Stockholm 1972, pp. 159-169.

Makarov, "Internationales Privatrecht und Rechtsvergleichung", in Rotondi, ed., *Inchieste*, pp. 467-480.

Malmström, "Jämförande rättsvetenskap. Synpunkter och riktlinjer", *Festskrift tillägnad Halvar Sundberg*, Uppsala 1959, pp. 270-288.

Malmström, "Rättsordningarnas system. Några synpunkter på ett klassifikationsproblem inom den jämförande rättsvetenskapen", *Festskrift till Håkan Nial*, Stockholm 1966, pp. 381-403. Also published in English: "The System of Legal Systems. Notes on a Problem of Classification in Comparative Law", 13 *Sc.St.L.* 127-149 (1969).

Malmström, "Quelques remarques sur le développement du droit comparé en Suède", *Livre du Centenaire de la Société de législation comparée*, vol. 2, Paris 1971, pp. 517-520.

Mansouri, "Approche méthodologique et fonctionelle du droit comparé", *Rev.dr.int.dr.comp.* 2006, pp. 173-196.

Markesinis, "The Destructive and Constructive Role of the Comparative Lawyer", *RabelsZ* 1993, pp. 438-448.

Markesinis, "Learning from Europe and Learning in Europe", in Markesinis, ed., *The Gradual Convergence. Foreign Ideas, Foreign Influences, and English Law on the Eve of the 21st Century*, London 1994, pp. 1-32.

Markesinis, "A Matter of Style", 110 *L.Q.R.* 607-628 (1994).

Markesinis, "Foreign Law Inspiring National Law. Lessons from *Greatorex* v. *Greatorex*", 61 *Cambridge L.J.* 386-404 (2002).

Markovits, "Civil Law in Eastern Germany – its Development and Relation to Soviet Legal History and Ideology", 78 *Yale L.J.* 1-51 (1968-1969).

Marsh, "Quelques réflexions pratiques sur l'usage de la technique comparative dans la réforme du droit national", *Rev.dr.int.dr.comp.* 1970, pp. 81-101.

Marsh, "Comparative Law and Law Reform", *RabelsZ* 1977, pp. 649-668.

Mattei, "Three Patterns of Law: Taxonomy and Change in the World's Legal Systems", 45 *A.J.C.L.* 5-44 (1997).

Mattei, "Comparative Law and Critical Legal Studies", in Reimann & Zimmermann, eds, *The Oxford Handbook*, pp. 815-836.

Matteucci, "Aperçu sommaire de l'état de l'unification du droit", *Rev.int.dr.comp.* 1973, pp. 865-872.

Mayda, "Quelques réflexions critiques sur le droit comparé contemporain", *Rev.int.dr.comp.* 1970, pp. 57-82.

McWhinney, "Toward the Scientific Study of Values in Comparative Law Research", *20th Century Comparative and Conflicts Law. Legal Essays in Honor of Hessel E. Yntema*, Leyden 1961, pp. 29-41.

von Mehren, "Choice-of-Law Theories and the Comparative-Law Problem", 23 *A.J.C.L.* 751-758 (1975).

von Mehren, "L'apport du droit comparé à la théorie et à la pratique du droit international privé", *Rev.int.dr.comp.* 1977, pp. 493-500.

Merryman, *The Loneliness of the Comparative Lawyer and Other Essays in Foreign and Comparative Law*, The Hague-London-Boston 1999.

Merryman, "Comparative Law and Scientific Explanation", *Law in the United States of America in Social and Technological Revolution. Reports from the United States of America on Topics of Major Concern as Established for the IXth Congress of the International Academy of Comparative Law*, Brussels 1974, pp. 81-104.

Merryman, "Comparative Law and Social Change: on the Origins, Style, Decline & Revival of the Law and Development Movement", 25 *A.J.C.L.* 457-491 (1977).

Merryman, "Law and Development Memoirs II: SLADE", 48 *A.J.C.L.* 713-729 (2000).

Michaels, "The Functional Method of Comparative Law", in Reimann & Zimmermann, eds, *The Oxford Handbook*, pp. 339-382.

Michaels, "Comparative Law by Numbers? Legal Origins Thesis, *Doing Business* Reports, and the Silence of Traditional Comparative Law", 57 *A.J.C.L.* 765-795 (2009).

Michaels, "Explanation and Interpretation in Functionalist Comparative Law – a Response to Julie de Coninck", *RabelsZ* 2010, pp. 351-359.

Miller, "A Typology of Legal Transplants: Using Sociology, Legal History and Argentine Examples to Explain the Transplant Process", 51 *A.J.C.L.* 839-885 (2003).

Mincke, "Eine vergleichende Rechtswissenschaft", *ZvglRW* 1984, pp. 315-328.

Modéer, "Optimala rättsliga kulturer? Om modernitet och kontinuitet i nationella och globala rättsliga kulturer", *JT* 1999-2000, pp. 71-87.

Møller, "Metoder til harmonisering og unifikation i Norden, EEC og USA", *NordTIR* 1974-1975, pp. 229-263.

Moss, "Russian Legislation and Foreign Models. Some Observations on Comparative Law", *TfR* 1997, pp. 766-791.

Moura Vicente, *Direito comparado, vol. I, introdução e parte geral*, ed. 2, Coimbra 2012.

Muir Watt, "La fonction subversive du droit comparé", *Rev.int.dr.comp.* 2000, pp. 503-527.

Müller-Römer, "Ziele und Methoden der Rechtsvergleichung zwischen beiden Teilen Deutschlands", *Recht in Ost und West* 1969, pp. 1-8.

Nelken, "Legal Transplants and beyond: of Disciplines and Metaphors", in Harding & Örücü, eds, *Comparative Law*, pp. 19-34.

Nelken, "Comparatists and Transferability", in Legrand & Munday, eds, *Comparative Legal Studies*, pp. 437-466.

Neuhaus & Kropholler, "Rechtsvereinheitlichung – Rechtsverbesserung?", *RabelsZ* 1981, pp. 73-90.

Neumayer, "Fremdes Recht aus Büchern, fremde Rechtswirklichkeit und die funktionelle Dimension in den Methoden der Rechtsvergleichung", *RabelsZ* 1970, pp. 411-426. Also published in French: "Law in the books, law in action et les méthodes du droit comparé", in Rotondi, ed., *Inchieste*, pp. 507-521.

Niglia, "Of Harmonization and Fragmentation: The Problem of Legal Transplants in the Europeanization of Private Law", *Maastricht Journal of European and Comparative Law* 2010, pp. 116-136.

Noda, "Quelques réflexions sur le fondement du droit comparé", *Aspects nouveaux de la pensée juridique. Recueil d'études en hommage à Marc Ancel*, vol. 1, Paris 1975, pp. 23-41.

Nordiskt institut för jämförande rättskunskap. Betänkande avgivet av samarbetande danska, finska, isländska, norska och svenska sakkunniga, *NU* 17/70, Stockholm 1970.

Oderkerk, "The Importance of Context: Selecting Legal Systems in Comparative Legal Research", *NILR* 2001, pp. 293-318.

Ogus, "Competition between National Legal Systems: A Contribution of Economic Analysis to Comparative Law", 48 *I.C.L.Q.* 405-418 (1999).

Ogus, "The Economic Approach: Competition between Legal Systems", in Örücü &Nelken, eds, *Comparative Law*, pp. 155-167.

Örücü, "Mixed and Mixing Systems: a Conceptual Search", in Örücü, Attwooll & Coyle, eds, *Studies*, pp. 335-352.

Örücü, "Law as Transposition", 51 *I.C.L.Q.* 205-223 (2002).

Örücü, "Family Trees for Legal Systems: Towards a Contemporary Approach", in Van Hoecke, ed., *Epistemology*, pp. 359-375.

Örücü, "Methodology of Comparative Law", in Smits, ed., *Elgar Encyclopedia*, pp. 442-454.

Örücü, "A General View of 'Legal Families' and of 'Mixing Systems'", in Örücü & Nelken, eds, *Comparative Law*, pp. 169-187.

Örücü, Attwooll & Coyle, eds, *Studies in Legal Systems: Mixed and Mixing*, The Hague-London-Boston 1996.

Örücü & Nelken, eds, *Comparative Law: A Handbook*, Oxford-Portland 2007.

Palmer, "From Lerotholi to Lando: Some Examples of Comparative Law Methodology", 53 *A.J.C.L.* 261-290 (2005).

Palmer, "Mixed Jurisdictions", in Smits, ed., *Elgar Encyclopedia*, pp. 467-475.

Palmer, "Two Rival Theories of Mixed Legal Systems", *E.J.C.L.*, vol. 12.1 (May 2008), www.ejcl. org.

Pålsson & Lando, *Bibliografisk introduktion till utländsk och komparativ rätt*, København 1968.

Pescatore, "Le recours, dans la jurisprudence de la Cour de Justice des Communautés européennes, à des normes déduites de la comparaison des droits des états members", *Rev. int.dr.comp.* 1980, pp. 337-359.

Peters & Schwenke, "Comparative Law beyond Post-Modernism", 49 *I.C.L.Q.* 800-833 (2000).

Pfersmann, "Le droit comparé comme interprétation et comme théorie du droit", *Rev.int. dr.comp.* 2001, pp. 275-288.

Philipps, *Erscheinungsformen und Methoden der Privatrechts-Vereinheitlichung*, Diss. Mainz 1963.

Picard, "Le droit et sa diversité nécessaire d'après les races et les nations", *Clunet* 1901, pp. 417-423.

Pihlajamäki, "Rättssystem i komparativrättsliga konstruktioner: det nordiska perspektivet", *Juridiska fakulteten i Uppsala årsbok 2011, Vänbok till Rolf Nygren*, Uppsala 2011, pp. 85-94.

Platsas, "The Functional and the Dysfunctional in the Comparative Method of Law: Some Critical Remarks", *E.J.C.L.*, vol. 12.3 (December 2008), www.ejcl.org.

Du Plessis, "Comparative Law and the Study of Mixed Legal Systems", in Reimann & Zimmermann, eds, *The Oxford Handbook*, pp. 477-512.

Ponthoreau, "Le droit comparé en question(s) entre pragmatisme et outil épistémologique", *Rev.int.dr.comp.* 2005, pp. 7-27.

Popescu, "Buts et méthodes de la comparaison dans le droit", *Rev.roumaine* 1974, pp. 63-71.

Pound, "Comparative Law in Space and Time", 4 *A.J.C.L.* 70-84 (1955).

Quigley, "Socialist Law and the Civil Law Tradition", 37 *A.J.C.L.* 781-808 (1989).

Rabel, "Rechtsvergleichung und internationale Rechtsprechung", *RabelsZ* 1927, pp. 5-47.

Raiser, "Das Eigentum als Rechtsbegriff in den Rechten West- und Osteuropas", *RabelsZ* 1961, pp. 230-237.

Recaséns-Siches, "Los métodos sociológicos en el derecho comparado", in Rotondi, ed., *Inchieste*, pp. 525-544.

Reimann, "The Progress and Failure of Comparative Law in the Second Half of the Twentieth Century", 50 *A.J.C.L.* 671-700 (2002).

Reimann & Zimmermann, eds, *The Oxford Handbook of Comparative Law*, Oxford 2006.

Reitz, "How to Do Comparative Law", 46 *A.J.C.L.* 617-636 (1998).

Reitz, "Legal Origins, Comparative Law, and Political Economy", 57 *A.J.C.L.* 847-862 (2009).

Ress, "Die Bedeutung der Rechtsvergleichung für das Recht internationaler Organisationen", *ZaöRV* 1976, pp. 227-279.

Reynolds, "Comparative Legal Dictionaries", 34 *A.J.C.L.* 551-558 (1986).

Reyntjens, "Note sur l'utilité d'introduire un système juridique 'pluraliste' dans la macro-comparaison des droits", *Rev.dr.int.dr.comp.* 1991, pp. 41-50.

Rheinstein, *Einführung in die Rechtsvergleichung*, München 1974.

Rheinstein, "Teaching Tools in Comparative Law", 1 *A.J.C.L.* 95-114 (1952).

Rheinstein, "Zur Einführung: Rechtsvergleichung", *Juristische Schulung* 1972, pp. 65-69.

Rheinstein, "Comparative Law – its Functions, Methods and Uses", in Rotondi, ed., *Inchieste*, pp. 547-556.

Riesenfeld & Pakter, *Comparative Law Casebook*, Ardsley N.Y. 2001.

Rodière, *Introduction au droit comparé*, Paris 1979.

Rotondi, ed., *Inchieste di diritto comparato 2. Buts et méthodes du droit comparé*, Padova-New York 1973.

Rotter, "Dogmatische und soziologische Rechtsvergleichung – eine methodologische Analyse für die Ostrechtsforschung", *Osteuropa-Recht* 1970, pp. 81-97.

Rozmaryn, "Les grandes controverses du droit comparé", in Rotondi, ed., *Inchieste*, pp. 579-591.

Sacco, "Legal Formants: a Dynamic Approach to Comparative Law", 39 *A.J.C.L.* 1-34 och 343-401 (1991).

Sacco, "Diversity and Uniformity in the Law", 49 *A.J.C.L.* 171-188 (2001).

Sacco, "Souvenirs d'un vieux comparatiste", *ZEuP* 2002, pp. 727-736.

Samuel, "Comparative Law and Jurisprudence", 47 *I.C.L.Q.* 817-836 (1998).

Samuel, "Epistomology and Comparative Law: Contributions from the Sciences and Social Sciences", in Van Hoecke, ed., *Epistemology*, pp. 35-77.

Sandrock, *Über Sinn und Methode zivilistischer Rechtsvergleichung*, Frankfurt a.M.-Berlin 1966.

Santa Pinter, "Etnopolítica jurídica comparada o sistemas legales contemporaneos", *Problèmes contemporains de droit comparé*, vol. 2, Tokyo 1962, pp. 357-372.

Sarfatti, "Les premiers pas du droit comparé", *Mélanges offerts à Jacques Maury*, vol. 2, Paris 1960, pp. 237-241.

Savatier, "Les bases sociales du droit comparé et l'accélération de l'histoire", *Problèmes contemporains de droit comparé*, vol. 2, Tokyo 1962, pp. 373-386.

Schlesinger, *Comparative Law. Cases – Texts – Materials*, ed. 3, Mineola N.Y. 1970.

Schlesinger, "Research on the General Principles of Law Recognized by Civilized Nations", 51 *A.J.I.L.* 734-753 (1957).

Schlesinger, "The Common Core of Legal Systems. An Emerging Subject of Comparative Study", *20th Century Comparative and Conflicts Law. Legal Essays in Honor of Hessel E. Yntema*, Leyden 1961, pp. 65-79.

Schlesinger, ed., *Formation of Contracts – a Study of the Common Core of Legal Systems*, vol. 1-2, New York-London 1968.

Schlesinger & Bonassies, "Le fonds commun des systèmes juridiques. Observations sur un nouveau projet de recherches", *Rev.int.dr.comp.* 1963, pp. 501-540.

Schmid, "Legitimacy Conditions for a European Civil Code", *Maastricht Journal of European and Comparative Law* 2001, pp. 277-298.

Schmidt, *The Ratio Decidendi. A Comparative Study of a French, a German and an American Supreme Court Decision*, Uppsala 1965.

Schmidt, "Komparativt rättsstudium", *TfR* 1951, pp. 473-483.

Schmitthoff, "The Science of Comparative Law", 7 *Cambridge L.J.* 94-110 (1941).

Schnitzer, *Vergleichende Rechtslehre*, ed. 2, vol. 1-2, Basel 1961.

Schnitzer, "Die Aufgabe der Rechtsvergleichung", *ZfRV* 1973, pp. 186-197.

Schnitzer, "Rechtsvergleichung, internationales Privatrecht und Völkerrecht im System des Rechts", *ZfRV* 1976, pp. 13-28.

Schoentjes-Merchiers, "L'apport du droit comparé à l'enseignement et à la recherche du droit", *Rev.dr.int.dr.comp.* 1977, pp. 70-84.

Scholler, "Bedeutung der Lehre vom Rechtskreis und die Rechtskultur", *ZvglRW* 2000, pp. 373-386.

Schulze, "Vergleichende Gesetzesauslegung und Rechtsangleichung", *ZfRV* 1997, pp. 183-197.

Schwarz-Liebermann von Wahlendorf, *Droit comparé. Théorie générale et principes*, Paris 1978.

Sefton-Green, "Compare and Contrast: monstre à deux têtes", *Rev.int.dr.comp.* 2002, pp. 85-95.

Selander, "Företagsjurister och deras arbetsuppgifter av internationell karaktär", *TSA* 1977, pp. 461-466.

Serick, "Über den Wert der Privatrechtsvergleichung in der Völkerrechtspraxis", i Rotondi, ed., *Inchieste*, pp. 635-658. Also published in *Rechtsvergleichung und Rechtsvereinheitlichung. Festschrift zum fünfzigjährigen Bestehen des Instituts für ausländisches und internationales Privat- und Wirtschaftsrecht der Universität Heidelberg*, Heidelberg 1967, pp. 215-232.

Sevastik, ed., *Legal Assistance to Developing Countries*, Stockholm 1997.

Shen, "Legal Transplant and Comparative Law", *Rev.int.dr.comp.* 1999, pp. 853-857.

Siems, "Statistische Rechtsvergleichung", *RabelsZ* 2008, pp. 354-390.

Siesby, "Om den sammenlignende retsvidenskabs formål og metode", *TfR* 1967, pp. 488-503.

Simmonds, "The International Encyclopedia of Comparative Law", 16 *I.C.L.Q.* 816-820 (1967).

Slapnicka, "Die Rezeption des Sowjetrechts in den europäischen Volksdemokratien", *Osteuropa-Recht* 1974, pp. 94-113.

Smits, "A European Private Law as a Mixed Legal System. Towards a Ius Commune through the Free Movement of Legal Rules", *Maastricht Journal of European and Comparative Law* 1998, pp. 328-340.

Smits, ed., *Elgar Encyclopedia of Comparative Law*, Cheltenham-Northampton 2006.

Smits, "On Successful Legal Transplants in a Future *Ius Commune Europaeum*", in Harding & Örücü, eds, *Comparative Law*, pp. 137-154.

Smits, "The Europeanisation of National Legal Systems: Some Consequences for Legal Thinking in Civil Law Countries", in Van Hoecke, ed., *Epistomology*, pp. 229-245.

Smits, "Comparative Law and its Influence on National Legal Systems", in Reimann & Zimmermann, eds, *The Oxford Handbook*, pp. 513-538.

Smits, "Convergence of Private Law in Europe: Towards a New Ius Commune", in Örücü & Nelken, eds, *Comparative Law*, pp. 219-240.

Smits, "Mixed Jurisdictions: Lessons for European Harmonisation?", *E.J.C.L.*, vol. 12.1 (May 2008), www.ejcl.org.

Smits, "Taking Functionalism Seriously: on the Bright Future of a Contested Method", *Maastricht Journal of European and Comparative Law* 2011, pp. 554-558.

Sola Cañizares, *Iniciación al derecho comparado*, Barcelona 1954.

Souto, *Da inexistência científico-conceitual do direito comparado*, Recife 1956.

Stanziane, "Considérations au sujet des méthodes du droit comparé", *Rev.int.dr.comp.* 1973, pp. 873-885.

Štefanovič, *Porovnávánie práva – socialistická právna komparatistika*, Bratislava 1987.

Strebel, "Vergleichung und vergleichende Methode im öffentlichen Recht", *ZaöRV* 1964, pp. 405-430.

Strömholm, *Allmän rättslära. En första introduktion*, ed. 3, Stockholm 1976.

Strömholm, "Legislative Material and Construction of Statutes. Notes on the Continental Approach", 10 *Sc.St.L.* 173-218 (1966).

Strömholm, "Användning av utländskt material i juridiska monografier. Några anteckningar och förslag", *SvJT* 1971, pp. 251-263.

Strömholm, "Har den komparativa rätten en metod?", *SvJT* 1972, pp. 456-465.

Strömholm, "Anm. av Zweigert/Kötz: Einführung in die Rechtsvergleichung auf dem Gebiete des Privatrechts", *SvJT* 1973, pp. 808-812.

Strömholm, "Comparative Legal Science – Risks and Possibilities", *Law under Exogenous Influences. Publications of the Turku Law School*, no. 1/1994, pp. 5-29.

Strömholm, "Le droit comparé en Suède au seuil du troisième millénaire", *Rev.int.dr.comp.* 1999, pp. 1033-1040.

Suksi, "Om komparativ juridik särskilt inom statsförfattningsrättens område", *FJFT* 1993, pp. 263-273.

Sundberg, "A Uniform Interpretation of Uniform Law", 10 *Sc.St.L.* 219-238 (1966).

Sundberg, "Civil law, Common Law and the Scandinavians", 13 *Sc.St.L.* 179-205 (1969).

Sweeney, "L'exposition du droit par le juge, source d'un malentendu sur le droit des Etats-Unis et le droit français", *Rev.int.dr.comp.* 1960, pp. 685-700.

Szabó, "La science comparative du droit", *Ann.Univ.Budapest.* 1964, pp. 91-134.

Szabó, "Le droit comparé de nos jours", *Act.Jur.Hung.* 1971, pp. 131-141.

Szabó, "Law Theory and Comparative Law", *Mélanges de droit comparé en l'honneur du doyen Åke Malmström*, Stockholm 1972, pp. 243-254.

Szabó, "La comparaison des institutions juridiques", *Act.Jur.Hung.* 1973, pp. 131-141.

Szabó, "Le droit comparé 'interne'", *Aspects nouveaux de la pensée juridique. Recueil d'études en hommage à Marc Ancel*, vol. 1, Paris 1975, pp. 59-67.

Szabó, "Theoretical Questions of Comparative Law", in Szabó & Péteri, eds, *A Socialist Approach*, pp. 9-44.

Szabó & Péteri, eds, *A Socialist Approach to Comparative Law*, Leyden-Budapest 1977.

Szirmai, "The Use of Soviet Law for the Western Lawmaker", in Rotondi, ed., *Inchieste*, pp. 661-684.

Tchkhikvadze & Zivs, "L'évolution de la science juridique et du droit comparé en U.R.S.S.", *Livre du Centenaire de la Société de législation comparée*, vol. 2, Paris 1971, pp. 581-600.

Teubner, "Legal Irritants: Good Faith in British Law or How Unifying Law Ends up in New Divergences", 61 *M.L.R.* 11-32 (1998).

Tokarczyk, *Wprowadzenie do komparatystyki prawniczej*, Lublin 1996.

Tolonen, "Om förhållandet mellan rättsordningen och det ekonomiska systemet", *FJFT* 1976, pp. 100-107.

Tontti, "European Legal Pluralism as a Rebirth of IUS commune", *Retfærd* 2001, no. 94, pp. 40-54.

Tunc, "Comparative Law, Peace and Justice", *20th Century Comparative and Conflicts law. Legal Essays in Honor of Hessel E. Yntema*, Leyden 1961, pp. 80-90.

Tunc, "La possibilité de comparer le contrat dans des systèmes juridiques à structures économiques différentes", *RabelsZ* 1962-1963, pp. 478-494.

Tunc, "La contribution possible des études juridiques comparatives à une meilleure compréhension entre nations", *Rev.int.dr.comp.* 1964, pp. 47-67.

Twining, "Globalization and Comparative Law", *Maastricht Journal of European and Comparative Law* 1999, pp. 217-243.

Valcke, "Comparative Law as Comparative Jurisprudence – The Comparability of Legal Systems", 52 *A.J.C.L.* 713-740 (2004).

Valladão, "Private International Law, Uniform Law and Comparative Law", *20th Century Comparative and Conflicts Law. Legal Essays in Honor of Hessel E. Yntema*, Leyden 1961, pp. 98-113.

Vallindas, "Droit uniforme international et droit comparé", *Ius et lex. Festgabe zum 70. Geburtstag von Max Gutzwiller*, Basel 1959, pp. 189-199.

Del Vecchio, "Les bases du droit comparé et les principes généraux du droit", *Rev.int.dr.comp.* 1960, pp. 493-499.

Del Vecchio, "Voraussetzungen und Bewertungskriterien in der Rechtsvergleichung", *ZvglRW* 1962, pp. 1-14.

Vogel, *Juridiska översättningar*, Lund 1988.

Waelde & Gunderson, "Legislative Reform in Transition Economies: Western Transplants – a Short-Cut to Social Market Economy Status?", 43 *I.C.L.Q.* 347-378 (1994).

Wahl, "Influences climatiques sur l'évolution du droit en Orient et en Occident. Contribution au régionalisme en droit comparé", *Rev.int.dr.comp.* 1973, pp. 261-276.

Warnander, *Om jämförande rättsforskning. Uppsats i tillämpade studier*, Stockholm 1966.

Watson, "Legal Transplants and Law Reform", 92 *L.Q.R.* 79-84 (1976).

Watson, "Comparative Law and Legal Change", [1978] *Cambridge L.J.* 313-336.

Watson, "Legal Transplants and European Private Law", *E.J.C.L.*, vol. 4.4 (December 2000), www.ejcl.org.

Weyl, "Marxisme et droit comparé", 12 *Comparative Law Review* (1977), no. 1.

Wigmore, *A Panorama of the World's Legal Systems*, vol. 1-3, St.Paul 1928.

Wijffels, "Le droit comparé à la recherché d'un nouvel *interface* entre ordres juridiques", *Rev. dr.int.dr.comp.* 2008, pp. 228-252.

Winizky, "De la technique comparative en droit", *Problèmes contemporains de droit comparé*, vol. 2, Tokyo 1962, pp. 511-534.

Winterton, "Comparative Law Teaching", 23 *A.J.C.L.* 69-118 (1975).

Xanthaki, "Legal Transplants in Legislation: Defusing the Trap", 57 *I.C.L.Q.* 659-673 (2008).

Yntema, "Comparative law and humanism", 7 *A.J.C.L.* 493-499 (1958). Also published in French: "Le droit comparé et l'humanisme", *Rev.int.dr.comp.* 1958, pp. 693-700.

Yokaris, "Problèmes méthodologiques et nature de la recherche comparative en droit international", *Revue hellénique de droit international* 1982-1983, pp. 65-96.

Zajtay, "Réflexions sur le problème de la division des familles de droits", *RabelsZ* 1973, pp. 210-216.

Zajtay, "Aims and Methods of Comparative Law", 7 *The Comparative and International Law Journal of Southern Africa* 321-330 (1974).

Zajtay, "Problèmes méthodologiques du droit comparé", *Aspects nouveaux de la pensée juridique. Recueil d'études en hommage à Marc Ancel*, vol. 1, Paris 1975, pp. 69-79.

Zemanek, "Was kann die Vergleichung staatlichen öffentlichen Rechts für das Recht der internationalen Organisationen leisten?", *ZaöRV* 1964, pp. 453-471.

Ziegert, "Juristische und soziologische Empirie des Rechts. Genese und Zukunft der Rechtsvergleichung als wissenschaftliches Problem des europäischen Rechts", *RabelsZ* 1981, pp. 51-72.

Zivs, "La méthode de recherche comparative dans la science juridique", *Act.Jur.Hung.* 1971, pp. 175-180.

Zlatescu, "Considérations sur la méthode comparative dans l'étude du droit", *Rev.roumaine* 1974, pp. 245-252.

Zlatescu, "En marge d'un débat sur le droit comparé socialiste", *Rev.roumaine* 1976, pp. 245-253.

Zwarensteyn, "Some Observations on the Comparison of Legal Institutions and the Concepts of Law in Different Societies", 10 *American Business Law Journal* 17-32 (1972-1973).

Zweigert, "Rechtsvergleichung als universale Interpretationsmethode", *RabelsZ* 1949-1950, pp. 5-21.

Zweigert, "Die Rechtsvergleichung im Dienste der europäischen Rechtsvereinheitlichung", *RabelsZ* 1951, pp. 387-397.

Zweigert, "Méthodologie du droit comparé", *Mélanges offerts à Jacques Maury*, vol. 1, Paris 1960, pp. 579-596.

Zweigert, "Zur Lehre von den Rechtskreisen", *20th Century Comparative and Conflicts Law. Legal Essays in Honor of Hessel E. Yntema*, Leyden 1961, pp. 42-55.

Zweigert, "Des solutions identiques par des voies différentes", *Rev.int.dr.comp.* 1966, pp. 5-18.

Zweigert, "Methodological Problems in Comparative Law", 7 *Israel L.R.* 465-474 (1972).

Zweigert, "Die kritische Wertung in der Rechtsvergleichung", *Law and International Trade. Festschrift für Clive M. Schmitthoff*, Frankfurt a.M. 1973, pp. 403-420.

Zweigert, "Die 'praesumptio similitudinis' als Grundsatzvermutung rechtsvergleichender Methode", in Rotondi, ed., *Inchieste*, pp. 737-758.

Zweigert, "Die soziologische Dimension der Rechtsvergleichung", *RabelsZ* 1974, pp. 299-316.

Zweigert, "Quelques réflexions sur les relations entre la sociologie juridique et le droit comparé", *Aspects nouveaux de la pensée juridique. Recueil d'études en hommage à Marc Ancel*, vol. 1, Paris 1975, pp. 81-93.

Zweigert & Kropholler, eds, *Sources of International Uniform Law*, vol. 1-3, Leyden 1971-1973.

Zweigert & Kötz, *Einführung in die Rechtsvergleichung auf dem Gebiete des Privatrechts*, vol. 1-2, Tübingen 1971-1969.

Zweigert & Kötz, *An Introduction to Comparative Law*, ed. 3, Oxford 1998.

Zweigert & Puttfarken, "Possibilities of Comparing Analogous Institutions of Law in Different Social Systems", *Act.Jur.Hung.* 1973, pp. 107-130.

Index